Annual 2017

TRUE PORTLAND

The unofficial guide for creative people

edit

BRIDGE LAB

Library of Congress
Cataloging-in-Publication Data

Names: Kurosaki, Teruo, author.
Title: True Portland : the unofficial
guide for creative people / by Ter-
uo Kurosaki.
Description: Portland, Oregon :
Hawthorne Books & Literary Arts,
[2017]
Identifiers: LCCN 2016041305 |
ISBN 9780997068306 (paperback)
Subjects: LCSH: Portland (Or.)–
Guidebooks. | Portland (Or.)–De-
scription and travel. | Portland
(Or.)–Social life and customs. |
BISAC: TRAVEL / United States
/ West / Pacific (AK, CA, HI, NV,
OR, WA).
Classification: LCC F884.P83 K87
2017 | DDC 979.5/49–dc23
LC record available at
https://lccn.loc.gov/2016041305

9 Hawthorne Books
8 & Literary Arts
7
6 2201 Northeast 23rd Avenue
5 3rd Floor
4 Portland, Oregon 97212
3 hawthornebooks.com
2
1 Printed in China

Set in Paperback

Introduction

2

True Portland is an annual Japanese publication that celebrates all things Portland. It was initially published in 2014 by Tokyo-based cultural luminary, designer, founder of Tokyo's Farmer's Market at United Nations University, and publisher Teruo Kurosaki and his hyper-creative team at Bridge Lab and Media Surf Communications, with the support of Travel Portland. The book has done so well in Japan that Kurosaki approached Hawthorne Books to publish an English version, and that is, of course, what you are holding. I was lucky enough to edit this book—removing businesses that had closed, refreshing its sections. What I resolutely did not do is change the essence of the book.

This is a love letter from Japan to Portland, well-curated by Kurosaki's team of hip, discerning Tokyoites, all honored on page 304. It includes Portland's best, including our celebrated restaurants and bars, live music venues and record labels, neighborhood boutiques, plus outdoor adventures and even urban wee-hour adventures. The book is, first and foremost, for Portland visitors, but it also allows us residents to feel like travelers in our own city, to see our city in new ways. I certainly learned a lot about Portland while working on it.

In recent months we've witnessed a political polarization between Americans as well as cultural xenophobia. Hawthorne Books champions inclusion and has been a longtime supporter of unsung heroes, outsider narratives, and international voices. We have published many loud and proud LGBTQ books, books that look closely and often uncomfortably at race relations, and books that grapple with patriotism and what it means to be American. *True Portland* embodies these values and enhances our catalogue. The Japan–Portland relationship grows steadily stronger, something we celebrate and encourage.

One of my first regular writing gigs in Portland was penning seasonal food and drink stories for the *Portland Tribune*. For several years I interviewed farmers, ranchers, and chefs who work with ingredients that thrive in the Willamette Valley and throughout Oregon, and shape our city's culinary culture. It is remarkable how many of those stories featured iconic Japanese ingredients that do well here, on our similar latitude—ginseng, ginger, wasabi, daikon, Kumamoto oysters, and more. I think that this is one of many reasons why Japanese folks feel so comfortable in the Portland area. The fact that snow-capped Mt. Hood, like Mt. Fuji, is almost always in sight, gracing our skyline, doesn't hurt.

In this book you get interviews with prominent Portlanders such as Nike's design director Dylan Raasch and Columbia Sportswear's chairman of the board and matriarch Gert Boyle. You also get the inside scoop on some of the city's iconic businesses such as The ReBuilding Center, Beast, Cinema 21, and Mississippi Records. And you will find interesting capsule reviews of less well-known but Portland-proud spots such as the Portland Museum of Modern Art and the world's smallest park (it's downtown!). Added bonus: there are fun 48-hour itineraries from Portland locals who make this city tick even if you don't yet

know their names. Other *True Portland* standouts include sections for LGBTQ businesses, skateboarding, tattooing, and trail running.

When I moved to Portland in 2002 the only Japanese spots on my radar were the handful of sushi restaurants (some good, a couple great, many mediocre) and the Japanese Garden. These days we have scores of ramen spots (some offshoots of Japan restaurants), izakayas, omakase, and kaiseki restaurants. We also have locally made Japanese wagashi (traditional Japanese confections), miso, tofu, sake, natto, Japanese traditional fabric businesses—the list goes on. These days Japan's influence is felt in every quadrant of the city. In fact, the Portland to Narita non-stop flight, first offered in 2004, is one of Portland International Airport's busiest daily flights, shepherding students, travelers, and business folks.

True Portland is our city's new, carefully designed compendium of Portland DIY and passion projects; all of these wonderfully niche businesses here that do one thing (or a few) extremely well. I am proud of our fair city. Proud that we are so welcoming, that we celebrate other cultures by way of food, festivals, and our college and university programs. Portland deserves an annual publication of this caliber that shines a light on all of that and more. Have fun with this book. We certainly had a great time putting it together. No matter how long you've lived here or how long you'll be visiting, there are many adventures detailed here to dive into. Tanoshinde!

True Portland English Edition
Editor   Liz Crain

3

A city's essence, its creativity

Every city has a particular essence and way. In Portland you experience firsthand the great value its residents place on things that embody CRAFT, HUMAN, and ORGANIC through its food and drink, architecture and design, art and music, street culture, and all the way down to the often smiling faces of its residents. Traveling often intensifies curiosity and to experience the realities of a city as if you are a resident rather than a tourist is rare. That is the purpose of this book. We will continue to visit Portland every year. It is a city that we deeply value and love.

Teruo Kurosaki
TRUE PORTLAND Author / Publisher

RAFT

UMAN

GANIC

TABLE OF CONTENTS

HERE ⎯⎯⎯⎯

BASIC INFORMATION *on* PORTLAND

Welcome to Portland

Portland's vibrant culture, friendly and welcoming locals, excellent food and drink, and limitless recreation opportunities make it a unique place to visit. You'll find retailers large and small, international and local within easy reach of downtown hotels. The nearby Pearl District is home to galleries, boutiques, chic restaurants, and the legendary Powell's City of Books. With no sales tax in the state of Oregon, Portland is a haven for shoppers.

An award-winning airport, efficient light rail system, and pedestrian-friendly city blocks in the city center make getting around town a real pleasure.

Portland is also home to over seventy breweries and counting—more than any other city on the planet, and myriad food carts, casual eateries, and fine dining restaurants where gutsy and creative chefs cook up some of the tastiest food around.

The city also offers easy access to many outdoor wonders, from urban hikes to the Pacific Coast just ninety minutes away to winter sports and camping on Mount Hood, the iconic destination only an hour from the city.

Whatever your interests, you're sure to find something that fascinates you in Portland.

travel PORTLAND

Travel Portland is a nonprofit organization that works to promote tourism in and around the Portland area. Its facilities include the Visitor Information Center in Pioneer Courthouse Square, which provides all sorts of useful advice.

Visitor Information Center

Ⓐ Pioneer Courthouse Square 701 SW 6th Ave.
 1-877-678-5263
Ⓣ (503) 275-8355
Ⓗ Mon-Fri 8:30 a.m.-5:30 p.m., Sat 1 a.m.-4 p.m.
 Sun(May-Oct. only) 10 a.m.-2 p.m.
Ⓦ travelportland.com

Facts

Population

Portland: 632,309
(2015 United States Census Bureau estimate)
Portland Metropolitan Area: 2,389,228
(2014 United States Census Bureau estimate)

Area

145 sq mi

Average elevation

183 ft

Time Zone

Pacific Standard Time (PST) (UTC -8 hours)
Pacific Daylight Time (PDT) (UTC -7 hours) *
*From the second Sunday in March through
the first Sunday in November

Sister City

Sapporo, Japan / Guadalajara, Mexico / Ashkelon, Israel /
Ulsan, South Korea / Suzhou, People's Republic of China /
Khabarovsk, Russia / Kaohsiung, Taiwan /Mutare, Zimbabwe /
Bologna, Italy / Kota Kinabalu, Malaysia / Utrecht, Netherlands

Alcohol Restrictions

Legal drinking age: 21
ID is required to purchase alcohol in bars and stores
Alcohol is licensed for sale 7:00 a.m.–2:30 a.m.
Drinking in parks and other public spaces is not permitted

Smoking

In accordance with the Smoke Free Workplace Law, Portland prohibits smoking in public spaces, including restaurants and bars, and within ten feet of all entrances, exits, accessibility ramps that lead to and from an entrance or exit, windows, and air-intake vents. As of January 2016, this law includes the use of e-cigarettes, vape pens, and other inhalant delivery systems.

	Jan	Feb	Mar	Apr	May	Jun	Jul	Aug	Sep	Oct	Nov	Dec
Maximum(°F)	44.6	50	55.4	60.8	60	73.4	80.6	80.6	75.2	64.4	51.8	46.4
Minimum(°F)	33.8	35.6	39.2	42.8	48.2	53.6	57.2	57.2	51.8	44.6	39.2	35.6
Rainfall(inch)	5.5	3.9	3.9	2.7	2.3	1.5	0.3	0.7	1.5	3.1	5.5	5.9

Maximum = Mean maximum temperature. **Minimum =** Mean minimum temperature.

Weather

Spring

Sudden showers continue even into spring, but there are occasional prolonged periods without rain. On a typical spring day, rain in the morning might be followed by fine weather and blue skies in the afternoon. From early March, as temperatures rise, flowers come into bloom.

What to wear: Layers with a light raincoat.

Summer

From July to September, the days get warmer (around 78.8°F on average), with comfortably low humidity. This period sees little rain, and from June–July you can enjoy the long summer evenings with good light until around 9 p.m.

What to wear: Summer clothes. But evenings can be cool, so be sure to carry a light jacket or sweater.

Autumn

The weather in October is comparatively stable, with frequent sunny days. As temperatures begin to fall, the leaves change color and there may even be some snow at higher elevations. Temperatures fall still further in November and December, when rainfall is common.

What to wear: Layers and a raincoat

Winter

While it never gets bitterly cold, each year sees several days on which temperatures drop below freezing, although snowfall is rare. When snow falls on Mt. Hood, it often rains in Portland.

What to wear: Coat, fleece, waterproof shoes, skiwear.

Getting to Portland

Portland International Airport (PDX)

Travelers love PDX for its convenience, amenities, and local food and drink.

Travelers named PDX the best airport in the United States in *Travel + Leisure* surveys for the past four consecutive years. Why do they love PDX? An easy light rail connection to downtown, free Wi-Fi, top local food and drink (including microbreweries and craft spirits), and tax-free shopping (with no markups) are just a few of the reasons.

Air service

PDX is currently served by seventeen international and domestic airlines, which feature longstanding international direct flights to Tokyo and Amsterdam. Recently, additional direct flights to and from Toronto and Calgary have made accessing Portland even simpler.

Getting to and from the airport

The airport is located nine miles northeast of downtown Portland and is conveniently connected to the city center via MAX light rail.

Light rail

The MAX light rail red line is the easiest way to travel to and from the airport. Here are some quick facts:

—The trip between the airport and downtown Portland takes about thirty-eight minutes.

—An adult ticket costs $2.50 (youth and senior citizens $1.25). MAX ticket machines return change in coins, so small bills are recommended.

—You can roll your luggage on board.

—The first train of the day arrives at PDX at 4:45 a.m. The last train departs PDX at 11:50 p.m.

—The MAX station and ticket machines are located on the lower level, next to the south baggage claim area (turn right at the bottom of the escalator).

For complete schedules and more information, visit trimet.org/schedules/maxredline. htm.

Taxis

The average taxi fare from the airport to downtown is approximately $35 before gratuity. Radio Cab offers a discount with coupons available on their website. The one-way trip takes twenty to forty minutes. Taxis wait in the center section of the airport terminal's lower roadway outside baggage claim; to get back to the airport from the city center, you can order a cab through the city's main operators or from a hotel with a dedicated taxi stand.

Rideshare companies

Uber, Lyft, and ReachNow all operate legally in Portland. Hail them via smartphone app and your ride will arrive in about five minutes at the same center island outside baggage claim where taxis wait. A ride downtown from the airport costs approximately $25.

Shuttles

The Downtown Airport Express runs every thirty minutes ($14 one-way and $24 roundtrip to downtown and Lloyd Center/Convention Center hotels). Other shuttle services are available, and many airport hotels provide free shuttles.

When leaving the airport, you can find the Downtown Airport Express and other hotel shuttle buses on the terminal's lower roadway (outside baggage claim) on the far side of Island #2, toward the parking garage.

Getting Around Portland

MAX Light Rail

Portland's efficient light rail system connects the metro area and downtown core.

At the heart of Portland's world-class public transportation system is MAX light rail, with ninety-seven stations and sixty miles of track connecting the city, airport, and region.

MAX lines

MAX has five lines, all of which run through downtown:

—Blue Line (Hillsboro/City Center/Gresham)
—Green Line (Clackamas/City Center/PSU)
—Red Line (Airport/City Center/Beaverton)
—Yellow Line (Expo Center/City Center/PSU)
—Orange Line (Oak Grove/City Center/PSU)

MAX trains arrive about every fifteen minutes most of the day, every day. Service is less frequent in the early morning, midday, and evening.

How to ride MAX

1. You must have a validated ticket, bus transfer receipt, or pass before boarding MAX. Ticket machines and validators are located at the station. There are no fare boxes onboard MAX. Before boarding, buy your ticket from a ticket machine or with the mobile ticketing app—or validate your previously purchased ticket in the validator located near the ticket machine. A validated ticket is your proof of payment, good for two hours on MAX, buses, and the Portland Streetcar. (Full-day tickets are also available.) Keep your ticket until you have completed your trip. If you have a TriMet pass or bus transfer receipt, just board MAX and have a seat. (Check the expiration time at the top of your transfer; you may board until that time.)

2. Signs at the station indicate where to wait and when the next train is due. Signs on the front of each train identify the line (Blue,

Green, Red, Yellow, or Orange) and destination.

3. MAX trains stop at every station, so you don't need to signal the operator to get on or off. The station name is announced before each stop and appears on an overhead reader board.

Where to go on MAX

In addition to all of downtown and the Old Town Chinatown district, you can ride MAX to the following attractions:

—Washington Park (Oregon Zoo, Portland Children's Museum, World Forestry Center, Discovery Museum, Hoyt Arboretum, Portland Japanese, Gardens) – Red and Blue lines
—Moda Center (NBA arena and concert venue) —all lines except for Orange line
—Union Station (Amtrak) —Green and Yellow lines
—Portland International Airport (PDX)—Red line
—Portland State University (PSU) —Green, Orange, and Yellow lines
—Lloyd Center (shopping center) —Blue, Green, and Red lines
—Clackamas Town Center (shopping center)— Green line
—Providence Park (soccer) —Blue and Red lines
—Oregon Convention Center —Blue, Green, and Red lines
—Portland Expo Center —Yellow line

Portland Streetcar

The Portland Streetcar carries passengers through downtown, the Pearl District, the Central Eastside, and more.

In 2001, Portland built the nation's first modern-day streetcar: the sleek and modern Portland Streetcar. The original line, now known as the North South (NS) Line, travels through downtown from Portland State University to the downtown from Portland State University to the Nob Hill neighborhood via the popular shopping and dining area of the Pearl District.

A second line, known as the Central Loop or CL line, opened in 2012, adding 3.3 miles and twenty-eight stops to the original line. The extension line crosses the Willamette River at the Broadway Bridge and heads south through the Lloyd District, Rose Quarter (home to the NBA's Trail Blazers), Oregon Convention Center, and the dynamic Central Eastside neighborhood before making a stop at the Oregon Museum of Science and Industry (OMSI). This line consists of the A Loop, which runs clockwise, and the B loop, which runs counter-clockwise.

Bike tours & rentals

Rent a bike or bring your own to enjoy Portland on two wheels.

Portland has more than three hundred miles of bike lanes, paths, and low-traffic streets designated as "bike boulevards," making cycling one of the best ways to see the city. Many of these bikeways run right through the heart of downtown and past popular attractions, shops, and restaurants.

For guided tours, two outfitters have you covered. Cycle Portland Bike Tours rides around the bridges, breweries, and parks of Portland; Pedal Bike Tours stretches farther afield, with downtown tours, coffee- and volcano-themed jaunts, and trips that explore the nearby wine country and the Columbia River Gorge. Both companies also provide custom tours.

Portland By Cycle, from the Portland Bureau of Transportation, offers free guided bike rides on Tuesday and Wednesday evenings in July and August, as well as other rides and classes in the spring and fall.

Or rent a bike and explore on your own. Necessary accessories — including a pump, a helmet, suggested routes, and a bike bag — are included. Bike maps are available at

the Travel Portland Information Center in downtown's Pioneer Courthouse Square or online. You'll find cyclist-submitted tours at Ride Oregon Ride, and the Portland Bureau of Transportation has a list of their nine best rides around Portland. Additionally, My City Bikes offers route maps and resources for beginning cyclists with their app for Android and iPhone.

In 2016, Nike partnered with the City of Portland to launch BIKETOWN, a bike-sharing program that allows riders to rent bikes for a small fee at over one hundred stations throughout interior Portland. These stations are painted orange and are ubiquitous in all heavily trafficked areas of the city.

Green signs and painted road symbols designate the most popular bikeways in Portland, including the downtown Waterfront Loop. This circular, three-mile route hugs both sides of the Willamette River, crossing over the Steel and Hawthorne bridges, both of which are extremely bike-friendly. Well-marked signs along this loop lead to easily bikeable neighborhoods, as well as to the popular Springwater Corridor Trail.

Mountain bikers will find an ample network of trails in Forest Park, a 5,157-acre urban wilderness just ten minutes from the city center. At the Fat Tire Farm bike shop, located near the park's NW Thurman Street trailhead, visitors can rent both trail and street bikes.

MAX LIGHT RAIL
AND
PORTLAND STREETCAR

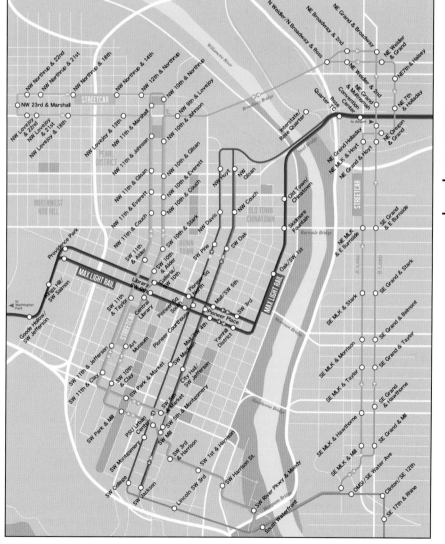

Central Eastside activities

Indoors and out, Portland's Central Eastside has everything
an urban explorer could hope to find.

Once a warehouse district, Portland's Central Eastside now offers all sorts of exciting ways to connect with natural wonders, innovative tastemakers, and great minds.

Located on the east bank of the Willamette River (and accessible via the Portland Streetcar), the Oregon Museum of Science and Industry (OMSI, p. 131) is a great bet for all-ages family entertainment. Check out permanent draws like a four-story movie theater, high-profile traveling displays like Body Worlds and Mythbusters, or special exhibits on everything from retro video games to nanotechnology.

In a titanic, century-old industrial laundry warehouse, Yale Union (YU, p. 126) boasts events, exhibits, and lectures that highlight emerging and established contemporary artists from around the globe. The Central Eastside's industrial aesthetic provides a fitting backdrop for Distillery Row (**1**), a collection of several neighborhood microdistilleries producing everything from homegrown cherry brandy to barrel-aged bourbon. Coffee is the only beverage sold at the Stumptown Annex (**2**), where beans are available for sale in bulk and tastings of their various blends come gratis.

Hipster biker bar White Owl Social Club (**3**) serves shoestring fries and rave-worthy beet burgers on its expansive patio, where patrons can roast s'mores on tabletop campfires. Housing hundreds of barrels filled with award-wining sour ales, Cascade Brewing Barrel House (p. 106) offers a tart tap list ripe with beers made with berries, apricots, and even local coffee.

Hosting nationally renowned headliners like Norm Macdonald and Maria Bamford, comedy battles, and weekly open mics, Helium Comedy Club (**4**) showcases some of the Northwest's best laughs in an intimate 275-seat venue where every seat is within sixty feet of the stage.

A 1.5-mile paved path along the banks of the Willamette, the Vera Katz Eastbank Esplanade (**5**) is a haven for bikers and joggers, offering panoramic city views and crossing a 1,200-foot floating walkway, the longest of its kind in the country, before linking up to the twenty-mile Springwater Corridor Trail (**6**). If you can't resist getting out on the water, Alder Creek Kayak (**7**) rents boats, and you can shove off from the dock near the Hawthorne Bridge.

1. Distillery Row
Ⓦ distilleryrowpdx.
com

2. Stumptown Annex
Ⓐ 100 SE Salmon St.
Ⓣ (503)808-9080
Ⓗ M-Sa 10 a.m.-4 p.m.
Ⓦ stumptowncoffee.
com

3. White Owl Social Club
Ⓐ 1305 SE 8th Ave.
Ⓣ (503)236-9672
Ⓗ 3 p.m.-2:30 a.m.
Ⓦ whiteowlsocialclub.
com

4. Helium Comedy Club
Ⓐ 1510 SE 9th Ave.
Ⓣ (888)643-8669
Ⓗ Tu-Th 6 p.m.-10 p.m.,
F-Sa 5:30 p.m.-12 a.m.
Ⓦ heliumcomedy.com

**5. Vera Katz
Eastbank Esplanade**
Ⓐ The Steel Bridge to
SE Caruthers St.
Ⓣ (503)823-7529

**6. Springwater
Corridor Trail**
Ⓐ SE Ivon St. to Boring

7. Alder Creek Kayak
Ⓐ 200 NE Tomahawk Island Dr.
Ⓣ (503)285-0464
Ⓗ M-Th 9 a.m.-6 p.m., F-Sa 9 a.m.-5 p.m.,
Su 9 a.m.-6 p.m.
Ⓦ aldercreek.com

Courtesy of Mt HoodTerritory.com

Travel Portland

Near Portland

Enjoy the bountiful natural wonders
that surround the Portland area

mthoodterritory.com

Mount Hood

Portland gives you access to the natural
beauty of Oregon, with each of the following
locations only one or two hours away by
bus or car. The Columbia River Gorge ranks
among the very few federally protected
National Scenic Areas in the United States. At
nearby Mount Hood—known among Japanese
tourists as "the American Mt. Fuji"—you can
enjoy hiking, skiing, snowboarding, and other
activities. Mt. Hood is a snowcapped gem
in western Oregon's verdant landscape, but
there is also the rugged and sublime coastline
as well as a bevy of state and national parks to
camp in and visit while touring the region.

The towering, 11,250-foot peak of this dormant volcano
stands around fifty miles east of Portland, among the Cascade Volcanic Arc. The mountain is also the site of Timberline Lodge (timberlinelodge.com), designated a National
Historic Landmark. The Timberline Lodge Ski Area is open
year-round, making for the longest ski season anywhere in
North America, and Mount Hood's many ski resorts also
include Mt. Hood Meadows, Cooper Spur Mountain Resort
and Ski Area, and Summit Ski Area, along with the Mt.
Hood Skibowl, North America's largest night ski park. And
aside from skiing and snowboarding, there are plenty of
other reasons to visit Timberline, from mountain climbing
to simply soaking up the sights.
mthoodterritory.com

Janis Misglavs

Janis Misglavs

Columbia River Gorge National Scenic Area

The nearest part of this sprawling, 291,000-acre canyon can be found just fourteen miles from Portland itself. With its breathtaking views, this is the ideal location for outdoor recreation, and the Historic Columbia River Highway, which threads the gorge, is a popular route for road trips. Moving east from Troutdale, the first highlight is Crown Point's Vista House observatory, which offers a panoramic view of the Columbia River Gorge. Built in 1916 and now listed on the National Register of Historic Places, Vista House is a memorial to the first pioneering settlers of Oregon and serves as both a rest stop for travelers and a tourist information center. The route of the Historic Columbia River Highway features numerous waterfalls big and small, including Oregon's largest and most famous: the 620-foot tall Multnomah Falls. Many of these waterfalls have their own hiking trails and picnic areas.
crgva.org

Heading along the gorge brings you to the town of Hood River. In winter, this outdoor paradise bustles with skiers, while popular summer pursuits include world-class windsurfing and kiteboarding. Hood River also has many art galleries and a host of craft breweries, including the renowned Full Sail Brewing Company (fullsailbrewing.com).
hoodriver.org

© Larry Geddis

The Oregon Coast

The cliffs of the Oregon Coast are a wonderland for photographers. Sometimes referred to as the "People's Coast," the entire shoreline of Oregon is designated as public lands. Places to visit include: Astoria, the oldest settlement west of the Rocky Mountains; Cannon Beach, a magnet for lovers of art and shopping; Tillamook, where the cheese factory attracts over a million visitors per year; Depoe Bay, popular for whale watching; Newport, home of the Oregon Coast Aquarium; and Florence, known for its sand dunes and the Sea Lion Caves, a network of caverns that form the breeding and wintering grounds for these aquatic mammals.
visittheoregoncoast.com

Willamette Valley Wine Country

Recent years have seen the popularity of Oregon wine grow. The Willamette Valley, a source of Oregon's best wines, occupies the same latitude as France's famous Burgundy region and is ideal for winemaking. Of Oregon's 700 wineries, 500 are in the Willamette Valley. This wine country is only nineteen miles from Portland, and many of the local vineyards offer tours and tasting rooms. The region is best known for Pinot Noir, but Chardonnay, Pinot Gris, and other grape varieties that favor a cool climate are also grown here, and regarded highly. Aside from grapes, the valley's fertile soil bears a diversity of produce that is served in fine restaurants across the region. Particularly common crops include hazelnuts, along with various berries. The rolling expanses of agricultural land also create memorable vistas.
willamettewines.com

How to Use This Book

How to Use

The information presented in this book was gathered between January and December 2016. We have done our best to ensure that this information is correct. However, in the time since publication, possible changes include business hours or locations of particular establishments. If you notice any such inconsistencies, please email us at info@truepdx.com.

18

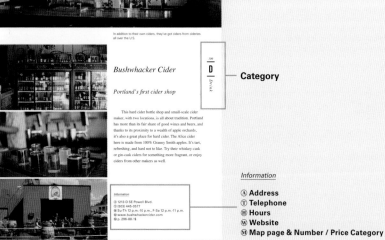

In addition to their own ciders, they've got ciders from cideries all over the U.S.

Bushwhacker Cider

Portland's first cider shop

This hard cider bottle shop and small-scale cider maker, with two locations, is all about tradition. Portland has more than its fair share of good wines and beers, and thanks to its proximity to a wealth of apple orchards, it's also a great place for hard cider. The Alice cider here is made from 100% Granny Smith apples. It's tart, refreshing, and hard not to like. Try their whiskey-cask or gin-cask ciders for something more fragrant, or enjoy ciders from other makers as well.

109
D
Drink

— **Category**

Information
Ⓐ 1212-D SE Powell Blvd.
Ⓣ (503) 445-0577
Ⓗ Su-Th 12 p.m.-10 p.m., F-Sa 12 p.m.-11 p.m.
Ⓦ www.bushwhackercider.com
Ⓜ p. 296-B8 / $

Information

Ⓐ **Address**
Ⓣ **Telephone**
Ⓗ **Hours**
Ⓦ **Website**
Ⓜ **Map page & Number / Price Category**

Abbreviations and Symbols
(Terms not included here not applicable)

*2 Addresses
Ave. – Avenue / Blvd. – Boulevard / Rd. – Road
St. – Street / Hwy. – Highway / Ct. – Court

*3 Price Categories
The system below is used to indicate prices for most dining establishments, bars, cafes, and accommodations. Although credit cards are accepted at most establishments, those with a "Buy Local" mark at the register generally prefer customers to pay by cash. By looking

around for special offers, it is often possible to find hotels at somewhat cheaper rates.

$-----------dining Under $10 / accommodations Under $100
$$ -------- dining $11–20 / accommodations up to $150
$$$------- dining $21– 40 / accommodations up to $250
$$$$----- dining Over $40 / accommodations up to $350

Although dining establishments do not charge taxes to customers, plan to leave a gratuity equal to 15%–20% of the overall bill.
* Depending on the number of rooms, some hotels may charge an accommodation tax of 11.5%–13.5%.

Area Guide

Portland is broadly divided into five main geographical districts. Each of these consists of several neighborhoods organized around a main street. To many visitors, the distinctive characteristics of the various neighborhoods are as much a part of Portland's charm as the city's many parks and museums.

SOUTHWEST (Map p.288)

Cultural District
The defining trait of this downtown area is its abundant greenery. The South Park Blocks are flanked on each side by high-rise apartment buildings, and several of the city's key cultural facilities are located here.

Pioneer District
The Pioneer Place Shopping Center and other department stores in this district carry a range of top brands. At the heart of the neighborhood is Pioneer Courthouse Square, known as "Portland's living room."

West End / Downtown
Until relatively recently, this part of downtown was not known as a hotspot for dining and culture. But since the opening of Ace Hotel and a streetcar route along 10th and 11th Avenues, the area has undergone a major resurgence.

NORTHWEST (Map p. 290)

Northwest Portland / Nob Hill
This district, known by locals as Nob Hill, sits at the foot of the West Hills, which is home to Portland's beloved hiking haven Forest Park. Forest Park is one of the largest urban forests in the United States. In addition to numerous gorgeous Victorian and Colonial mansions, the tree-lined streets of this area boast many modern apartment buildings, as well as plenty of popular shops, restaurants, and bars.

Old Town / Chinatown
Beneath these streets run the Shanghai Tunnels. According to local lore, these subterranean passageways were where local men were transported against their will to serve as labor on ships coming in and out of port. Nowadays, this bustling district is known for art.

Pearl District
This area is a model for mixed-use urban redevelopment. A former industrial area was transformed into a hub of sophistication, with swathes of buildings with LEED-designated status.

NORTH / NORTHEAST (Map p. 292 / Map p. 294)

Alberta Arts District / Killingsworth
The grassroots development of this culturally diverse district accommodates artists, businesspeople, creatives, young families, and students. Most of the fun and activity in terms of bars, restaurants, shops, and galleries is centered on NE Alberta Street between Martin Luther King Boulevard and NE 33rd Avenue.

North Mississippi Avenue
A great area to stroll around, window shop, and enjoy street food. The district has an arty, youthful vibe, combining renovated old buildings and new structures built to eco-friendly specifications.

North Williams
Since this neighborhood's designation as a cycle-friendly "bike corridor" several years ago, it has become a hub for eco-friendly apartments and stores.

SOUTHEAST (Map p. 296)

Hawthorne and Belmont
With its freewheeling vibe, Hawthorne Boulevard has historically been the heart of Portland's hippie culture. Today hippies, hipsters, and a diverse population live, work, and play in this area (including Belmont street to the north) that is home to the nearby beautiful, historic, 28-acre Laurelhurst Park as well as many independent and vintage shops, cafes, bars, and food carts.

Central Eastside
Among the warehouses and railway tracks of this district, which is home to Portland's historic Produce Row, are all sorts of restaurants, bars, clubs, furniture shops, and more. The industrial bays blend seamlessly with a hip community atmosphere. Development has hastened since the opening of the Central Loop streetcar line in 2012.

East Burnside
Until the last decade, this district was characterized in large part by industry. Since then it has been transformed by an influx of new breweries, restaurants, shops, and food carts. All of this development coincides with the opening of the stylish Jupiter Hotel and its subterranean music venue the Doug Fir in 2004.

Division/Clinton
This historic neighborhood lies south of Hawthorne Boulevard. SE Division Street, primarily between 10th and 50th Avenues, is crammed with shops and some of the city's most acclaimed restaurants, making for a lot of foot-traffic all hours of the day. Although Clinton Street is mainly a residential area, it is also home to several funky, independently-owned businesses.

28th and Burnside Street
The tree-lined half-mile of 28th Avenue from NE Glisan Street to SE Stark Street is packed with popular restaurants, bars, and shops—perfect for a leisurely walk with plenty of fun stops along the way.

The lobby of downtown's Ace
Hotel is a fixture of Portland's
hip yet inclusive scene. It's a
place where anyone can walk
in off the street and hang out
— an urban theater of people
coming and going, meeting
friends, drinking Stumptown
Coffee, reading, working, and
perfectly embodying the spirit
of Portland.

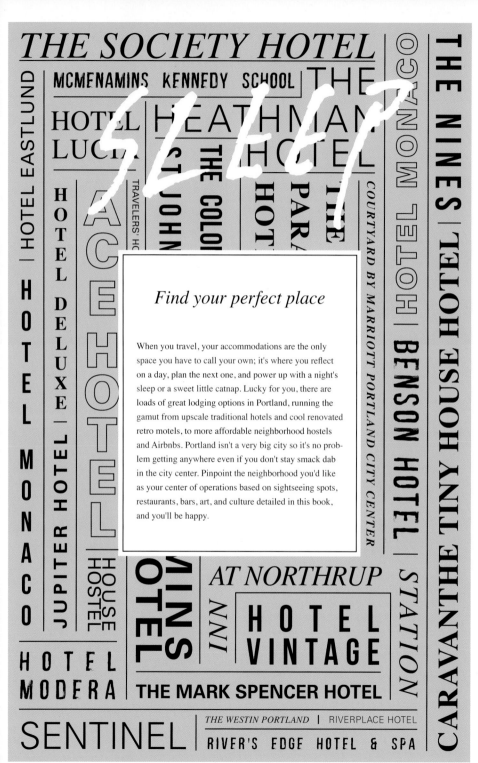

THE SOCIETY HOTEL

SLEEP

MCMENAMINS KENNEDY SCHOOL · THE HEATHMAN HOTEL · HOTEL LUCIA · HOTEL EASTLUND · HOTEL DELUXE · ACE HOTEL · TRAVELERS' HO... · THE COLO... · ST JOHN... · THE PAR... · HOTEL MONACO · THE NINES · HOTEL MONACO · BENSON HOTEL · COURTYARD BY MARRIOTT PORTLAND CITY CENTER · CARAVAN THE TINY HOUSE HOTEL · JUPITER HOTEL · HOUSE HOSTEL · HOTEL MONACO · ...AINS ...OTEL · INN AT NORTHRUP STATION · HOTEL VINTAGE · THE MARK SPENCER HOTEL · HOTEL MODERA · SENTINEL · THE WESTIN PORTLAND · RIVERPLACE HOTEL · RIVER'S EDGE HOTEL & SPA

Find your perfect place

When you travel, your accommodations are the only space you have to call your own; it's where you reflect on a day, plan the next one, and power up with a night's sleep or a sweet little catnap. Lucky for you, there are loads of great lodging options in Portland, running the gamut from upscale traditional hotels and cool renovated retro motels, to more affordable neighborhood hostels and Airbnbs. Portland isn't a very big city so it's no problem getting anywhere even if you don't stay smack dab in the city center. Pinpoint the neighborhood you'd like as your center of operations based on sightseeing spots, restaurants, bars, art, and culture detailed in this book, and you'll be happy.

The Society Hotel

Bridging the gap between hotel and hostel

Information

Ⓐ 203 NW 3rd Ave.
Ⓣ (503)445-0444
Ⓦ thesocietyhotel.com
Ⓜ p. 290-47 / $$

The Mariners Building, built in 1881 by the Portland Seamen's Friend Society, originally opened as a safe boarding house for sailors (void of booze and red light activities) who came through Portland. Jessie Burke, Jonathan Cohen, Matt Siegel, and Gabe Genauer acquired the Old Town/Chinatown Portland building in 2013, and after undergoing a full renovation, during which they retained the original cast-iron facade, they re-launched it as the artful Society Hotel.

The hotel boasts private modern rooms and suites as well as the coolest bunk room you'll likely ever set foot in. The Bunk Room's twenty-four bunk beds each have their own curtain, outlets for charging, and personal reading lights for about $40/night per person.

The top floors of the building hadn't been touched since 1945, so when the management team that purchased the building stepped into this area after 68 years, they felt like time travelers. This hotel is the symbol of modern Portland. It's hip, modern, casual, and central.

The first floor cafe is ideal for a bit of relaxation or to meet up with friends. You can also head up to the rooftop to enjoy beautiful views of downtown. The front desk staff is very friendly and helpful. We highly encourage you to consider The Society Hotel when booking your next trip to Portland.

The rooms at Ace feature lowkey design and cleverly incorporate decor from pre-renovation such as salvaged industrial furnishings and military surplus items. There are two types of rooms: those with shared bathrooms and those with private ones.

Ace Hotel

An ultracool Portland take on what a hotel should be

Information

Ⓐ 1022 SW Stark St.
Ⓣ (503) 228-2277
Ⓦ acehotel.com/portland
Ⓜ p. 288-16 / $$$

Ace Hotel raised its global profile when the hotelier opened a property in Panama in 2013 and in London's Shoreditch in 2014. Like the Shoreditch Ace, downtown Portland's Ace lobby is open to the public, and you will find people there working, reading, drinking coffee, and killing time in an impromptu community. There's also a photo booth in the lobby where it's fun to snap photos before heading out on the town. Despite its international cachet, Ace Hotel is firmly rooted in Portland, and it's known as one of the coolest spots to stay downtown because of details such as record players and vinyl in many rooms. The hotel is a block from Powell's Books, a block from the Pearl, and it's right next to the ever-popular restaurant Clyde Common with its exceptional bar. The Ace has reimagined the modern hotel, making it fun, ultracool, and full of art. With popularity has come steeper rates, but we still highly recommend it. Oh, and you can bring your dog along. They'll even provide dog treats.

Hotel Modera

Sleek, central, and tranquil

This sleek, modernist hotel in the heart of Portland's theater district has a spacious lobby and a distinctive central courtyard featuring outdoor firepits. The room decor is subdued and calming with well-designed monotone fabrics, finishes, and local artwork. Some rooms and suites offer great views of Portland. The hotel's restaurant and bar, Nel Centro, serves tasty cuisine inspired by southeastern France and northern Italy, and the adjoining bar is a great place to meet friends, especially to gather around the courtyard firepits. Added bonus to staying at Hotel Modera: excellent public transit access.

Information

Ⓐ 515 SW Clay St.
Ⓣ (503) 484-1084
Ⓦ hotelmodera.com
Ⓜ p. 288-69 / $$

Sentinel Hotel

A century of history and European style give this hotel gravitas

The Sentinel is listed on the National Register of Historic Places and traces its roots back to the Seward Hotel built in 1909. The building was renovated in 1997 and operated as the Governor Hotel until 2014 when it got a fresh redesign as The Sentinel with everything from honey-producing beehives on the rooftop to newly-acquired modern art throughout the building. There are all sorts of plush rooms and suites to choose from. Some of the swankier ones even have private rooftop firepits and wet bars. On the first floor you can dine at the old-school classy restaurant Jake's Grill or head over to the new chic bar/lounge Jackknife, which features DJs most nights.

Information

Ⓐ 614 SW 11th Ave.
Ⓣ (503) 224-3400
Ⓦ sentinelhotel.com
Ⓜ p. 288-51 / $$$

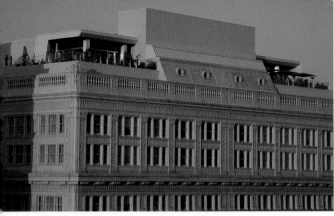
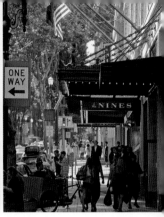

The Nines

Luxury hotel with impressive dining and views

Information

Ⓐ 525 SW Morrison St.
Ⓣ (877) 229-9995
Ⓦ thenines.com
Ⓜ p. 288-59 / $$$

The Nines was originally a department store facing Pioneer Courthouse Square; now it's a swank hotel with a gorgeous atrium and a balance of classic and modern art and elements. It doesn't get more central than this with many Portland tourist destinations within walking distance. The top floor houses executive chef Gregory Gourdet's popular Asian-fusion restaurant and lounge Departure, plus some of Portland's best views.

The Jupiter Hotel

Renovated trendy motel attached to music venue

The Jupiter Hotel is a 1950s-era motel on Lower East Burnside remodeled into a stylish hotel and cultural hub for creatives and a mostly younger crowd. The Jupiter has its own bar and dining room and one of the city's most beloved music venues, the Doug Fir Lounge (p. 143). In every hotel room one wall is adorned with a floor-to-ceiling graphic design ranging from a portrait of Marilyn Monroe to one of John Lennon. Keep in mind that the club vibe often spills outside to the firepit on show nights so it can get loud on the bar side of the hotel in the wee hours. Guests get free bus passes which is a nice combo of sustainability plus hospitality. Ask about the 420 hotel cannabis package if you are so inclined.

Information

Ⓐ 800 E Burnside St.
Ⓣ (503) 230-9200
Ⓦ jupiterhotel.com
Ⓜ p. 296-4 / $$

The Colony St. Johns

Creative space in St. Johns with lodging

The Colony is a renovated 1950s funeral parlor located in the St. Johns neighborhood on the east side of the river, north of downtown. The space itself is a little bit hard to define because there so many things available. There is an event space with a large ballroom and dance studio, conference rooms, a well-equipped commercial kitchen available for hourly or monthly use, and of course, lodging. The Colony's three units include two stylish apartments (Bones & Arrows and The Landing Pad) and a funky late-seventies RV trailer with a king size bed and compact fridge (The Hide Away). This is the place to stay if you want Portland flavor but don't want to be too close to the hustle and bustle.

Information

Ⓐ 7525 N Richmond Ave.
Ⓣ (503) 206-7051
Ⓦ thecolonystjohns.com / $$

Caravan
The Tiny House Hotel

Stay here for a test run of scaled-down living

Information

Ⓐ 5009 NE 11th Ave.
Ⓣ (503) 288-5225
Ⓦ tinyhousehotel.com
Ⓜ p. 294-10 / $$$

The U.S. has seen a booming trend in recent years in tiny houses that support simple, downsized, low-cost living, and easy-on-the-planet lifestyles. At Caravan on NE Alberta Street, six different houses of varying tininess (120-170 square feet) sleep from one to four on an urban lot with a communal firepit (all-you-can-eat s'mores provided while you stay!) ping pong, a barbecue, and more. Each unit has a hot shower, flush toilet, kitchen, and electric heat. This is a fun and lively neighborhood to stay in with plenty of food carts, co-ops, galleries, shops, restaurants, and bars to explore.

McMenamins Kennedy School

Kathleen Nyberg

Stay at one of Portland's most unique, fun hotels that occupies a former elementary school and serves its own beer, coffee, and wine in the old classrooms, auditorium, and gym.

Ⓐ 5736 NE 33rd Ave. / ⓣ (503) 249-3983
Ⓦ mcmenamins.com
Ⓜ p. 294-5 / $$

Hotel Lucia

This modern, centrally-located, cushy boutique hotel just down from Pioneer Square is filled with art, including photos by Pulitzer Prize-winning photographers.

Ⓐ 400 SW Broadway
ⓣ (503) 225-1717
Ⓦ hotellucia.com / Ⓜ p. 288-34 / $$$

Benson Hotel

Built in 1913, this downtown luxury hotel is known for hosting U.S. Presidents and treating all of its guests with the same respective regal hospitality.

Ⓐ 309 SW Broadway / ⓣ (503) 228-2000
Ⓦ bensonhotel.com
Ⓜ p. 288-31 / $$$$

Hotel Eastlund

This former Red Lion Inn near the Oregon Convention Center, was snazzed up and reborn in 2015, adding Altabira City Tavern on the rooftop.

Ⓐ 1021 NE Grand Ave.
ⓣ (503) 235-2100
Ⓦ hoteleastlund.com
Ⓜ p. 294-31 / $$$

The Heathman Hotel

Built in 1927, this downtown luxury hotel boasts its own high-end chocolate shop, destination fine dining, and Russian tea service in its Tea Court Lounge from chef Vitaly Paley.

Ⓐ 1001 SW Broadway / ⓣ (503) 241-4100
Ⓦ portland.heathmanhotel.com
Ⓜ p. 288-57 / $$$

Hotel Monaco

Originally the Lipman Wolfe Department Store, which opened in 1912, the Hotel Monaco is now a lavish, sophisticated boutique hotel with the Red Star Tavern.

Ⓐ 506 SW Washington St. / ⓣ (503) 222-0001
Ⓦ monaco-portland.com
Ⓜ p. 288-37 / $$$$

Inn at Northrup Station

Every room is a suite with a kitchen and satellite television at this Nob Hill hotel with colorful pop furnishings and decor.

Ⓐ 2025 NW Northrup St.
ⓣ (503) 224-0543
Ⓦ northrupstation.com
Ⓜ p. 290-7 / $$$

Courtyard by Marriott Portland City Center

This urban chic, centrally-located Marriott Hotel has a 24-hour fitness center and the open-late new take on a diner: The Original Dinerant.

Ⓐ 550 SW Oak St.
ⓣ (503) 505-5000
Ⓦ courtyardportlandcitycenter.com
Ⓜ p. 288-36 / $$$

McMenamins Crystal Hotel

Torsten Kjellstrand / travelportland.com

Every room in this super funky, fun hotel is inspired by a song or performance at the adjacent Crystal Ballroom music venue and includes admission to the below street-level saltwater soaking pool.

Ⓐ 303 SW 12th Ave. / ⓣ (503) 972-2670
Ⓦ mcmenamins.com/mcmenamins
Ⓜ p. 288-7 / $$

The Paramount Hotel

The rooms and suites at this upscale hotel, which is a 4-minute walk from the Portland Art Museum, are well-equipped, and you can upgrade to ones with whirlpool bathtubs and balconies.

Ⓐ 808 SW Taylor St. / Ⓣ (503) 223 -9900
Ⓦ portlandparamount.com
Ⓜ p. 288-54 / $$$

River's Edge Hotel & Spa

Stephen Cridland

If you want to decompress, yet still be central, this stylish hotel offers a quieter setting with views of the Willamette River and its own spa.

Ⓐ 0455 SW Hamilton Ct.
Ⓣ (503) 802-5800
Ⓦ riversedgehotel.com
$$

Travelers' House Hostel

This is Portland's newest hostel in a fun Northeast Portland neighborhood that opened in 2014. It's bike friendly (bike maps, rentals, and tours) and boasts a large, well-designed kitchen.

Ⓐ 710 N Alberta St. / Ⓣ (503) 954-2304
Ⓦ travelershouse.org
Ⓜ p. 292-13 / $

The Westin Portland

If you stay at downtown's Westin Hotel you can enjoy the fitness studio, in-room spa treatments, and food and drink from the Daily Grill.

Ⓐ 750 SW Alder St.
Ⓣ (503) 294-9000
Ⓦ westin.com/portland
Ⓜ p. 288-55 / $$$$

RiverPlace Hotel

Views of the city lights and Willamette River are the draw here, along with nearby Tom McCall Waterfront Park and the Tilikum Crossing pedestrian and light-rail bridge that takes you to OMSI.

Ⓐ 1510 SW Harbor Way / Ⓣ (503) 228-3233
Ⓦ riverplacehotel.com
Ⓜ p. 288-70 / $$$$

Hotel Vintage

This chic downtown hotel has all of the amenities you'd expect as well as rooms with outdoor hot tubs, beds for pets, a daily wine hour featuring local wineries, and dining at Pazzo Ristorante.

Ⓐ 422 SW Broadway / Ⓣ (503) 228-1212
Ⓦ hotelvintage-portland.com
Ⓜ p. 288-35 / $$$

29

S

Sleep

The Mark Spencer Hotel

Centrally located, modern hotel with 101 rooms and suites and all sorts of guest perks including a complimentary continental breakfast, afternoon tea, and evening wine reception.

Ⓐ 409 SW 11th Ave. / Ⓣ (503) 224-3293
Ⓦ markspencer.com
Ⓜ p. 288-11 / $$

Hotel deLuxe

The 1912 Hotel deLuxe is glamorous yet modern, with a Hollywood heyday feel. It's home to Gracie's Restaurant and the popular retro cocktail lounge the Driftwood Room.

Ⓐ 729 SW 15th Ave.
Ⓣ (503) 219-2094
Ⓦ hoteldeluxeportland.com / Ⓜ p. 288-2 / $$

Atelier Ace

A cultural platform that fosters fresh ideas, engaged dialogue, and compassionate curiosity

Information
@atelierace.com

Interview with

RYAN BUKSTEIN *Vice President of Brand*

Please tell us what Atelier Ace does?

Atelier Ace is the studio, workshop, and creative services arm behind Ace Hotel Group. From its headquarters in Portland, OR and New York, NY, Atelier Ace provides architecture, interior, graphic and product design, marketing, PR, development, digital presence, events, storytelling, and cultural engineering for each Ace Hotel location. We don't outsource our creative and marketing efforts. Instead, we choose to handle them internally, as a close knit team of people who know and understand Ace well — and care deeply about even its smallest details.

Comprised of a motley crew of multi-disciplinary thinkers, writers, artists, interior designers, architects, web developers, and conceptualists, Atelier Ace makes it possible for Ace to provide an inspiring, cohesive,

and meaningful experience for guests and friends.

How did the Atelier Ace start and do you feel the city of Portland has been changed since then?

When Ace Hotel started in Seattle in 1999, it was the brainchild of the original partners: Alex Calderwood, Wade Weigel, and Doug Herrick. Atelier Ace started in 2007, when the team was working on Ace Hotel Portland. It originally operated out of a tiny mezzanine room above Ace Hotel Portland's 1,200-square-foot event space. Yes, the city of Portland has changed immensely, but that's what cities do, and it's one of the reasons we love them. There is an ever-evolving quality about Portland, and that brings with it new ways of looking at the city. It's bittersweet, too, of course, but we've welcomed

new restaurants, new art, and new culture to our home. Change is inevitable, and it's ultimately pretty exciting.

What do you think about the Ace Hotel's role in cities?

We've come to recognize that the more we grow, the more vital and active our role in cities will be. We're both honored and humbled by that responsibility, and we're learning more about how we can give back to our communities in each city we inhabit. The funds can only be spent within the city, so it comes full circle. We're always looking for ways to engage, connect with, and sustain each other.

What is the DNA of Ace?

We appreciate the honesty of materials and the spirit of the cities we live in. We like buildings with good bones and we have an affinity for soulful craft and engineering. At

our core is collaboration; we work alongside artists and friends we love, following our instincts and sharing stories. We hope to act as a conduit for creativity — a cultural platform that fosters fresh ideas, engaged dialogue, and compassionate curiosity.

What is Atelier Ace's upcoming projects?

In 2016, we cut the ribbons on both Ace Hotel Pittsburgh and Ace Hotel New Orleans. It's been an incredibly exciting and fulfilling experience. Recently we worked with the team behind New York's Grand Banks to open Seaworthy, an oyster and cocktail bar a few doors down from Ace New Orleans. We're also collaborating with a number of brands for our online shop and front desk retail, including a pair of slippers with the leather artisans Hender Scheme and a collection of travel bags with the cult brand Porter by Yoshida Kaban.

31

Airbnb

Airbnb gives travelers the option to stay in residential homes or apartments belonging to folks rooted in Portland. As a result, booking an Airbnb can make your trip feel a bit more grounded, as if you are actually a Portlander, not just a visitor. Portland has plenty of charming hosts as well as an Airbnb office that opened in 2014. Since the Portland lifestyle is such a big part of the city's appeal, Airbnb is certainly worth considering.

Sleep | S | 32

Interview with

REBECCA ROSENFELT
Growth Product Manager, Airbnb, San Francisco

Please explain to us the role of the Portland office.

Airbnb is headquartered in San Francisco, and the Portland office is the hub for North America customer service operations. It's just a short flight from San Francisco, so it's great to have the team so close so we can collaborate.

What are the unique characteristics and the concept of the office?

The office is like nothing I've ever seen —it's an innovative mix of different kinds of work spaces. There are stand-up booths, communal tables, and little huts you can work inside. I'm actually most impressed with the acoustics engineering. Since this is a customer service office, people are generally on the phone with customers, but it's amazingly quiet in the office. They've done a great job thinking not just about the visuals, but also the audio component.

What makes Portland attractive as a city?

Speaking from my personal point of view, the appeal of Portland is its immense livability. It's just an easy place to be—the city is incredibly progressive in terms of zoning and planning, so there's fantastic public transit, it's great for biking, and overall it's more affordable than many major US cities. On top of that, the great quality of life has inspired people to move there and open restaurants, cocktail bars, and coffee shops, so the food is world-class. There's also a world-famous bookstore called Powell's City of Books (p. 236)—visitors often can spend a full day there browsing. You won't get the hustle and bustle of New York City or Tokyo, but in my view, you get all the perks of a major city with the benefits of a very livable town.

What are the differences in Airbnb features/ services in Portland as compared to other cities in the US?

One thing I notice that's different about Airbnb in Portland, again based on my personal experience, is how enthusiastic Portland hosts are about helping guests find the best local experiences. I think part of that has to do with the culture of quality food and quality life—hosts are really excited to share tips with guests. The city has also done a lot to enable residents to host, which is so great.

33

S

Sleep

Airbnb

We asked Rebecca Rosenfelt of Airbnb to name her top five favorite listings. Each host has something unique to offer. Check the Airbnb website for more information.

PDX's Famous Atomic Ranch on Mt Tabor-King Beds!

This spacious flat is located right at the base of Mount Tabor. Situated on a 1,400-square-foot lot, it even has a private patio. A bus stop one block away will take you downtown in fifteen minutes. On top of that, there's a pair of super comfy king-size beds; the best that money can buy, according to the host.

<u>Information</u>

Ⓐ SE Thorburn St.
Property type: House
Room type: Entire home/apt
Ⓦ airbnb.com/rooms/2552957

> *Rebecca's Comment*
> I've stayed here before. It's really well styled, and close to hiking. A good option for larger groups.

Carriage House on Urban Farm

This 1,000-square-foot apartment is located on a one-acre urban farm. This is the place to stay if you're looking for a balance between urban excitement and privacy to relax. Public transportation is within walking distance.

<u>Information</u>

Ⓐ NE Going St.
Property type: Apartment
Room type: Entire home/apt
Ⓦ airbnb.com/rooms/981753

> *Rebecca's Comment*
> Urban farming is very popular in Portland, and here's a way to experience it up close!

Serene & Elegant
North Tabor Home

This private backyard oasis is located near Laurelhurst & Mt. Tabor. The elegant and serene ambience of this quiet home provides a respite from your busy activities touring and playing in Portland. Close to public bus routes, and the MAX is a 12-15 minute walk.

Information

Ⓐ NE 52nd Ave.
Property type: House
Room type: Entire home/apt
Ⓦ airbnb.com/rooms/3379249

Rebecca's Comment

This host from Portland offers a true experience of "living like a local."

Handcrafted
Japanese Carpentry Too

This unique, handcrafted building is located in the hip Mississippi Arts District. The building itself reflects a love of Old World and natural elements. The detailed woodwork complements the modern furniture and arty interior design. Its location is perfect for walking around town.

Information

Ⓐ N Michigan Ave.
Property type: House
Room type: Entire home/apt
Ⓦ airbnb.com/rooms/4546296

Rebecca's Comment

This host is really into Japanese carpentry, which is beautiful. I'd love to learn more about their passion.

Portland Pearl District
1BR Apt

Located on a quiet street across from a park, the lively Pearl District is just down the street. It's a great location for business and vacation rentals. The bedrooms are more spacious than your typical listing. It's a luxurious apartment with high-end decor and thoughtful amenities.

Information

Ⓐ NW Park Ave.
Property type: Apartment
Room type: Entire home/apt
Ⓦ airbnb.com/rooms/2429195

Rebecca's Comment

This place is a great spot right downtown.

The James Beard Awards, the "Oscars" of food, recognize restaurants that contribute to U.S. culinary culture. In 2016, eighteen Oregon chefs and establishments made it to the semifinals. Beloved pastry chef Kristen Murray of Màurice was a semifinalist for Outstanding Pastry Chef.

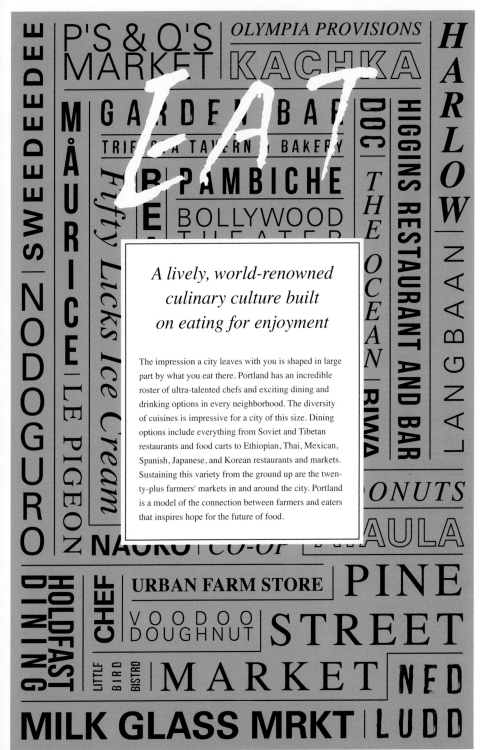

SWEEDEEDEE | P'S & Q'S MARKET | OLYMPIA PROVISIONS | KACHKA | HARLOW

MAURICE | GARDEN BAR | DOC | HIGGINS RESTAURANT AND BAR

Fifty Licks Ice Cream | TRIFECTA TAVERN & BAKERY | PAMBICHE | BOLLYWOOD THEATER

OZODOGURO | LE PIGEON | THE OCEAN | RIWA | LANGBAAN

EAT

A lively, world-renowned culinary culture built on eating for enjoyment

The impression a city leaves with you is shaped in large part by what you eat there. Portland has an incredible roster of ultra-talented chefs and exciting dining and drinking options in every neighborhood. The diversity of cuisines is impressive for a city of this size. Dining options include everything from Soviet and Tibetan restaurants and food carts to Ethiopian, Thai, Mexican, Spanish, Japanese, and Korean restaurants and markets. Sustaining this variety from the ground up are the twenty-plus farmers' markets in and around the city. Portland is a model of the connection between farmers and eaters that inspires hope for the future of food.

NAURU | CO-OP | PAULA | ONUTS

HOLDFAST DINING | CHEF | URBAN FARM STORE | PINE

LITTLE BIRD BISTRO | VOODOO DOUGHNUT | STREET

MARKET | NED

MILK GLASS MRKT | LUDD

Pine Street Market

Portland's first diverse food hall

WIZBANGBAR
SALT & STRAW

Soft Serve Flavors 3.25
Vanilla Custard
Chocolate Fudge
Sea Salt & Caramel
Hops & Garam Masala
Roasted Strawberry Coconut

Dipped Cones 4.25
Single Origin Chocolate Shell
Oregon Black Raspberry Shell
Toasted White Chocolate &
Cardamom Shell

Special Sundaes 8.50
• Peanut Butter & Jelly
  w/ PB Cereal & Vanilla Custard
• Brown Butter Blondie & Hot Fudge
  w/ Pralined Hazelnut Crunch &
  Chocolate Fudge Soft Serve
• Rhubarb Sour Straws
  w/ Rosé Lemon Curd &
  Vanilla Custard Soft Serve
• Ritz Pie a la mode
  w/ Apples, Sea Salt &
  Caramel Soft Serve

Concretes
Homemade Cookies &
Salted Almond
Salted Malted
Chip Cookie D

Extras
Waffle Cone, Ho
Caramel, Ho
Sprinkles, Por

Opened in spring of 2016 to much buzz and acclaim, 10,000-square-foot Pine Street Market is a crowed-pleasing modern, high-end food hall located downtown near the Willamette River in a historic building. Pine Street takes the mall food court to a whole new level. First, there's booze. Excellent booze. Second, most of the small counter-service restaurants and cafes in Pine Street's communal seating open floor plan are beloved independent Portland businesses with other larger, more established locations around town. The lineup at Pine Street includes everything from Korean food to pizza and burgers, rotisserie chicken, frankfurters, ramen, and even fancypants soft serve ice cream.

Nine of Portland's best and brightest call Pine Street home including coffee-centric Barista's Brass Bar, Kim Jong Grillin's Kim Jong Smokehouse, Kure Juice Bar, Tokyo's Marukin Ramen, Olympia Provisions' Wurst, Josh Scofield's Pollo Bravo, Ken Forkish's Trifecta Annex, and Salt & Straw's Wiz Bang Bar. It's a beautifully renovated space with towering skylights, historic exposed brick, chunky wood beams, and so many tasty choices. There really is something for everyone at Pine Street, open daily from 8 a.m. to 11 p.m.

Information

Ⓐ 126 SW 2nd Ave.
Ⓗ 8 a.m.-11 p.m. daily
Ⓦ pinestreetpdx.com
Ⓜ p. 288-42

Sweedeedee

From-scratch,
small but mighty North Portland cafe

Sweedeedee is a super sweet, full-of-character, delicious counter-service cafe in North Portland. It's named after a song by Astoria, Oregon-based folk musician Michael Hurley who is very close to the folks around the corner at Portland-record-haven Mississippi Records (p. 136). Vinyl and cassette tape music is on constant rotation at Sweedeedee and there's also a permanent slow-down-and-enjoy-the-day vibe to the place that makes you want to stay even after you've finished your food.

Cafe owner Eloise Augustyn is a Portland native. According to her, "I pursued a dream of opening a country-style cafe for many years. I wanted it to be homey, a place for locals. A place where people come to unwind and enjoy healthy, conscientious food. That was the concept behind this business."

She succeeded. An always-changing handwritten menu hangs on the wall, housemade preserves line the shelves, and simple, delicious, unfussy fare is prepared in the small exposed kitchen.

As soon as the cafe opens its doors, patiently waiting patrons filter in. Lines are common even on weekdays. Don't fret, it gives you a chance to look over the menu and the display of freshly baked pastries and figure out your order.

Bottom right: The ever-popular Sweedeedee Breakfast Plate ($10). Bottom left: Honey Cake with Fruit & Cream ($5); naturally the preserves are made in house. Other options include Granola ($6.50), sandwiches (from $7), etc. Coffee is on the get-a-cup-at-the-counter-and-pour-your-own system.

Says Augustyn, "A lot of small-scale farms in the Willamette Valley grow amazing produce. I'm thrilled to be able to put that produce to the best possible use by cooking and serving it to my customers here. It's very important to know where the food you eat comes from. We don't put anything on the menu here, no dish, no ingredient, without careful thought."

The space reflects Augustyn's priorities: Many of the objects in it are handmade, the decor is full of character, and everything is environmentally friendly and artful. Augustyn adds, "The community of people who eat at this cafe is growing all the time. I feel lucky to be able to make food for them."

If you are lucky enough to dine at Sweedeedee try make time to stop by some of the other lovely businesses right around the corner, such as Mississippi Records (p. 136), Cherry Sprout Produce, and The Red Fox Bar.

Information

Ⓐ 5202 N Albina Ave.
Ⓣ (503) 946-8087
Ⓗ M-Th 9 a.m.-3 p.m., F-Sa 8 a.m.-3 p.m.,
   Su 8 a.m.-2 p.m.
Ⓦ sweedeedee.com
Ⓜ p. 292-10 / $$

Harlow

*Supercharge your body
with fresh-pressed wheatgrass shots*

Information

Ⓐ 3632 SE Hawthorne Blvd.
Ⓣ (971) 255-0138
Ⓗ M-Sa 8 a.m.-9 p.m., Su 8 a.m.-3 p.m.
Ⓦ harlowpdx.com
Ⓜ p. 296-65 / $$

Portland is pretty fantastic these days for vegans and vegetarians. High-quality organic fruits, vegetables, and grains are readily available, and plenty of chefs in recent years have moved away from meats and toward veggie-centric menus. Harlow doesn't serve any meat or fish, and it's always packed with health-conscious diners. One menu highlight is a wheatgrass shot ($3), freshly pressed from the tender leaves of young wheat shoots. When you place an order, a swath of wheatgrass is harvested from what looks like a patch of lawn on the counter (facing page, top left). Freshly juiced wheatgrass has a surprising sweetness with a lot of green tea flavor and very little bitterness. After a brilliant kelly-green wheatgrass shot, many people feel energized. We're making no health claims here, but there are plenty of associated ones.

In addition to fresh, housemade juices, Harlow's menu offers a wide range of bowls, with tempeh or brown rice topped with colorful veggies. Its sister restaurant, Prasad, located downtown (925 NW Davis St.) shares its space with a yoga studio.

Above, center left: the luscious red drink is the Ruby ($6), with grapefruit, carrot, beet, and ginger. The green drink is the Popeye ($6),a spinach smoothie. Bottom left: Granola ($6). Bottom right: Apple Walnut Flapjacks ($8).

E

Eat

Måurice

Kristen Murray's dreamy downtown pastry-driven cafe

Information

ⓐ 921 SW Oak St.
ⓣ (503) 224-9921
ⓗ Tu-Sa 10 a.m.-7 p.m.
ⓦ mauricepdx.com
ⓜ p. 288-24 / $$

Måurice is one of downtown's most charming and delicious cafes serving up fresh-baked pastries of the pies-and-tarts variety and meals crafted from fresh seasonal ingredients. It reflects the personal vision of its stylish owner, Kristen Murray, of an unfussy eatery that people can casually wander into.

"I moved to Portland from the East Coast eight years ago. I was soon captivated by a lifestyle full of unexpected encounters at every turn. I wanted to open an eatery like an extension of my personal dining room, offering lots of great pastries with a French and Norwegian accent."

The food at Måurice is lovingly handcrafted at every stage, from the pie crusts to the sauces. The menu, handwritten every day, conveys the same welcoming spirit.

Let yourself be ushered into Murray's oasis of domestic meets public mealtime bliss and you won't regret it. Every meal is memorable here.

Mâurice chef-owner Kristen Murray looking dapper here in her quirky glasses and French striped shirt, was a semifinalist for the 2016 James Beard Outstanding Pastry Chef Award. Her chocolate mousse is to die for.

Milk Glass Mrkt

Nancye Benson's sweet and savory North Portland cafe

Nancye Benson's sweet little corner cafe with a full bar in North Portland's Overlook neighborhood serves Moxie Rx favorites (Moxie Rx was Benson's beloved food cart that specialized in pastries). Milk Glass Mrkt also serves tasty breakfast/brunch/lunch dishes such as fried fava beans, a smoked trout plate, and housemade bread pudding. There's a small selection of take-home treats like Umi Organic ramen noodles and good wines in the pint-sized market section of the cafe.

50

E

Eat

Information

Ⓐ 2150 N Killingsworth St.
Ⓣ (503) 395-4742
Ⓗ Tu-Sa 9 a.m.-4 p.m., Su 9 a.m.-3 p.m.
Ⓦ milkglassmrkt.com
Ⓜ p. 292-7 / $$

Top: Buttermilk biscuit with sheep's milk cheese and tomato marmalade (a sour-sweet delight) ($5). Middle: ever-so-moist vanilla poppy seed muffin with whipped cream ($7).

Top left: The impressive, colorful, and diverse salad spread at Garden Bar.

Garden Bar

Casual salad bar featuring local produce

At its six Portland locations (this one is our favorite) Garden Bar serves up large made-to-order salads (big enough for two if you aren't terribly hungry). You can choose from their signature salads such as the Vietnamese Banh Mi salad ($11) with jicama, roasted chicken, fresh herbs, and sriracha aioli, or you can create your own ($9). Many of the ingredients here are sourced from local purveyors and the tables are made of Oregon-grown bamboo. In other words, the keep-it-local ethic is strong. If you need something warm, try the soup of the day ($4).

Information

Ⓐ 25 NW 11th Ave.
Ⓣ (971) 888-5263
Ⓗ M-Su 10:30 a.m.-9 p.m.
Ⓦ gardenbarpdx.com
Ⓜ p. 290-32 / $$

P's and Q's Neighborhood Market and Deli

Convenience and authenticity

This small, sweet neighborhood cafe and grocery store features high-quality, local, organic food and from-scratch menu items loaded with good old-fashioned flavors. There's a full deli, and we recommend the barbecued brisket and roast beef. Their sandwiches and baked goods are all super tasty. On weekdays, happy hour goes from 3-6pm, and they also serve dinner. This market is a fun and friendly place to eat and linger with friends.

Information

Ⓐ 1301 NE Dekum St.
Ⓣ (503) 894-8979
Ⓗ M-F 11 a.m.-9 p.m., Sa-Su 9 a.m.-9 p.m.
Ⓦ psandqsmarket.com
Ⓜ p. 294-1 / $$

52

E

Eat

Trifecta

The sound of firewood being chopped sometimes echoes through this prized bakery-pub-restaurant

Ken Forkish, the man behind Ken's Artisan Bakery and Ken's Artisan Pizza, opened his third, and most fun, business in late 2013. His cookbook *Flour Water Salt Yeast*, published in 2012, quickly became a bestseller, propelling him to nationwide fame. The concept of a tavern with a full bakery menu was a long time in the making. Now it's here, bringing one of our favorites—the Pimento Double-Cheeseburger ($15): two patties and spreadable cheddar cheese with a kick on a brioche bun with fries. What really sets these gourmet burgers apart is that the buns come from the head and heart of a true bread master. Also worthy of special mention are the expertly chosen and prepared seasonal veggies and tasty steaks from Trifecta's wood-fired oven, the top-notch cocktails, and the awesome fresh seafood selection, especially the raw oysters.

Information

Ⓐ 726 SE 6th Ave.
Ⓣ (503) 841-6675
Ⓗ M 5 p.m.-9 p.m., Tu-Th 5 p.m.-10 p.m.,
   F-Sa 4 p.m.-10:30 p.m., Su 4 p.m.-9 p.m.
Ⓦ trifectapdx.com
Ⓜ p. 296-35 / $$$

An hour before dinner begins, Trifecta starts selling bread, baked from Forkish's recipes developed specifically for this eatery using a blend of wheats. They even churn their own butter!

Ataula

Fabulous tapas from a Spanish chef

The man with the big smile is chef Jose Chesa, who started his culinary career at fifteen years old, working in the Barcelona restaurant of his chef-owner father. Later, Chesa worked in New York, then moved to Portland in 2010. In the summer of 2014, he finally opened his own place, serving next-level tapas with stunning presentation. The Pulpo ($12), served on a wooden board, is thin slices of grilled octopus over mashed potatoes, topped with a black olive sauce. Golden globules of pomegranate vinegar sauce provide the final flourish. Then there is the Cua de Bou ($10), steamed oxtail on a bun with a spicy sauce that Chesa picked up from a Korean friend. You'll have fun here.

Information

Ⓐ 1818 NW 23rd.
Ⓣ (503) 894-8904
Ⓗ Tu-Sa 4:30 p.m.-10 p.m.
Ⓦ ataulapdx.com
Ⓜ p. 290-3 / $$

55

E | *Eat*

Upper left: Paamb Xocolatai Oli d'Oliva ($7) deploys Jacobsen Salt Co. (p. 90) to highlight the sweetness of the chocolate mousse.
Lower left: Cojonudo ($6), chorizo presented lollipop style.

Kachka

Soviet Portland rises

Ask the staff at Kachka if they serve Russian food and you'll get a firm Nyet. This, the comrades will proudly tell you, is Soviet cuisine. Rewind to the Cold War and let your taste buds defect across the Iron Curtain via this restaurant that's star is on the rise. Depicted on the upper left is Herring Under A Fur Coat ($9), a traditional salad with seven beautiful layers: pickled herring, potato, onion, carrot, beet, mayonnaise, and egg. A more modern interpretation of the same is seen at lower left: Salat Mimoza ($9). Bottom middle are Ukrainian-style dumplings (from $10); the dough is made fresh daily on the premises, with various fillings. This is a restaurant that will open up your tastebuds and your mind to new flavors and experiences, potentially more or less so if down a few delicious chilled vodkas while you're at it.

The ambient music that plays in Kachka is Russian pop punctuated by Soviet military anthems and folk songs of Mother Russia. The walls are adorned with Soviet propaganda posters for that coveted gulag-chic look, while the logo is an orange cartoon duck showing the cuddly side of the Eastern Bloc.

Information

ⓐ 720 SE Grand Ave.
ⓣ (503) 235-0059
ⓗ 4 p.m.-12 a.m. daily
ⓦ kachkapdx.com
ⓜ p. 296-32 / $$$

Eat **E**

Top: View from the seating area into the kitchen. The candles and red-and-white checked curtains add to the romantic atmosphere.

DOC

Italy meets the Northwest with an impressive wine program

Northwest ingredients meet Italian cuisine at this charming little, romantic Northeast neighborhood restaurant. When entering through the front door you may at first feel alarmed, as if you've accidentally walked through the back door, since the intimate, exposed kitchen flanks the entrance. Don't fret, you're at the right place. The chef and cooks are just a part of the welcoming committee. We highly recommend submitting to your server's recommendations when it comes to wine here because it is a large part of the sit down, relax, and stay awhile (hopefully for the five-course tasting menu with wine pairings) DOC dining experience. Even though the tasting menu is advised, a la carte is available as well. Vegetarians and walk-ins are always welcome.

59

E | *Eat*

Information

Ⓐ 5519 NE 30th Ave.
Ⓣ (503) 946-8592
Ⓗ Tu-Sa 6 p.m.-10 p.m.
Ⓦ docpdx.com
Ⓜ p. 294-4 / $$$$

Chef-owner Akkapong Earl Nimson is on the left in the facing photo, chef Rassamee Ruaysuntia is on the right.

Langbaan

Transcendent Thai
in a secret hideaway

Information

Ⓐ 6 SE 28th Ave.
Ⓣ (971) 344-2564
Ⓗ Th-Sa seatings at 6 p.m. & 8:45 p.m.,
  Su seatings at 5:30 p.m. & 8:15 p.m.
Ⓦ langbaanpdx.com
Ⓜ p. 296-12 / $$$$

Chef/owner Akkapong Earl Nimson is on a roll. His reservation-only (reservations need to be placed months in advance) non-standard Thai tasting-menu restaurant Langbaan came in at number two in *GQ Magazine*'s 2015 list of the best restaurants in America, and that same year he made it to the James Beard Award semifinals. After that, the wait for reservations for this Thursday through Saturday dining room went from weeks to months and the restaurant started opening on Sundays to accommodate demand. Langbaan, which means "behind the house" in Thai, has no street entrance; it's tucked away behind a discreet door in Nimson's other acclaimed midscale Thai restaurant PaaDee, through which you are ushered into a tiny, private dining room. At this hideaway, you get to enjoy the freshest of local ingredients combined with special, uncommon Thai flavors, recipes, and techniques handed down from Thai grandmas.

Beast

Chef Naomi Pomeroy's tasting-menu beauty

Naomi Pomeroy is one of Portland's most esteemed and celebrated chefs, and if you can get a reservation at her Northeast Portland tasting menu, communal, reservation-only restaurant Beast, which she opened in 2007, you should jump on it. If you can't get a dinner reservation, consider the Sunday brunch with three seatings. Self-taught (and in large part, she says, cookbook-taught) chef Pomeroy won the James Beard Award for Best Chef Pacific Northwest in 2014, and she was also named as Best New Chef in Food & Wine in 2009. Her cookbook *Taste & Technique* came out in late 2016. Beast is one of our favorite Portland restaurants. If you dine there visit Pomeroy and her husband's cocktail lounge Expatriate (p. 115) just across the street.

Information

Ⓐ 5425 NE 30th Ave.
Ⓣ (503) 841-6968
Ⓗ W-Sa 6 p.m. & 8:45 p.m., Su 7 p.m. dinner seatings,
    Su 10 a.m., 11:30 a.m., 1p.m. brunch seatings
Ⓦ beastpdx.com
Ⓜ p. 294-7 / $$$$

The two dinner seatings have fixed starting times, so make sure of your reservation times. Weekend brunch is as highly regarded as dinner.

Le Pigeon

Food redolent with the spirit of independence

Cross the Burnside Bridge from downtown and you will run smack into this restaurant run by two-time James Beard Award-winner Gabriel Rucker. (Sister eatery Little Bird Bistro is covered on p. 66) Known for its inventive preparations of squab and excellent tasting menus, the foie gras profiteroles for dessert are also a draw. Le Pigeon offers up fine dining in an intimate yet relaxed dining room.

Information

Ⓐ 738 E Burnside St.
Ⓣ (503) 546-8796
Ⓗ 5 p.m.-10 p.m. daily
Ⓦ lepigeon.com
Ⓜ p. 296-3 / $$$

Olympia Provisions

Elias Cairo, Olympia Provisions co-owner and salumist, did a meat curing apprenticeship in Switzerland when he was eighteen years old and years later, after he returned to the U.S., he opened this low-lit, charming Southeast Portland industrial restaurant in order to revive traditional meat-processing methods and serve these cured meats (Oprah's favorite!) alongside a diverse menu of primarily European food. Many high-end food retailers carry Olympia Provisions' cured USDA organic salamis and sausages. A second Olympia Provisions restaurant opened in 2011 across the river in Northwest Portland.

Information

Ⓐ 107 SE Washington St.
Ⓣ (503) 954-3663
Ⓗ M-F 11 a.m.-10 p.m., Sa-Su 9 a.m.-10 p.m.
Ⓦ olympiaprovisions.com
Ⓜ p. 296-27 / $$

Dreamy cured meats and European fare on the ground floor of an old cereal mill building

Trailblazing locavore landmark

Higgins Restaurant and Bar

Information

Ⓐ 1239 SW Broadway
Ⓣ (503) 222-9070
Ⓗ M-Th 11:30a.m.-2 p.m., 5 p.m.-9:30 p.m.,
    F 11:30a.m.-2 p.m., 5 p.m.-10:30 p.m.,
    Sa 5 p.m.-10:30 p.m., Su 4 p.m.-9:30 p.m.
Ⓦ higginsportland.com
Ⓜ p. 288-68 / $$$$

These days, everyone knows that Portland chefs value close ties with local farmers, foragers, ranchers, and fishers as essential for a robust food culture. One of the chefs who founded this reverence for local ingredients was Greg Higgins when he opened his eponymous downtown restaurant in 1994. Higgins is one of Portland's most esteemed chefs and his restaurant is a Rose City institution. Go here to celebrate the local bounty of fiddlehead ferns, chanterelle and morel mushrooms, wild game, salmon, Pinot Noir, and other quintessential Pacific Northwest fare.

Ned Ludd

Wood-fired rustic cooking from Jason French

Billing itself as an "American craft kitchen," chef-owner Jason French's Ned Ludd is all about simple, rustic, locally-sourced foods. Most menu items are cooked in the wood-fired oven (whole roasted trout, spiced flatbreads) that is the heart of the dining room. In 2014, French opened up Elder Hall next door as a space for communal dining and community events, ranging from photo exhibitions to cooking workshops.

Information

Ⓐ 3925 NE MLK Jr. Blvd.
Ⓣ (503) 288-6900
Ⓗ 5 p.m.-10 p.m. daily
Ⓦ nedluddpdx.com
Ⓜ p. 294-21 / $$$$

Holdfast Dining

Below, top: Parboiled egg yolk topped with roe and black garlic. Below, center: The open kitchen encircled by tables.

Conceptualizing the restaurant as an event

Information

Ⓐ 537 SE Ash St. #102
Ⓣ (503)504-9448
Ⓗ F-Su 7 p.m. seating, Reservation only
Ⓦ holdfastdining.com
Ⓜ p. 296-14 / $$$$

Will Preisch and Joel Stocks are young chefs now in the spotlight after making their names running their own pop-up restaurant at KitchenCru while honing their chops at big-name restaurants in Portland and beyond. In late 2014, they opened their own reservation-only restaurant, open Friday through Sunday with one 7 p.m. seating per night. Holdfast also hosts various collaboration dinners with local cooks and chefs. Dining is prix fixe here (nine courses) with an emphasis on pairing food and booze (or nonalcoholic beverages). Book reservations via their website.

Indian street food infused with a chef's French training

Bollywood Theater

Chef-owner Troy MacLarty's frist step with his counter-service Indian restaurant Bollywood Theater was a trip to India to study street food, where he absorbed the energy and spontaneity of the food culture. Back in Portland he filtered that experience through his haute cuisine skillset and created a cross-cultural culinary gem with full-flavored Indian dishes served on steel plates, as is custom in Mumbai. At Bollywood Theater (two locations: Northeast and Southeast) MacLarty brings delicious Indian street food to lucky Portlanders and travelers. Both locations have ample outdoor seating.

Information

Ⓐ 3010 SE Division St.
Ⓣ (503) 477-6699
Ⓗ 11 a.m.-10 p.m. daily (both locations)
Ⓦ bollywoodtheaterpdx.com
Ⓜ p. 296-89 / $$

66

E

Eat

Little Bird Bistro

Unsnobby French cuisine downtown

If French cuisine strikes you as snobby, then you'll enjoy correcting those assumptions at Little Bird Bistro, Le Pigeon's lovely downtown sister restaurant. A good choice is the charcuterie board, a wooden plank heaped with outstanding hors d'oeuvres. The macaroni gratin is one of our favorite side dishes. Little Bird is open for lunch Monday through Friday, and dinner seven nights a week.

Information

Ⓐ 215 SW 6th Ave.
Ⓣ (503) 688-5952
Ⓗ M-F 11:30 a.m.-12 a.m., Sa-Su 5 p.m.-12 a.m.
Ⓦ littlebirdbistro.com
Ⓜ p. 288-33 / $$

¿Por Qué No?

A Mexican pit stop to refuel while exploring

Step inside this pretty little pink building (there's often a line but it moves quickly) and you are welcomed by the festive, colorful Mexican ambiance. Start with the housemade guacamole and chips, then pick from multiple taco fillings (chorizo, fried cod, barbacoa) nestled in housemade corn tortillas. And why not have a tequila cocktail while you're at it? Por Qué No is a fun, tasty spot with an additional Southeast location.

Information

Ⓐ 3524 N Mississippi Ave.
Ⓣ (503) 467-4149
Ⓗ M-Sa 11 a.m.-10 p.m., Su 11 a.m.-9:30 p.m.
Ⓦ porquenotacos.com
Ⓜ p. 292-30 / $$

Pambiche

Information

Ⓐ 2811 NE Glisan St.
Ⓣ (503) 233-0511
Ⓗ M-Th 11 a.m.-10 p.m., F 11 a.m.-12 a.m., Sa 9 a.m.-12 a.m., Su 9 a.m.-10 p.m.
Ⓦ pambiche.com
Ⓜ p. 294-37 / $$

Cuba has a rich culinary culture, blending Spanish and African influences with the tropical fruits and vegetables that thrive in the island's Caribbean climate. We really like the yucca frita served with a garlicky sauce, all of the croquetas and empanadas, and the oxtail stew. Finish your meal with the chocolate rum truffle cake, in the shape of a cigar, for total Cuban indulgence. The desserts are exceptional here.

A vibrant mural marks this festive Cuban eatery

Salt & Straw

*People may not literally scream
for this ice cream,
but they do line up for it*

Information

Ⓐ 3345 SE Division St.
Ⓣ (503) 208-2054
Ⓗ 10 a.m.-11 p.m. daily
Ⓦ saltandstraw.com
Ⓜ p. 296-74 / $

This ice cream parlor's rise from food cart to Portland institution has generated plenty of media coverage and put it on the itineraries of many tourists. Salt & Straw now has locations on NW 23rd, Alberta Street, and the restaurant row of Division Street, and has even made the leap to L.A. Each location serves a unique selection of flavors. The ice cream parlor's "farm-to-cone" philosophy leads to truly delectable frozen dairy treats. Even though the line will likely snake down the block when you visit, that's just more time to gaze hungrily at the menu. One secret to Salt & Straw's popularity is the easygoing and helpful ice cream servers.

Each location also sells a selection of small-batch Oregon products with charming packaging that make for great souvenir gifts.

Fifty Licks Ice Cream

A food chemist formulates ice cream for all

Owner Chad Draizin was drawn to Portland for its beer brewing, but now he makes ice cream, limited to the amount that can be made by hand on premises. Ultra-picky about ingredients, he even makes his own gluten-free waffle cones. This is the only scoop shop in Portland that's nut free, so even nut allergy sufferers can get their delicious licks with peace of mind here.

Information

Ⓐ 2021 SE Clinton St.
Ⓣ (503) 395-3333
Ⓗ M-Th 2 p.m.-10 p.m. F-Su 1 p.m.-11 p.m.
Ⓦ fifty-licks.com
Ⓜ p. 296-80 / $

69

E

Eat

The Meadow

Gourmet chocolate, salt, and bitters from around the world

Information

Ⓐ 3731 N Mississippi Ave.
Ⓣ (503) 974-8349
Ⓗ 11 a.m.-8 p.m. daily
Ⓦ themeadow.com
Ⓜ p. 292-25

This pint-sized shop stocks salt (prepare to be astonished at the amazing variety of specialty salts from around the world), gourmet chocolate bars, bitters, and vermouths, all carefully curated by author-owner Mark Bitterman. It's a wonderland for food nerds and we love it. A second location can be found in the shopping mecca of NW 23rd Avenue, and if you're in New York there's even a Meadow there.

Blue Star Donuts

Luxe ingredients go into gourmet donuts

Who wouldn't want a doughnut shop that uses local ingredients and fries up seasonal doughnuts? The wheat that comprises Blue Star's high-grade flour is Oregon-grown and so is the fruit used in many of the gourmet doughnuts here. All six Blue Star locations fry their doughnuts fresh daily starting at 3 a.m. There is no effort spared for the shop's traditional brioche dough in the style of southern France. Once it's prepared, Blue Star molds it into exotic selections such as the Brulée Cointreau and Blueberry Bourbon Basil doughnuts. In classic Portland fashion, Blue Star closes when the day's doughnuts sell out.

Information

Ⓐ 1237 SW Washington St.
Ⓣ (503) 265-8410
Ⓗ 7 a.m.-8 p.m. daily
Ⓦ bluestardonuts.com
Ⓜ p. 288-8 / $

SOCIAL MEDIA EXPLAINED
twitter- im eating a #donut
facebook- i like donuts
foursquare- this is where i eat donuts
instagram- here is a photo of my donut
youtube- here i am eating a donut
linkedin- my skills include donut eating
pinterest- here's a donut recipe
spotify- now listening to 'donuts'
g+- i'm a google employee who eats donuts

BLUE ⭐ STAR
QUALITY over
QUANTITY

E

Eat

Voodoo Doughnut

Weird, crazy popular, late-night doughnut shop

Information

Ⓐ 22 SW 3rd Ave.
Ⓣ (503) 241-4704
Ⓗ 24 hours every day
Ⓦ voodoodoughnut.com
Ⓜ p. 288-40 / $

Go to this cash-only, wacky doughnut spot at night. The garish neon sign and weird interior lighting make it that much more compelling as if outrageous doughnuts with names like the Tex-Ass and Dirty Snowball, with appearances to match, weren't compelling enough. First-timers might want to try one of our favorites – the Bacon Maple Bar. Voodoo also sells pedestrian doughnuts like French crullers for the less adventurous. There's a Northeast location and several other Voodoo locations in Oregon and other states.

Among the offerings are Mexican street tacos from Uno Mas, butcher shop lunches from Tails & Trotters, and the cute Pie Spot serving good ol' American pie.

The Ocean

Introducing
the micro-restaurant

Information

Ⓐ NE 24th Ave. & Glisan St.
Ⓦ slowburger.net,
thesudra.com, unomastaquiza.com,
24thandmeatballs.com,
tailsandtrotters.com,
pie-spot.com
Ⓜ p. 294-33 / $

According to a 2008 study done at Portland State University, the average annual take of food carts, which leverage the cheap space and minimal restrictions in vacant lots and parking lots, is $36,000–$60,000. The downside of the carts is that accessibility is heavily influenced by weather and unpredictable hours. To solve those issues, a developer came up with the novel financing and land-use solution of The Ocean micro-restaurant pod, a local favorite. There are six sit-down eateries to serve customers out of the elements, and they share fixed hours. Considering how many culinary stars have emerged from the food cart scene, some of these micro-restaurants might be launch pads for tomorrow's leading restaurateurs.

Shizuku by Chef Naoko

Authentic Japanese Cuisine by Chef Naoko

Chef Naoko Tamura moved to Portland from Japan in 2008 to open a downtown bento box cafe (which is now a beautifully redesigned restaurant by Kengo Kuma), and she has enriched Portland's Japanese food culture immensely since. Her commitment to organic ingredients and seasonal flavors has even won her a deal from Delta Airlines to supply Japanese cuisine in first and business class on flights from Portland to Tokyo.

Information

Ⓐ 1237 SW Jefferson St.
Ⓣ (503) 227-4136
Ⓗ Tu-F 11:30 a.m.-2 p.m., 6 p.m.-9:30 p.m.,
   Sa 5 p.m.-9:30 p.m.
Ⓦ shizukupdx.com
Ⓜ p. 288-65 / $$

Biwa

Fun, late-night Japanese izakaya

    An izakaya is the Japanese equivalent of a gastropub, serving Japanese comfort food favorites like yakitori, ramen, sushi, and sashimi to wash down with sake and shochu. Owners, Gabe Rosen and Kina Voelz, remodeled the original Biwa and opened their Japanese cocktail bar, Parasol, in its place in 2016. Parasol is inspired by busy Japanese train station restaurants and serves soba, udon, and curry rice. Parasol and Biwa are in the same building, different hours.

Information

Ⓐ 215 SE 9th Ave.
Ⓣ (503) 239-8830
Ⓗ W-M 5 p.m.-10 p.m.
Ⓦ biwaizakaya.com
Ⓜ p. 296-18 / $$$

Nodoguro

Reservation-only Japanese omakase tasting menu

Information

Ⓐ 2832 SE Belmont St.
Ⓗ tickets required
Ⓦ nodoguropdx.com
Ⓜ p. 296-58 / $$$$

    Japanese-speaking gutsy and creative chef Ryan Roadhouse serves up eleven-course dinners of haute Japanese cuisine based on local ingredients. Tickets to dinner seatings sell out well in advance, so book ahead.

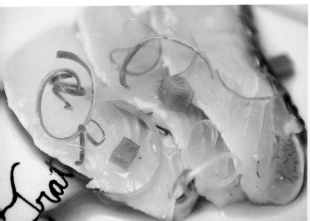

The Side Yard Farm & Kitchen

The farm-to-table ideal made real

A lot of the food consumed in Portland comes from producers near the city, and at Side Yard you can see how that works firsthand. Urban farmer and chef-owner Stacey Givens started this residential district farm in NE Portland in 2009. In the farm kitchen, Givens and her staff and volunteers prepare many delicious and inspired dishes from foods that they cultivate and harvest on site for their supper club, weekend brunches, and catered events. You can also find Side Yard Farm produce in local shops and restaurants. Volunteers have contributed immensely to the farm's success over the years. Check out the website to get a sense of this urban wonderland where Portland's natural bounty and urban agriculture shine.

Information

Ⓐ 4800 NE Simpson St.
Ⓣ (503) 957-4588
Ⓦ thesideyardpdx.com
Ⓜ p. 294-9 / $$$

A current field that came into service in 2015 features an Air-stream kitchen, a big step toward Givens' dream of touring the West Coast while serving fantastic, farm-fresh food.

People's Food Co-op

A progressive community grocer with strong social ties

You see the word "cooperative" a lot around Portland, and it's often attached to small independent, worker-owned-and-run businesses such as grocery stores, bike shops, printers, or taxi companies. People's Food Co-op (open since 1969) is one of them, selling natural and organic food, home, and garden products. Anybody can become a member, but you don't have to be a member to shop here. Members volunteer at the co-op, learn how it runs, and receive a discount equal to the labor that they contribute. There is a farmers' market in front of the store every Wednesday and regular co-op organized farm tours. Everything is geared to shift thinking from mere consumption to personal involvement.

Information

Ⓐ 3029 SE 21st Ave.
Ⓣ (503) 674-2642
Ⓗ 8 a.m.-10 p.m. daily
Ⓦ peoples.coop
Ⓜ p. 296-85

A great selection of fresh produce and packaged foods—minimally packaged or sold in bulk as much as possible to reduce packaging.

E

Eat

Urban Farm Store

All sorts of urban homesteading supplies including seedlings and baby chicks

Plenty of Portlanders have gardens and grow their own food. If you aspire to that lifestyle or are already an edible gardener, this is the store for you. It's stocked with seeds, potting soil, soil amendments, seedlings, and everything else needed for vegetable cultivation. Urban Farm Store also sells a wide variety of chicken breeds. The store can hook you up with a coop, chicken feed, how-to-keep-chickens guides, and so on to get your home poultry operation up and running for a steady supply of your own chicken eggs and a funny new pet or two–or three.

Information

Ⓐ 1108 SE 9th Ave.
Ⓣ (503) 234-7733
Ⓗ Check out the seasonal opening hours on the website
Ⓦ urbanfarmstore.com
Ⓜ p. 296-47

It's not purely hardcore agriculture supplies; even casual gardeners like you or someone on your gift list could use stuff like biodegradable planters, DIY cheese kits, and more.

Farmers Markets of Portland

BIO

Yusuke Tanaka
Born in Tokyo in 1985. Involved in the establishment of Media Surf Communications services such as the Farmer's Market @ UNU and COMMUNE 246 in Tokyo. Always visits local markets when travelling. Chief editor of this book's "Drink" section despite being a teetotaler until just a few years ago. Equally fond of both eating and drinking now.
farmersmarkets.jp

Start your Saturday morning at the PSU Portland Farmers Market

The global farmers' market movement that puts farmers and urban residents into direct contact has gained a lot of ground in recent years, and the U.S. is no exception, with the number of farmers' markets nationwide growing almost five-fold over the past two decades, with over 8,000 markets currently. Portland and the greater Portland area has a particularly robust farmers' market culture with forty or so markets of varying size to call its own.

One great farmers' market to check out takes place every Saturday year-round on the Portland State University (PSU) campus. It's the largest of seven such markets organized around the city by the local nonprofit Portland Farmers Market. As the city's largest farmers' market, the PSU market presents the wares of 140 producers. In addition to the expected fruits, vegetables, and flowers, the mouth-watering range of offerings includes fresh meat and fish, as well as specialty foods such as pâté and jam. Walking among the stalls, you're sure to find something that will stir your appetite. For breakfast, you can enjoy locally roasted coffee and fresh fruit, or you can head to one of the numerous on-site vendors for cooked street food prepared with market ingredients.

Other days of the week you can check out farmers' markets in other parts of the city, each with its own distinctive character. Wednesday's Shemanski Park Farmers Market (just a hop and skip from the Ace Hotel) is a great one in the shade of grand old elm, oak, and maple trees. It's a lovely environment even for those without the urge to shop. Northwest Market caters to local preferences by opening in the afternoon rather than the morning. Hollywood Farmers Market is tucked into the parking lot of a Northeast Portland budget supermarket.

At all of Portland's markets, you will find live music, chef demonstrations, and cooking lessons for kids in environments that blend entertainment and education seamlessly. Recycling waste is taken seriously at all of the markets, so visitors should note the receptacles for compostable and recyclable materials.

Each market's hours and active seasons vary, so before you head out, be sure to check the Portland Farmers Market website.

WEEKLY SCHEDULE

Portland Farmers Market
portlandfarmersmarket.org

Monday

Pioneer Courthouse Square
Place: SW Broadway & SW Morrison St.
Schedule: Mid-June–Late September,
10 a.m.-2 p.m.

Wednesday

Shemanski Park
Place: SW Park Ave. & SW Salmon St.
Schedule: Early May–Late November,
10 a.m.-2 p.m.

Kenton
Place: N Denver Ave. & N McClellan St.
Schedule: Early June–Late September,
3 p.m.-7 p.m.

Thursday

Northwest
Place: NW Everett St. & NW 19th Ave.
Schedule: Early June–Late September,
2 p.m.-6 p.m.

Saturday

Portland State University
Place: SW Park Ave. & SW Montgomery St.
(Near 1717 SW Park Ave.)
Schedule:March–October, 8:30 a.m.-2 p.m.
November–February, 9 a.m.-2 pm

Sunday

King
Place: NE Wygant St. & NE 7th Ave.
Schedule: Early May–Late November,
10 a.m.-2 p.m.

Lents
Place: SE 91st Ave and Foster Rd.
Schedule: Early June–Late October,
9 a.m.-2 p.m.

OTHER NEIGHBORHOOD MARKETS

Wednesday

People's Farmers' Market
peoples.coop/farmers-market

Saturday

Hollywood Farmers Market
hollywoodfarmersmarket.org

Sunday

Hillsdale Farmers' Market
hillsdalefarmersmarket.com

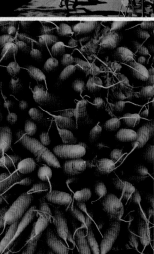

E
Eat

Scenes from Portland State University, King, and Hollywood farmers' markets. Each market boasts a wealth of farm-fresh foods, and is lively with culinary conversations between producers and customers.

Ken's Artisan Bakery

The Nob Hill bakery run by Ken Forkish, renowned artisan baker and author of the award-winning cookbook *Flour Water Salt Yeast*.

Ⓐ 338 NW 21st Ave. / Ⓣ (503) 248 -2202
Ⓗ M 7 a.m.-9:30 p.m., Tu-Sa 7 a.m-6 p.m., Su 8 a.m.-5 p.m.
Ⓦ kensartisan.com / Ⓜ p. 290-53 / $

Pearl Bakery

Delicious croissants, sandwiches, pastries, breads, and other baked goods are offered at this open-early breakfast and lunch spot.

Ⓐ 102 NW 9th Ave. / Ⓣ (503) 827-0910
Ⓗ M-F 6:30 a.m.-5:30 p.m., Sa 7 a.m.-5 p.m., Su 8 a.m.-4 p.m.
Ⓦ pearlbakery.com / Ⓜ p. 290-37 / $

Tabor Bread

This bakery goes the extra mile, even milling their own flour in-house and baking everything in wood-fired brick ovens.

Ⓐ 5051 SE Hawthorne Blvd.
Ⓣ (971) 279-5530
Ⓗ Tu-Su 8 a.m.-6 p.m.
Ⓦ taborbread.com / Ⓜ p. 296-61 / $

Little T American Baker

Enjoy Little T's tasty collaborations with other artisan foodmakers such as cookies made with Woodblock Chocolate (p. 86) at this diverse Southeast Portland bakery.

Ⓐ 2600 SE Division St. / Ⓣ (503) 238-3458
Ⓗ M-Sa 7 a.m.-5 p.m., Su 8 a.m.-2 p.m.
Ⓦ littletbaker.com / Ⓜ p. 296-76 / $

Nuvrei Fine Cakes & Pastries

Highlights here include the plum brioche, almond croissants, macarons, and, well, pretty much everything on the menu. Go here!

Ⓐ 404 NW 10th Ave.
Ⓣ (503) 972-1700
Ⓗ M-Sa 7 a.m.-5 p.m., Su 8 a.m.-5 p.m.
Ⓦ nuvrei.com / Ⓜ p. 290-21 / $

Saint Cupcake

These purveyors of yummy little designer cupcakes also cater event and special occasions from their four locations.

Ⓐ 1138 SW Morrison St. / Ⓣ (503) 473-8760
Ⓗ M-F 9 a.m.-6 p.m., Sa 10 a.m.-6 p.m. Su 11 a.m.-5 p.m.
Ⓦ saintcupcake.com / Ⓜ p. 288-49 / $

Lovejoy Bakers

Their Pearl District bakery (there are two locations) is part of the fabric of life in the neighborhood. Pick up some takeout to savor in nearby Jamison Park.

Ⓐ 939 NW 10th Ave. / Ⓣ (503) 208-3113
Ⓗ 6 a.m.-6 p.m. daily
Ⓦ lovejoybakers.com / Ⓜ p. 290-12 / $

Spielman Bagels

This small, family-run place with three locations makes bagels from scratch with fanatical dedication to quality, including their wild yeast sourdough starter.

Ⓐ 2200 NE Broadway / Ⓣ (503) 477-9045
Ⓗ 6 a.m.-4 p.m. daily
Ⓦ spielmanbagels.com / Ⓜ p. 294-26 / $

Crema Coffee & Bakery

Crema is a beautiful bakery, full of natural light, and a vibe that fosters community and supports local artists. It's a great place to get breakfast or lunch and hang out for a while.

Ⓐ 2728 SE Ankeny St. / Ⓣ (503) 234-0206
Ⓗ 7 a.m.-6 p.m. daily
Ⓦ cremabakery.com / Ⓜ p. 296-16 / $

Lardo

This pig-focused sandwich joint's generous pork meatball banh mi goes great with beer, and the dirty fries are unforgettable at both locations.

Ⓐ 1205 SW Washington St.
Ⓣ (503) 241-2490
Ⓗ 11 a.m.-10 p.m. daily
Ⓦ lardosandwiches.com / Ⓜ p. 288-9 / $

Eb & Bean

Housemade frozen yogurt with artisanal toppings from organic ingredients is the treat here and at their NE Broadway Street location.

Ⓐ 1425 NE Broadway
Ⓣ (503) 281-6081
Ⓗ 12 p.m.-10 p.m. daily
Ⓦ ebandbean.com / Ⓜ p. 294-25 / $

Pine State Biscuits

Start with the fried chicken and biscuits and load on bacon, gravy, and other Southern comfort food at Pine State's three locations.

Ⓐ 2204 NE Alberta St.
Ⓣ (503) 477-6605
Ⓗ 7 a.m.-3 p.m. daily
Ⓦ pinestatebiscuits.com / Ⓜ p. 294-17 / $

Bunk Sandwiches

A pioneer of the gourmet sandwich boom with five locations, Bunk's plugged-in founders also partnered with a record label guru for Bunk Bar, which hosts live music.

Ⓐ 211 SW 6th Ave. / Ⓣ (503) 328-2845
Ⓗ M-F 8 a.m.-3 p.m., Sa-Su 9 a.m.-3 p.m.
Ⓦ bunksandwiches.com / Ⓜ p. 288-32 / $

Little Big Burger

When you are jonesing for a burger—even a vegan one—come straight here (several locations) for fast food burgers with a conscience. And beer. And truffle oil fries.

Ⓐ 122 NW 10th Ave. / Ⓣ (503) 274-9008
Ⓗ 11 a.m.-10 p.m. daily
Ⓦ littlebigburger.com / Ⓜ p. 290-35 / $

Canteen

If you're looking to eat healthy, the veggie bowls and organic smoothies and juices here are just the ticket.

Ⓐ 2816 SE Stark St.
Ⓣ (503) 922-1858
Ⓗ 9 a.m.-9 p.m. daily
Ⓦ canteenpdx.com / Ⓜ p. 296-30 / $

81

E

Eat

HOTLIPS Pizza

This pizza joint with several locations uses earth-friendly ingredients and promotes sustainability. They even have their own line of all-natural fruit sodas.

Ⓐ 721 NW 9th Ave.
Ⓣ (503) 595-2342
Ⓗ 11 a.m.-10 p.m. daily
Ⓦ hotlipspizza.com / Ⓜ p. 290-13 / $

Nong's Khao Man Gai

The lure of Thai khao man gai by chef Nong Poonsukwattana, a simple but flavorful chicken and rice dish with legendary sauce, generates long lines at the three locations.

Ⓐ 1003 SW Alder St. / Ⓣ (971) 255-3480
Ⓗ M-F 10 a.m.-4 p.m.
Ⓦ khaomangai.com / Ⓜ p. 288-20 / $

Oven and Shaker

If you have a craving for the great combo of wood-fired pizza and top-notch cocktails, go here. Their original house cocktails are the best.

Ⓐ 1134 NW Everett St. / Ⓣ (503) 241-1600
Ⓗ Su-Th 11:30 a.m.-11 p.m.,
    F-Sa 11:30 a.m.-12 a.m.
Ⓦ ovenandshaker.com / Ⓜ p. 290-31 / $$$

Pok Pok

With star-chef owner Andy Ricker this Thai street food spot is a favorite. Get on the list, then head across the street to the Whiskey Soda Lounge, same chef, for a cocktail and small bites.

Ⓐ 3226 SE Division St. / ⓣ (503) 232-1387
Ⓗ 11:30 a.m.-10 p.m. daily
Ⓦ pokpokpdx.com / Ⓜ p. 296-78 / $$$

Broder Nord

Start your day at one of Broder's three locations with Swedish pancakes, Swedish meatballs, Swedish hash with smoked trout...you get the idea.

Ⓐ 2240 N Interstate Ave. Ste #160
ⓣ (503) 282-5555
Ⓗ 8 a.m.-3 p.m. daily
Ⓦ broderpdx.com / Ⓜ p. 292-40 / $$

Tasty n Sons

A prime brunch and dinner spot serving skillet-centric new-American and international cuisine inspired by chef-owner John Gorham's culinary travels.

Ⓐ 3808 N Williams Ave. Suite C
ⓣ (503) 621-1400
Ⓗ Su-Th 9 a.m.-10 p.m., F-Sa 9 a.m.-11 p.m.
Ⓦ tastynsons.com / Ⓜ p. 292-27 / $$

Old Salt Marketplace

Old Salt's tasty deli / butcher counter serves lunch by day and at night it becomes a restaurant/bar with a full dinner menu. Brunch is served on weekends.

Ⓐ 5027 NE 42nd Ave. / ⓣ (971) 255-0167
Ⓗ M-Th 11 a.m.-11 p.m., F 11 a.m.-12 a.m.,
Sa 9 a.m.-12 a.m., Su 9 a.m.-11 p.m.
Ⓦ oldsaltpdx.com / Ⓜ p. 294-14 / $$

Ox

The finest local beef and fish, grilled over wood and served up Argentine-style. The smoked beef tongue is amazing.

Ⓐ 2225 NE Martin Luther King Jr Blvd.
ⓣ (503) 284-3366
Ⓗ Su-Th 5 p.m.-10 p.m., F-Sat 5 p.m.-11 p.m.
Ⓦ oxpdx.com / Ⓜ p. 294-23 / $$$

Lúc Lác Vietnamese Kitchen

You won't feel out of place dining solo at this yummy counter-service Vietnamese place. It can get busy at night; Lúc Lác is open into the wee hours.

Ⓐ 835 SW 2nd Ave. / ⓣ (503) 222-0047
Ⓗ M-Th 11 a.m.-2:30 p.m., 4 p.m.-12 a.m.,
F-Sa 11 a.m.-2:30 p.m., 4 p.m.-4 a.m.
Su 4 p.m.-12 a.m.
Ⓦ luclackitchen.com / Ⓜ p. 288-62 / $$

Eat

Luce

This cute Italian place is a sister eatery to the popular Navarre. Check the menu board before ordering.

Ⓐ 2140 E Burnside St.
ⓣ (503) 236-7195
Ⓗ 11 a.m.-10 p.m. daily
Ⓦ luceportland.com / Ⓜ p. 296-11 / $$$

Departure Restaurant + Lounge

Fresh local ingredients go into the Asian fusion cuisine of this restaurant located on the top floor (amazing view) of The Nines hotel (p. 26).

Ⓐ 525 SW Morrison St. / ⓣ (503) 802-5370
Ⓗ Su-Th 4 p.m.-12 a.m., F-Sa 4 p.m.-1 a.m.
Ⓦ departureportland.com / Ⓜ p. 288-60 / $$$

Apizza Scholls

The Apizza Amore and Caesar salad are don't-miss choices from the dinner menu of this much-loved-by-locals pizzeria.

Ⓐ 4741 SE Hawthorne Blvd. / ⓣ (503) 233-1286
Ⓗ M-F 5 p.m.-9:30 p.m.,
Sa-Su 11:30 a.m.-2:30 p.m., 5 p.m.-9:30 p.m.
Ⓦ apizzascholls.com / Ⓜ p. 296-60 / $$

KitchenCru

This culinary incubator boasts a lavish 4,800-square-foot commercial kitchen that rents space by the hour. If you think you have the chops to start your own catering company, bake your own breads or pastries to peddle to Portland's cafes, or open your own pop-up restaurant, this can be your launch pad. From ovens to ice cream makers, KitchenCru has the equipment to turn any recipe you create into reality. Jacobsen Salt Co. (p. 90) and Holdfast Dining (p. 65) are among its talented alumni.

Information

Ⓐ 337 NW Broadway
Ⓣ (503) 226-1400
Ⓦ kitchencru.biz
Ⓜ p. 290-27 / $$

E

Eat

Portland's Culinary Workshop

Portland's Culinary Workshop is a place for locals to enjoy cooking workshops and classes in an inviting, homey atmosphere. Go by yourself or take advantage of kid-, family-, or couple-oriented classes. Topics span all types of ethnic foods, vegetarian cuisine, baking, pairing wine and cheese, and more. Click around their website and you're sure to find something that suits your interests.

Information

Ⓐ 807 N Russell St.
Ⓣ (503) 512-0447
Ⓦ portlandsculinaryworkshop.com
Ⓜ p. 292-36 / $$

Oregon Culinary Institute

This Portland culinary school offers programs in culinary arts, baking, pastry, and restaurant management that run from eight to sixteen months. Local restaurants and chefs actively engage with the Institute's students to ensure that the Portland ethos of farm-to-fork sustainability is instilled in its students.

Information

Ⓐ 1701 SW Jefferson St.
Ⓣ (503) 961-6200
Ⓦ oregonculinaryinstitute.com
Ⓜ p. 288-4 / $$

QUIN

Information

Ⓐ 1025 SW Stark St
Ⓣ (971) 300-8395
Ⓗ M-Sa 11 a.m.-6 p.m., Su 11 a.m.-5 p.m.
Ⓦ quincandy.com
Ⓜ p. 288-13

Old-time American candies reinvented
with modern foodie magic

QUIN owner-chef Jami Curl once ran a cupcake bakery in Portland. In 2013, she opened her contemporary take on the classic American candy shop. It started in her bakery days, when she decided to make treats that could sit by the register to tempt sweet-toothed impulse buyers. Her caramels were such a hit with customers that people constantly asked her for the recipe. Next, she decided to give lollipops a shot, made with whole fresh berries from local farms. It spiraled from there, as Curl kept coming up with ideas and trying recipes, winning rave reviews. Eventually she decided to sell her bakery and go all-in by opening a candy shop.

Caramels, lollipops, marshmallows, gumdrops . . . she stocks ten or more regular candies, plus two or three limited-edition candies that rotate seasonally. QUIN's flagship product is the fruit-flavored "Dreams Come Chew"—inspired by a dream Curl had of the ultimate fruit candy. She woke up in the middle of the night and scribbled down her sugary vision, then went into the kitchen the next morning to create it.

All QUIN candies are unique, and they were all invented serendipitously, as Curl's cupcake-baking skill was applied to classic American candies whenever inspiration struck. Every QUIN candy tugs at the heartstrings of childhood memories but is reimagined for discerning modern palates. Nothing but the finest all-natural ingredients (and many syrups made in-house) ensure impeccable flavor, aroma, color, and texture. An insistence on freshness is why QUIN makes all of its candies by hand in small batches.

Now more than one hundred retail outlets in the U.S. and Canada carry QUIN candies, and the business was built the hard way, via in-person sales calls. Even today, the only place you can buy every flavor of QUIN's candies is at the original store in Portland.

At QUIN's candy factory, scrumptious smells and music waft around the happy candy-makers. An on-site retail outlet is planned for the factory.

Woodblock's combined retail outlet and chocolate factory offers the chance to sample and identify the perfect match for your "choc tooth." The chocolate wig (bottom center) is, alas, not for sale.

Woodblock Chocolate

Information

ⓐ 1236 SE Oak St.
ⓣ (503) 477-5262
ⓗ M-F 10 a.m.-3 p.m., Sa 11 a.m.-4 p.m.
ⓦ woodblockchocolate.com

Bean-to-bar artisan chocolate deals Portland its cacao fix

A real-life Charlie and the Chocolate Factory. Charley Wheelock, that is. Wheelock moved to Portland ten years ago with his wife Jessica and their two kids. They had been living in New York, where Wheelock worked as an interior designer, but the cost of living there was exorbitant. When the couple took a trip to Portland to attend the wedding of friends who run Rex Hill Winery outside town, they immediately fell in love with the city and its vibrant design community.

After relocating, amid the chaos of working and raising kids, they yearned to find a more sustainable way of life for their family. Their winery-owning friends urged them to try something at the intersection of food and design. The Wheelocks brainstormed while working at Rex Hill for three consecutive harvests and they started making chocolates while Wheelock was working on his third vintage there. Because their involvement with winemaking had further educated their palates, they noted the many points in common between wine and chocolate.

The next epiphany was that the craft-brewed beer and artisan coffee sectors were experiencing wild growth—but nobody was doing artisan chocolate. In Portland of all places, an epicenter of artisan food, existing chocolatiers were simply melting down and processing imported chocolate; no one was making it from scratch starting with cacao beans. The more the Wheelocks studied chocolate, the more apparent its depth of possibilities became. Charging ahead at the vanguard of an American artisan chocolate movement seemed a good bet to win over Portland foodies.

While attending classes at UC Davis Wheelock adopted the approach of winemakers, giving meticulous attention to the terroir of particular cacao fields and the growing methods used. From four scrupulously selected growing regions—Trinidad, Peru, Ecuador, and Madagascar—he sourced beans with dramatically different characteristics. To bring the unadulterated flavor of the cacao through, they decided that Woodblock's chocolate bars would include no dairy products or other additives—only cacao and pure cane sugar.

Everything is done by hand, from roasting beans to packaging the bars, to produce the company's line of three single-origin bars and six double-origin (blended) bars, as well as bars with intriguing flavors such as salt and sesame. It's tempting to buy the whole range of bars to sample the whole spectrum of chocolate possibilities.

Alma Chocolate

Information

Ⓐ 140 NE 28th Ave.
Ⓣ (503)517-0262
Ⓗ M–Sa 11 a.m.–6 p.m., Su 12 p.m.-5 p.m.
Ⓦ almachocolate.com
Ⓜ p. 294-47

In pursuit of a world of chocolate

Around 2004, Sarah Hart thought, "Why is it that there is a lot of low quality chocolate bunnies at Easter?" This simple question was what led her into the world of chocolate. In 2005, Hart started doing her own chocolate research —meeting Ian Titterton, who became her teacher. For months, Hart honed her chocolate-making skills and increased the quality of her chocolates. She opened her first store in 2006.

Hart does not make or sell any chocolate that does not match her brand's core values so, she crafts Alma Chocolates with organic, single-origin cacao. As for community support Hart says, "I am not sure I would have been able to come as far as I have come, if I had started my business in a city other than Portland."

Alma Chocolate is beloved by Portland and the city is very supportive of the business—a cultural element that is unique to Portland. As a general rule, Portland residents are happy to consistently purchase local brands, dine at local restaurants and bars, and support local entrepreneurs. "I believe this is what helps a brand grow," says Hart.

Alma Chocolate is known as a flavor innovator, which is certainly true, but this is not actually what Alma aims to be. Instead, Hart's focus is on drawing out the best flavors from top-notch ingredients—a perfectly-balanced combination of cacao and organic cream, butter, sugar, nuts, fresh herbs, and spices. Stop by and sample some Alma Chocolate bon bons, toffees, chocolates, and drinking chocolate at the Northeast or Southeast shops and purchase some of the beautiful edible gold leaf chocolate icons for gifts while you are there.

Ben Jacobsen and Damian Magista immediately formed a mutual respect when they met.

Jacobsen Salt Co. & Bee Local

Information

Jacobsen Salt Co.
Ⓐ 602 SE Salmon St.
Ⓣ (503) 719-4973
Ⓗ M-F 9 a.m.-5 p.m.
Ⓦ jacobsensalt.com
Ⓜ p. 296-51

Bee Local
Ⓐ 602 SE Salmon St.
Ⓣ (503) 719-4973
Ⓗ M-F 11 a.m.-5 p.m.
Ⓦ beelocal.com
Ⓜ p. 296-50

Making your own salt and honey

Chef Gregory Gourdet of Departure Restaurant and Lounge (p. 82) firmly advised us to put Portland-made foods in the spotlight in this edition of *True Portland*. He specifically suggested Jacobsen Salt Co. and Bee Local, which are co-located. You've heard about Portland coffee and craft beer, but have you heard about Portland salt and honey?

So how did Ben Jacobsen of the eponymous Salt Co. and Damian Magista of Bee Local get started making their respective products in Portland?

Jacobsen was studying in Copenhagen when he came across some salt that he found especially delicious. At the time, despite all the great foods coming out of the Pacific Northwest, salt wasn't one of them, and Portlanders were buying their salt from places like France, the U.K., and Japan. Jacobsen wanted to change that so he started making salt in 2011. He tasted seawater at twenty different locations up and down the Washington and Oregon coasts and settled on the seawater in Oregon's Netarts Bay, where the

company now hand-makes its salt.

Magista started making honey the same year Jacobsen started making salt. The previous year, he'd placed beehives at community sites, and noticed how dramatically the honey harvested varied from area to area, not just in flavor but even in color. Bee Local's mission is to supply the healthiest, most distinctive, and flavorful honey using the most sustainable beekeeping methods.

The two brands and two founders share a space they moved into and renovated mostly themselves in 2014. It includes a retail store and test kitchen, office, and shipping facilities. Sharing a range of functions is a big advantage, Jacobsen affirms, because the products may be different, but they are largely carried by the same retailers. Most importantly, Jacobsen Salt and Bee Local share a philosophy of providing people, whether dining at home or at a restaurant, with the finest quality "elemental cooking ingredients," which they can feel good about cooking with and eating. That inspires the respect they have for

E

Eat

E

Eat

each other's products and beliefs.

A strong footing of cooperation enabled Jacobsen and Magista to overcome various challenges, like no heat in the new building for their first six months, which included winter. As the area where their businesses are located undergoes rapid urban evolution that—as in many parts of Portland—shows no signs of stopping, cheesemakers, distilleries, ice cream makers, and many other artisan food operations have sprung up.

Jacobsen says that Portland reminds him of the Northern European cities he's lived in, both in terms of its scale and how its citizens engage with the outdoors. In many big cities, it takes a long drive just to reach greenery, but drive fifteen or twenty minutes in practically any direction from Portland, and you're along a river, in the forest, in the mountains, or at a park. This promotes healthy lifestyles that, Magista adds, have nurtured the two brands.

Another ingredient to their success is that Portland is very tolerant of change. In the context of the city's collaboration-friendly, easygoing culture, people support each other's projects. Jacobsen Salt, for example, has worked with top chefs and restaurants, coffee roasters, and more. It's the people who make the city. Magista says that Portlanders are what make Portland so appealing for anyone with a crazy business idea that might not fly anywhere else, and he and Jacobsen are perfect examples. Their salt and honey are both cultural products of Portland. The creativity and community of the city has carried the two brands to success.

Their airy retail space has a panoply of salts, honeys, and caramels on display. Elsewhere on the premises are the test kitchen, offices, storage, and shipping facilities, all shared.

The Commons Brewery's original location. The sleek, silvery tanks stand out against the textured brick walls. Captivating contrasts like this are part of Portland's appeal.

DRINK

A city brimming with great libations

There's no two ways about it: Portland is a great place to have a drink. Not only is it a gathering place for third-wave coffee aficionados, it's also home to more breweries than any other city in the world. And the number of breweries continues to grow steadily. Just when you thought there were enough coffee roasters in town, another one pops up. Portland's obsession with all manner of libations may have something to do with the fact that its urban and suburban areas are rich with green spaces, and there's a nearly endless supply of clean water flowing from the snowy peak of Mt. Hood. Portland's deeply ingrained DIY culture continues to nurture new generations of alcoholic and non-alcoholic beverage makers. Whatever the reason, there is always something new (and tasty) brewing in Portland.

The Commons Brewery

People gather around great beer

In 2015, this brewery and taproom moved to a new location that's nearly three times larger than their previous space. It's one of Portland's most dynamic breweries, and, with a motto like "gather around beer," it's clear that the owners believe in beer's power to bring people together.

Their most popular beer is the Urban Farmhouse Ale. It's a saison ale made from mostly local ingredients that features a crisp finish.

The new taproom usually has twelve beers on tap. In addition to their classic and seasonal beers, you can also choose beers made in collaboration with other breweries.

Steve Jones, an award-winning cheese expert, runs a small kitchen called the Cheese Annex inside the brewery, where he serves cheese boards and cured meats. All the bread on the menu is baked at Little T American Baker (p. 80), which is made from the same yeast used for the Urban Farmhouse Ale.

Information

Ⓐ 630 SE Belmont St.
Ⓣ (503) 343-5501
Ⓗ 12 p.m.-10 p.m. daily
Ⓦ commonsbrewery.com
Ⓜ p. 296-46 / $$

D

Drink

Plenty of natural light floods the taproom, which shares the same floor as the brewery.

Multnomah Whiskey Library

*The handsome,
old-timey feel pairs well
with top-shelf whiskey*

Information

Ⓐ 1124 SW Alder St.
Ⓣ (503) 954-1381
Ⓗ M-Th 4 p.m.-12 a.m., F-Sa 4 p.m.-1 a.m.
Ⓦ mwlpdx.com
Ⓜ p. 288-48 / $$$

The Multnomah Whiskey Library opened in 2014, and since then, you'd be hard-pressed to find a Portland bar with more bottles of the brown stuff on the wall. In fact, we don't think it exists. Order a dram of whiskey, scotch, or bourbon and watch as your suited bartender rolls a large library ladder along the towering bar wall to fetch it. Bottles on hand for your enjoyment include whiskey distilled in Portland, Scotch whiskey, Irish whiskey, Japanese whiskey, bourbon, and spirits from Mexico. An in-house curator is constantly adding to the menu of over 1,600 bottles from around the world.

If you are sitting at a table or couch, cocktails are prepared tableside or seat-side from a well-equipped bar cart. While membership is not required, the $600 fee buys access to many special tasting events. When designing the bar's relaxed and refined interior, the owners looked to the architecture of English gentlemen's clubs. The walls are decorated with portraits of distillers from around the world.

98

D

Drink

Reservations can only be made by members, however, it's still possible to get a table as a walk-in, especially right after they open. There's plenty of good food on the menu.

Courier Coffee Roasters

Fantastic coffee, friendly staff

Portland's coffee scene is constantly changing. Popular roasters often choose to expand and there's always a new kid in town. But Courier Coffee, located just down the street from downtown's Powell's City of Books, has somehow resisted the urge to change all that much. It still seems very much the same as it was when it first opened. The owner, Joel Domreis, has other things on his mind beyond the pursuit of corporate growth. The Courier staff is very friendly and more than happy to recommend places to visit for out of town travelers. With its fantastic coffee and friendly staff, this is a place you'll want to stop by again and again. Pastries are baked fresh every morning. Courier also delivers, but only as far as they can get by bicycle.

Information

Ⓐ 923 SW Oak St.
Ⓣ (503) 545-6444
Ⓗ M-F 7 a.m.-6 p.m., Sa-Su 9 a.m.-5 p.m.
Ⓦ couriercoffeeroasters.com
Ⓜ p. 288-23 / $

You'll find only light and medium roasts on the menu. The canelé, a pastry with a soft custard center, is definitely worth trying (right, second from the bottom). It's popular, though, so get there early.

Tea Bar

*Tea that brings people together
and encourages revitalization*

Four blocks north of the vibrant NE Alberta
Street, is NE Killingsworth Street. Here you'll find Tea
Bar, a tea shop and house that opened in 2014 that's at
the forefront of an up-and-coming trend in Portland:
Asian tea. Owner, Erica Indira Swanson, first fell in
love with tea at the age of sixteen, when she was living
in China. After returning home, she opened Tea Bar on
the ground floor of a building owned by her family's
real estate company, Little Beirut Properties. Swanson
says she did everything herself on a limited budget,
including designing the store's interior. She even
researched the city's Pedestrian Master Plan when pick-
ing a location. All of her hard work seems to have paid
off: She opened two other locations on SE Division
Street and NW Northrup Street.

Information

Ⓐ 1615 NE Killingsworth St.
Ⓣ (503) 477-4676
Ⓗ 8 a.m. - 8 p.m. daily
Ⓦ teabarpdx.com
Ⓜ p. 294-3 / $

(Left) Erica Indira Swanson buys her matcha green tea from a small farm in Kyoto, Japan. Lavender boba is one of their best sellers. A great place to grab a stylish cup of tea.

Ex Novo Brewing Co.

Making the world a better place through beer

What kind of business do you imagine when someone says "nonprofit?" We're guessing not a brewery. Well, Ex Novo Brewing Co. was the 55th brewery to open its doors in Portland, and it's also the only one so far that's a nonprofit. All Ex Novo profits go to charity.

Ex Novo founder Joel Gregory used to work in solar energy as an engineer. He became interested in beer after getting into homebrewing. His goal of "effecting positive social change" eventually brought him to the idea of starting a nonprofit brewery. When asked what his future goals are, he simply says he wants to make good beer. It's pretty sweet that the good in his beer isn't just about the taste.

104

D

Drink

Information

Ⓐ 2326 N Flint Ave.
Ⓣ (503) 894-8251
Ⓗ M-Th 3 p.m.-10 p.m., F 3 p.m.-11 p.m.,
    Sa 10 a.m.-11 p.m., Su 10 a.m.-10 p.m.
Ⓦ exnovobrew.com
Ⓜ p. 292-38 / $

Gregory is originally from New Mexico. He came to Portland in search of nature and culture.

In addition to their popular pilsner, they brew other kinds of beer year-round. Ganum is also the co-founder of the Old Salt Market-place (p. 82).

Upright Brewing

Home of Portland's 2015 Beer of the Year

    This small brewery is in the basement of an old building just across the Broadway Bridge from downtown. Their farmhouse open-fermentation beers are some of the most popular among Portlanders, with the *Willamette Week* newspaper picking their pilsner as its 2015 Beer of the Year.

    With a typically Portland outlook on business, owner, Alex Ganum, says he simply just brews the beers that he wants to drink. After all, what's better than making people happy doing something you love? Stop by, listen to some records, and sip a tasty pint.

Information

Ⓐ 240 N Broadway, Suite 2
Ⓣ (503) 735-5337
Ⓗ Th 5 p.m.-9 p.m., F 4:30 p.m.-9 p.m.,
   Sa 1 p.m.-8 p.m., Su 1 p.m.-6 p.m.
Ⓦ uprightbrewing.com
Ⓜ p. 292-41 / $

Cascade Brewing Barrel House

Embrace sour power

This brewery specializes in sour barrel-aged beers that are often made by adding fruit during the aging process. The strawberry, blueberry, and apricot are all delicious and we think that their beer sampler is a good place to start. But be careful; these tart brews typically come with a higher alcohol content.

Information

Ⓐ 939 SE Belmont St.
Ⓣ (503) 265-8603
Ⓗ Su–Th 12 p.m.-11 p.m., F-Sa 12 p.m.-12 a.m.
Ⓦ cascadebrewingbarrelhouse.com
Ⓜ p. 296-40 / $$

D

Drink

Baerlic Brewing Company

Sundry beers in a simple setting

Information

Ⓐ 2235 SE 11th Ave.
Ⓣ (503) 477-9418
Ⓗ M-Th 4 p.m.-10 p.m., F 2 p.m.-11 p.m.,
   Sa 12 p.m.-11 p.m., Su 12 p.m.-9 p.m.
Ⓦ baerlicbrewing.com
Ⓜ p. 296-90 / $

This brewery quickly made a name for itself after opening in 2014. They feature ten beers on tap in the taproom, and while they don't have a food menu, you can bring your own food. The brewery is occasionally open for tours, so if you're interested in seeing how beer is made, check out the schedule on their website.

Burnside Brewing Co.

Experimental brews
from a true beer laboratory

Information

Ⓐ 701 E Burnside St.
Ⓣ (503) 946-8151
Ⓗ Su-Tu 11 a.m.-10 p.m., W-Th 11 a.m.-11 p.m.,
    F-Sa 11 a.m.-12 a.m.
Ⓦ burnsidebrewco.com
Ⓜ p. 294-41 / $$

This creative brewery isn't afraid of taking risks. In fact, they've thrown out the rulebook in an effort to make beer you've never tasted before. As a result, over half the beers on their menu are seasonal. Their food menu is also good.

D

Drink

Gigantic Brewing Company

Check out the labels
designed by local artists

This brewery's all about hoppy IPAs. All non-IPA beers are limited runs, and most of those are brewed only once. The Ume Umai was introduced in 2015. Made with black rice and plums, it was originally created for a Japanese izakaya festival in Portland. The label was designed by Tokyo native Yu Suda.

Information

Ⓐ 5224 SE 26th Ave.
Ⓣ (503) 208-3416
Ⓗ M-W 3 p.m.-9 p.m., Th-F 2 p.m.-10 p.m.,
    Sa 12 p.m.-10 p.m., Su 12 p.m.-9 p.m.
Ⓦ giganticbrewing.com / $

Reverend Nat's Hard Cider

Tradition and innovation

Information

Ⓐ 1813 NE 2nd Ave.
Ⓣ (503) 567-2221
Ⓗ Tu-Th 4 p.m.-10 p.m., F 4 p.m.-11 p.m.,
 Sa 10 a.m.-11 p.m., Su 10 a.m.-7 p.m.
Ⓦ reverendnatshardcider.com
Ⓜ p. 294-24 / $

In the past few years hard cider has become many people's drink of choice in Portland. Reverend Nat West has played the largest role in that. West has been making delicious cider ever since he took some apples from a friend's backyard tree years ago and pressed and fermented his first batch. After a stint of home cider making in his basement and garage, he moved into his current cidery in 2013. You can now find Reverend Nat Ciders all along the West Coast and British Columbia, in Hawaii, Alaska, Japan, and Singapore. In addition to award-winning traditional hard ciders made from 100% apples, West experiments with the addition of hops, apricots, and ginger. If you're in the mood to taste a few of the Reverend's ciders, we highly recommend the sampler. The Reverend Nat tasting room is one of our very favorites in Portland.

Behind the bar are the stainless steel tanks where the Reverend brews his cider.

In addition to their own ciders, they've got ciders from cideries all over the U.S.

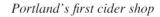

Bushwhacker Cider

Portland's first cider shop

This hard cider bottle shop and small-scale cider maker, with two locations, is all about tradition. Portland has more than its fair share of good wines and beers, and thanks to its proximity to a wealth of apple orchards, it's also a great place for hard cider. The Alice cider here is made from 100% Granny Smith apples. It's tart, refreshing, and hard not to like. Try their whiskey-cask or gin-cask ciders for something more fragrant, or enjoy ciders from other makers as well.

Information

Ⓐ 1212-D SE Powell Blvd.
Ⓣ (503) 445-0577
Ⓗ Su-Th 12 p.m.-10 p.m., F-Sa 12 p.m.-11 p.m.
Ⓦ bushwhackercider.com
Ⓜ p. 296-88 / $

Because it used to be a body shop, the building is open and airy, and there's even space to park your bicycle inside.

Coopers Hall

A must-visit urban winery

This 8,000 square-foot urban winery and taproom occupies a giant building in Southeast Portland that used to be an auto body shop. Enjoy your meal paired with delicious wine while surrounded by barrels of fermenting wine. The wall behind the bar is lined with forty-four wine spouts because Coopers Hall is dedicated to crafting and serving wine from kegs as opposed to bottle conditioning it. They produce more than fifteen kinds of wine and offer additional "guest taps" that vary seasonally. If you're interested in tasting a lot of different wines, you can order samples from as little as two ounces. And, of course, they've got beer and hard cider on the menu, too. Wines are also available by the bottle, so you might take one back to your hotel room to round off the evening.

Information

Ⓐ 404 SE 6th Ave.
Ⓣ (503) 719-7000
Ⓗ M-Sa 4 p.m.-10 p.m.
Ⓦ coopershall.com
Ⓜ p. 296-23 / $$$

ENSO Winery

Authentic old-world-style wines

Founder Ryan Sharp started ENSO because of his desire to bring wine production to the doorstep of Portland wine drinkers. He first fell in love with wine-making after helping out at a winery in nearby Salem. Soon after, he began making wine at home using local grapes. ENSO Winery is the culmination of his passion.

The winery itself is located right behind the bar so you often catch glimpses of production. Sample Sharp's wines (all price levels) as well as other tasty West Coast wines at ENSO, the food menu includes local bread, cheese, and meats.

Information

Ⓐ 1416 SE Stark St.
Ⓣ (503) 683-3676
Ⓗ M-Th 4 p.m.-10 p.m., F 4 p.m.-11 p.m.,
  Sa 1 p.m.-11 p.m., Su 1 p.m.-10 p.m.
Ⓦ ensowinery.com
Ⓜ p. 296-29 / $$

111

D

Drink

Sharp and his staff, in the middle of wine production in late summer. ENSO Winery uses grapes from Oregon, California, and Washington.

F. H. Steinbart Co.

A one-stop shop for homebrewers

Founded in 1918, this is one of the oldest wine and beer-making supply stores in the U.S. They sell all the equipment and ingredients you need here for home beer, wine, cider, and soda-making, including malt by the ounce, yeast, and hops. They even have all-in-one kits for the first-time home brewer as well as in-store classes on the basics of homebrewing. Naturally, the staff is incredibly knowledgeable and always quite helpful.

Information

Ⓐ 234 SE 12th Ave.
Ⓣ (503) 232-8793
Ⓗ M-W 8:30 a.m.-6 p.m., Th-F 8:30 a.m.-7 p.m.,
Sa 9 a.m.-4 p.m., Su 10 a.m.-4 p.m.
Ⓦ fhsteinbart.com
Ⓜ p. 296-19

D

Drink

See See Motor Coffee Co.

A cafe for motorcycle lovers

This motorcycle depot/cafe hybrid is a must for motorcycle enthusiasts. Check out their original gear, or head to the garage behind the shop, where you can have your custom bike built. The cafe serves Stumptown Coffee.

Information

Ⓐ 1642 NE Sandy Blvd.
Ⓣ (503) 894-9566
Ⓗ M-F 7 a.m.-7 p.m., Sa-Su 8 a.m.-6 p.m.
Ⓦ seeseemotorcycles.com
Ⓜ p. 294-43 / $$

The Toffee Club

Dedicated to all football lovers

This stylish, modern English pub for football fans (soccer lovers to Americans) opened in 2016 with several large flat-screen TVs and plenty of savory pies and UK and European beers. Three football lovers—Niki Diamond, her husband Pete Hoppins, and his brother Jack Hoppins—founded the joint in the former Hawthorne Strip strip club space. It's a great central spot to gather and watch a game (screenings are regularly updated on their website); eat some tasty fish & chips, a Scotch egg, or bangers and mash; and toss back a couple craft pints from across the pond. Minors are welcome until 8 p.m.

Information

Ⓐ 1006 SE Hawthorne Blvd.
Ⓣ (971) 254-9518
Ⓗ M-Th 11:30 a.m.-12 a.m.,F 11:30 a.m.-2 a.m.,
  Sa 7 a.m.-2 a.m., Su 8 a.m.-12 a.m.
Ⓦ toffeeclubpdx.com
Ⓜ p. 296-87 / $$

113

D

Drink

Heart Roasters

Coffee of uncompromising quality

Finnish pro snowboarder Wille Yli-Luoma opened this roastery and cafe in 2009 and the downtown location in 2013. He doesn't specialize in light or dark roasts; instead he prefers to do the right roast for each bean, guaranteeing an amazing cup of coffee each time. Some of the downtown cafe's furniture is produced by The Good Mod (p. 194).

Information

Ⓐ 2211 E Burnside St.
Ⓣ (503) 206-6602
Ⓗ 7 a.m.-6 p.m. daily
Ⓦ heartroasters.com
Ⓜ p. 294-45 / $

Sip Juice Cart

Organic juice every day

This juice business now has a storefront on Alberta Street in addition to its original cart at People's Food Co-op (p. 76). On the menu are juices and smoothies made from all sorts of local, organic ingredients. Lucky for you, both locations are open seven days a week from 9 a.m. Check out their offshoot restaurant, Canteen (p. 81).

Information

Ⓐ 2210 NE Alberta St.
Ⓣ (503) 680-5639
Ⓗ Su-Th 9 a.m.-4 p.m., F-Sa 9 a.m.-6 p.m.
Ⓦ sipjuicecart.com
Ⓜ p. 294-18 / $

D

Drink

Steven Smith Teamaker

Home of a true tea master

Information

Ⓐ 1626 NW Thurman St.
Ⓣ (503) 719-8752
Ⓗ 10 a.m.-6 p.m. daily
Ⓦ smithtea.com
Ⓜ p. 290-4 / $$

The late Steven Smith introduced a whole generation to the world of tea through his company Tazo Tea and other tea ventures, and he became famous, as the *New York Times* noted, as the "Marco Polo" of American tea. After selling Tazo Tea to Starbucks, Smith moved to France. Inspired by the country's artisanal culture, he vowed to open a tea company in Portland where he could focus on creating the teas he really wanted to make, expertly blended ones. Both locations have lovely tasting rooms serving Smith's teas so you can sip and shop. Smith sadly passed away in 2015, and the company is now run by his right-hand man, Tony Tellin.

Angel Face

What's on the menu? Nothing!

Information

Ⓐ 14 NE 28th Ave.
Ⓣ (503) 239-3804
Ⓗ Su-Th 5 p.m.-12 a.m., F-Sa 5 p.m.-1 a.m.
Ⓦ angelfaceportland.com
Ⓜ p. 294-48 / $$$

That's right, this bar has no cocktail menu. Tell the bartender what type of cocktail you're in the mood for (there's wine and beer as well) and leave the rest up to them. Typically, you'll be served up an expert version of a classic cocktail. There is also a wide selection of vermouths and brandies to tipple.

Expatriate

Expert cocktails and Naomi Pomeroy's Asian-inspired menu

Chef Naomi Pomeroy (Beast, p. 62) and her husband Kyle Webster are co-owners of this gorgeous Northeast cocktail lounge just across the street from her restaurant Beast. Webster runs the much lauded cocktail program, and the dreamy, largely Asian-inspired menu is, of course, helmed by Pomeroy. Expatriate is one of the tastiest and beautifully moody bars in Portland. It was named 2014's Bar of the Year by local newspaper *Willamette Week*.

Information

Ⓐ 5424 NE 30th Ave.
Ⓣ (503) 805-3750
Ⓗ 5 p.m.-12 a.m. daily
Ⓦ expatriatepdx.com
Ⓜ p. 294-8 / $$$

Stumptown Coffee Roasters

Third-wave coffee served at five locations, including inside Ace Hotel. They have a roasting facility and a retail annex inside their headquarters on Salmon Street.

Ⓐ 3356 SE Belmont St.
Ⓣ (855) 711-3385
Ⓗ M-F 6 a.m.-7 p.m., Sa-Su 7 a.m.-7 p.m.
Ⓦ stumptowncoffee.com / Ⓜ p. 296-55 / $

Coava Coffee Roasters

Great coffee served in a large industrial space. Check out their newer location on SE Hawthorne Boulevard, open since 2014.

Ⓐ 1300 SE Grand Ave.
Ⓣ (503) 894-8134
Ⓗ M-F 6 a.m.-6 p.m., Sa-Su 7 a.m.-6 p.m.
Ⓦ coavacoffee.com / Ⓜ p. 296-52 / $

Extracto Coffee Roasters

This small-batch roaster with tasty single origin espresso has two locations in Northeast Portland: its original roastery and cafe as well as this second coffeehouse.

Ⓐ 1456 NE Prescott St. / Ⓣ (503) 284-1380
Ⓗ 7 a.m.-6 p.m. daily
Ⓦ extractocoffee.com / Ⓜ p. 294-20 / $

Albina Press

One of Portland's most beloved spots to grab a cup of exquisite joe with regular exhibitions by local artists. Albina Press put Portland on the coffee map.

Ⓐ 4637 N Albina Ave.
Ⓣ (503) 212-5214
Ⓗ 6 a.m.-8 p.m. daily / Ⓜ p. 292-16 / $

Barista

This multi-roaster coffee shop has five locations including Brass Bar in Pine Street Market (p. 38). The extremely skilled baristas began roasting some of their own coffee as well in 2016.

Ⓐ 1725 NE Alberta St. / Ⓣ (503) 208-2568
Ⓗ M-F 6 a.m.-6 p.m., Sa-Su 7 a.m.-6 p.m.
Ⓦ baristapdx.com / Ⓜ p. 294-12 / $

Pépé Le Moko

In the basement of the Ace Hotel is this gem of a small cocktail bar. Everything is perfection here including cocktails made with Stumptown Coffee.

Ⓐ 407 SW 10th Ave.
Ⓣ (503) 546-8537
Ⓗ 4 p.m.-2 a.m. daily
Ⓦ pepelemokopdx.com / Ⓜ p. 288-19 / $$

Donnie Vegas

Grab an on-tap cocktail and specialty hot dog (Seoul Dog, Banh Mi Dog...) at this bar founded by former Ned Ludd (p. 64) employees.

Ⓐ 1203 NE Alberta St.
Ⓣ (503) 477-7244
Ⓗ M-F 4 p.m.-2:30 a.m., Sa-Su 12 p.m.-2:30 a.m.
Ⓦ donnie.vegas / Ⓜ p. 294-11 / $

Rum Club

It's in the name: Rum Club is all about great rum and tasty craft cocktails at reasonable prices. Start off with their popular Rum Club Daiquiri.

Ⓐ 720 SE Sandy Blvd.
Ⓣ (503) 265-8807
Ⓗ 4 p.m.-2 a.m. daily
Ⓦ rumclubpdx.com / Ⓜ p. 296-28 / $$

Church

You don't have to be religious to enjoy this cocktail bar. Stop in to listen to the gospel according to their DJ or make a "confession" in the photo booth.

Ⓐ 2600 NE Sandy Blvd.
Ⓣ (503) 206-8962
Ⓗ 4 p.m.-2 a.m. daily
Ⓦ churchbarpdx.com / Ⓜ p. 294-34 / $$

Base Camp Brewing Company

Enjoy the urban outdoors from their large outdoor seating area with various food carts to choose from.

Ⓐ 930 SE Oak St.
Ⓣ (503) 477-7479
Ⓗ Su–W 12 p.m.-10 p.m., Th–Sa 11 a.m.-12 a.m.
Ⓦ basecampbrewingco.com
Ⓜ p. 296-24 / $

PINTS Brewing Company

This Old Town brewery/taproom doubles as a cafe in the morning.

Ⓐ 412 NW 5th Ave.
Ⓣ (503) 564-2739
Ⓗ M-F 11:30 a.m.-11 p.m., Sa 10 a.m.-11 p.m., Su 10 a.m.-9 p.m.
Ⓦ pintsbrewing.com
Ⓜ p. 290-28 / $$

Hopworks Urban Brewery

Organic beer at three locations made with a commitment to sustainability and energy efficiency. The bikes decorating the bar are made by a local manufacturer.

Ⓐ 2944 SE Powell Blvd. / Ⓣ (503) 232-4677
Ⓗ Su-Th 11 a.m.-11 p.m., F-Sa 11 a.m.-12 a.m.
Ⓦ hopworksbeer.com / Ⓜ p. 296-86 / $$

Bailey's Taproom

This beer bar has more than 100 delicious brews on the menu (26 on tap) making it an ideal place to try something new.

Ⓐ 213 SW Broadway / Ⓣ (503) 295-1004
Ⓗ 12 p.m.-12 a.m. daily
Ⓦ baileystaproom.com
Ⓜ p. 288-29 / $

Saraveza

Choose from more than 250 bottled beers at this bottle shop/beer bar. There's a limited food menu specializing in British pasties, and bottles are discounted if you buy them to go.

Ⓐ 1004 N Killingsworth St.
Ⓣ (503) 206-4252 / Ⓗ 11 a.m.-12 a.m. daily
Ⓦ saraveza.com / Ⓜ p. 292-8 / $$

The Oregon Public House

"Have a pint. Change the world." That's the motto of this brewery, where all profits go to charity.

Ⓐ 700 NE Dekum St.
Ⓣ (503) 828-0884
Ⓗ Tu-Th 11:30 a.m.-10 p.m., F-Sa 11:30 a.m.-11 p.m., Su 11:30 a.m.-10 p.m.
Ⓦ oregonpublichouse.com / Ⓜ p. 294-2 / $$

117

D

Drink

Willamette Valley Wineries

Portland is located in the Willamette Valley, which stretches for 150 miles and is home to more than 500 wineries. Take a weekend trip south and explore.

Ⓦ willamettewines.com

Southeast Wine Collective

Discover a wide variety of wines, many of which have been made by collective members in the 5,000-square-foot urban winery space.

Ⓐ 2425 SE 35th Pl. / Ⓣ (503) 208-2061
Ⓗ M 4 p.m.-9 p.m., W-F 4 p.m.-10 p.m., Sa 1 p.m.-10 p.m., Su 1 p.m.-9 p.m.
Ⓦ sewinecollective.com / Ⓜ p. 296-75 / $$

Bull Run Distilling Company

Lee Medoff's Nob Hill distillery focuses on dark spirits including his pure malt whiskey that you can sample in the tasting room.

Ⓐ 2259 NW Quimby St.
Ⓣ (503) 224-3483
Ⓗ W-Su 12 p.m.-6 p.m.
Ⓦ bullrundistillery.com / Ⓜ p. 290-6 / $$

Commentary

RED GILLEN

Beer Blogger

"Must try" drinks for Portland newewcomers

Red Gillen blogs in Japanese about the Portland craft beer scene and provides tours of Portland breweries. oshuushu.com

One thing that makes the Portland beer and alcoholic beverage scene so fantastic is that in addition to established players, a new crop of breweries, cideries, urban wineries, and distilleries emerges every year. Like Portland's dynamic restaurant scene, this offers drinkers the choice of revisiting delicious favorites or trying something new that might amaze them. Here are some recommendations for new Portland spots that have grabbed my attention and taste buds.

Labrewatory

This brewpub, with its modern, attractive decor, located in an industrial part of Portland, is unlike any other I've ever been to. The small (five-barrel) brewing system in the back is used by Labrewatory, and other breweries, to try out new recipes, tweak old recipes, or create experimental beers. The first beer I had there was a cranberry and squid ink beer that went on to win a Portland beer award. Fear not—a wide, changing menu of more traditional beers are available, including sours, Belgian-style ales, and a Japanese lager that made me want to eat sushi immediately.

Ⓐ 670 N Russell St. / Ⓣ (971) 271-8151 / Ⓗ Tu-Th 11 a.m.-9 p.m., F-Sa 11 a.m.-11 p.m., Su 11 a.m.-7 p.m. / Ⓦ labrewatory.com

Great Notion Brewing

This small brewery in Portland's funky Alberta Arts District was putting out award-winning IPA-style beers within a few months of its launch. Great Notion's IPAs are far different from the bitter, citrusy IPAs typically found in Portland. Great Notion makes IPAs marked by light-colored clarity, a fruity rather than bitter taste, and a very hoppy nose. I highly recommend trying out a pint or two in Great Notion's flowery, laid-back beer garden area.

Ⓐ 2204 NE Alberta St. #101. / Ⓣ (503) 548-4491 / Ⓗ Su-Th 12 p.m.-10 p.m., F-Sa 12 p.m.-11 p.m. / Ⓦ greatnotionpdx.com

Hi-Wheel Fizzy wine Co.

Rather than beer, Hi-Wheel makes other kinds of alcoholic beverages I'd never tried before. I like to call them "artisanal wine coolers," but they're much better than what you remember from college. Described by Hi-Wheel as "fizzy wines," these refreshing drinks are citrus-based and include a number of ingredients such as ginger, lavender, carrots, even habanero peppers. They are very popular and are available throughout Portland in bottles or on tap.

Ⓐ 6719 NE 18th Ave. / Ⓣ (503) 928-5723 / Ⓗ Tu-F 5 p.m.-10 p.m., Sa 12 p.m.-10 p.m., Su 12 p.m.-9 p.m. / Ⓦ hiwheelwines.com

Profile

NATALIE ROSE BALDWIN

Brewer

Born in Colorado, moved to Portland in 2012. Hobbies include hiking, bicycling, travel, and making stuff. Formerly worked as a brewer at Burnside Brewing. Currently working at Breakside Brewery.

Portland's economy is buzzed on homebrewing

You can't discuss Portland's vaunted beer culture without talking about homebrewing. Natalie Rose Baldwin started out as a homebrewer and worked her way up to become one of the few women in the ranks of the city's professional brewers.

She got into homebrewing several years ago. Having studied biochemistry in college, and being an aficionado of cheese and beer, she wanted to try her hand at making her favorite drink herself. She loaded up on homebrewing supplies at breweries or stores like F. H. Steinbart (p. 112), and got together with fellow homebrewers for yeast-exchange parties. Her first beer making efforts made it obvious that home brewing was more difficult than expected, but in no time she was expanding her horizons beyond homebrewing, collaborating with professional brewers to craft beers for contests, and aiming to join their ranks.

She officially set out on the path to become a pro brewer when she took a job as an assistant at Burnside Brewing (p. 107) in October 2014. In February 2015, a brewer position opened up at the company, but she didn't think she had enough experience to apply for it until the brewery owner and

chief brewer urged her to go for it. She got the job and for more than a year she handled the brewing of Burnside's regular beers while exploring her own recipes. She also sold beer at events and filled orders from far-flung locales like Japan, Malaysia, Spain, and Brazil while at Burnside. Baldwin currently works at Breakside Brewery.

Portland has so much community support for brewing delicious beers that public-sector funding is even available for start-up breweries. Baldwin believes that the ever-growing number of Portland breweries is good for the industry because competition drives everyone to craft better beers. Plus, since each brewery has its own style, people aiming to become brewers can garner a wide range of experience. The competition to land paying jobs as a brewer is also intense, with homebrewers making the rounds with their proudly brewed beers, asking if there are any openings at breweries.

Baldwin's ambition now is to hone her craft so she can brew even more delicious beers and someday have her own little brewery.

119

D

Drink

INSKEEP GALLERY

The Portland Art Museum is located downtown. It has a large selection of art from around the world, ranging from prehistoric to modern.

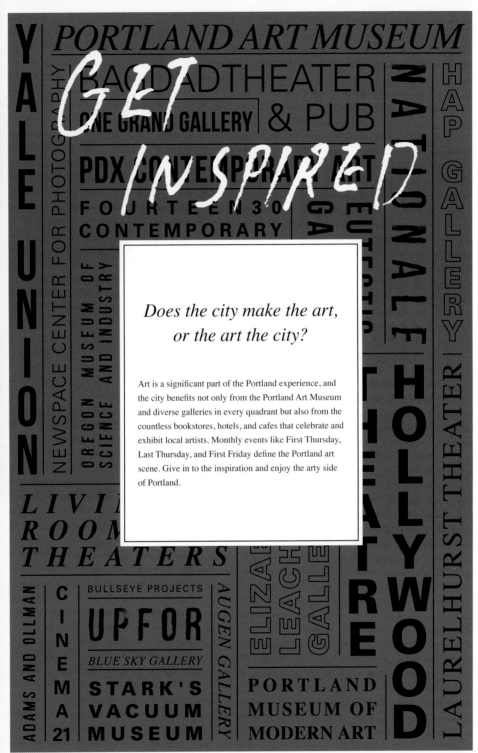

GET INSPIRED

Does the city make the art, or the art the city?

Art is a significant part of the Portland experience, and the city benefits not only from the Portland Art Museum and diverse galleries in every quadrant but also from the countless bookstores, hotels, and cafes that celebrate and exhibit local artists. Monthly events like First Thursday, Last Thursday, and First Friday define the Portland art scene. Give in to the inspiration and enjoy the arty side of Portland.

Portland Art Museum

One of America's oldest museums boasts a fantastic art collection

Founded in 1892, The Portland Art Museum has more than 45,000 objects in its collection. It was the seventh museum to open in the U.S. and the first on the West Coast. Its collection of Native American art is particularly impressive as is its Northwest collection with 10,000 works by artists from the region. The museum hosts artwork by important female artists and artists of color, including Carrie Mae Weems, Robert Colescott, Helen Frankenthaler, Wendy Red Star, and Kehinde Wiley. In addition, there are paintings by Monet, Renoir, Cézanne, and Picasso, sculptures by Rodin, and pieces by Marcel Duchamp and Andy Warhol. There's also a sizable collection of Asian art, which includes Japanese scrolls and ukiyo-e woodblock prints, and Chinese pottery and tomb objects. In other words, it's best to carve out a few hours to take in all that the Portland Art Museum has to offer. Take a break from exploring the exhibits and collections at the Museum Grounds Cafe next to the gift shop, or get a breath of fresh air in the adjoining outdoor sculpture garden.

Information

Ⓐ 1219 SW Park Ave.
Ⓣ (503) 226-2811
Ⓗ Tu-W 10 a.m.-5 p.m., Th-F 10 a.m.-8 p.m.,
   Sa-Su 10 a.m.-5 p.m.
Ⓦ portlandartmuseum.org
Ⓜ p. 288-67

In addition to its fine art collection, the Portland Art Museum also holds exhibitions highlighting Portland culture, including exhibitions about bicycles and tattoos.

Nationale

Cozy Southeast Portland gallery and shop for emerging artists

Information

Ⓐ 3360 SE Division St.
Ⓣ (503) 477-9786
Ⓗ W-M 12 p.m.-6 p.m.
Ⓦ nationale.us
Ⓜ p. 296-79

This unique art gallery and specialty shop focuses on exhibiting the works of emerging artists, art and design gifts and books, and a unique merchant-in-residence program. Nationale is one of the preeminent small galleries in Portland with plenty of artwork for sale at reasonable prices.The owner, May Barruel, has chosen a beautiful selection of fragrances, accessories, and artful products from local brands to sell in the shop. Born in Grenoble, France, Barruel is a an art and literature lover. She moved to Portland in 2000 and began working as an art curator downtown while keeping a part-time gig as a barista at Stumptown Coffee. Nationale opened its doors in 2008.

After you've checked out the exhibition space, take a peek at the collection of art books and other crafts on sale in the shop. Everything from the art on the walls to the items on sale feels like it was curated with the utmost care.

Upfor

A spacious gallery for new and digital media

Upfor is one of the only galleries in the Pearl District focusing on new and digital media. It is run by famed speculative fiction writer Ursula K. Le Guin's son Theo Downes-Le Guin. Downes-Le Guin is a fixture in Portland's contemporary art community and was formerly a think tank market and policy researcher. Many of the exhibits and performances here explore the theme of technology as an art medium.

Information

Ⓐ 929 NW Flanders St.
Ⓣ (503) 227-5111
Ⓗ Tu-Sa 11 a.m.-6 p.m.
Ⓦ upforgallery.com
Ⓜ p. 290-22

Adams and Ollman

Get inspired by self-taught artists

Information

Ⓐ 209 SW 9th Ave.
Ⓣ (503) 724-0684
Ⓗ W-Sa 11 a.m.-5 p.m.
Ⓦ adamsandollman.com
Ⓜ p. 288-26

This art gallery, a block away from the downtown Powell's Books, specializes in twentieth century self-taught and contemporary artists from around the country. Gallery owner, Amy Adams, is a self-taught artist herself and she opened the gallery with John Ollman, owner of Fleisher/Ollman Gallery in Philadelphia. The two galleries often hold collaborative events.

Yale Union

An experimental art gallery in an old commercial laundry building

This nonprofit center for contemporary art is "led by a desire to support artists, propose new modes of production, and stimulate the ongoing public discourse around art." Check their website in advance for the schedule of events and exhibitions. The art library is open by appointment only. Located in the newly renovated Yale Union Laundry Building, which was constructed in 1908, the building is now listed in the National Register of Historic Places.

Information

Ⓐ 800 SE 10th Ave.
Ⓣ (503) 236-7996
Ⓗ call for exhibition
Ⓦ yaleunion.org
Ⓜ p. 296-41

Portland Museum of Modern Art

Super funky North Portland basement museum

Located in the basement of Mississippi Records (p. 136) the Portland Museum of Modern Art is tiny but mighty. The national and international art and conceptual projects on display are excellent and often reside at the intersection of fine art and music. A recent exhibit included the paintings of legendary avant-garde guitarist John Fahey. What this museum lacks in traditional museum atmosphere, it more than makes up for with Portland attitude.

Information

Ⓐ 5202 N Albina Ave.
Ⓗ 12 p.m.-7 p.m. daily
Ⓦ portlandmuseumofmodernart.com
Ⓜ p. 292-12

Get Inspired

Disjecta Contemporary Art Center

Renowned nonprofit art center with community events

This North Portland nonprofit contemporary art center, located inside an old renovated bowling alley, focuses on visual and performance art. In addition to their curator-in-residence program, funded by the Andy Warhol Foundation for the Visual Arts, they hold events, such as the Portland Biennial, that showcases local artists and the annual Quiet Music Festival of Portland.

Information

Ⓐ 8371 N Interstate Ave.
Ⓣ (503) 286-9449
Ⓗ F-Su 12 p.m.-5 p.m.
Ⓦ disjectaarts.org
Ⓜ p. 292-2

Tickets are sold at the box office window next to the entrance. Get there early and grab a drink or a bite to eat before the show starts.

Living Room Theaters

Go to the movies and relax just like at home

This popular downtown theater was the first in the nation to use digital projectors exclusively. Popular new releases, independent movies, and international films can all be enjoyed for $10 ($8 for matinees). The food isn't the usual movie theater fare either—pizza, shish ka-bobs, panini sandwiches, and sushi are all served at the lounge with a full bar, and your order is brought directly to your theater seat. Lean back in the plush seats with a hot meal, cold beer or cocktail, and enjoy the show. A jazz band plays in the bar area on Fridays and Saturdays.

Information

Ⓐ 341 SW 10th Ave.
Ⓣ (971) 222-2010
Ⓗ 11:30 a.m.-late night daily
Ⓦ pdx.livingroomtheaters.com
Ⓜ p. 288-15

Laurelhurst Theater

1923 art deco-style movie theater

The Laurelhurst Theater became part of Portland's cultural and architectural history when it first opened in 1923. The original single-screen auditorium could seat 650 people and was one of the first art deco-style theaters of the period. Laurelhurst Theater now has four screens that show second-run modern cinema, independent, art, and classic films all for the low price of $4 a ticket (just $3 for matinees!). The menu includes beer, wine, and pizza. twenty-one and over only after 5:30 p.m.

Information

Ⓐ 2735 E Burnside St.
Ⓣ (503) 232-5511
Ⓗ call for movie schedule
Ⓦ laurelhursttheater.com
Ⓜ p. 294-46

Get Inspired

Cinema 21

Beloved Nob Hill independent theater

Information

Ⓐ 616 NW 21st Ave.
Ⓣ (503) 223-4515
Ⓗ call for movie schedule
Ⓦ cinema21.com
Ⓜ p. 290-8

Cinema 21 is a mainstay of Portland cinema arts. It was recently renovated; two new screens were added and the old 1920s screen was replaced. This theater hosted the premiere and after party for the 2014 film version of Cheryl Strayed's bestselling memoir *Wild* starring Reese Witherspoon and Laura Dern. For the past twenty-plus years the theatre has also been home to the Queer Film Festival (formerly known as the Portland Lesbian & Gay Film Festival) every year in October. Showings after 6 p.m. are $9.50 for adults, matinees $7.50.

Elizabeth Leach Gallery

First opened in 1981, this Pearl District art gallery features prominent contemporary artists from around the world.

Ⓐ 417 NW 9th Ave.
Ⓣ (503) 224-0521
Ⓗ Tu-Sa 10:30 a.m.-5 p.m.
Ⓦ elizabethleach.com / Ⓜ p. 290-23

Augen Gallery

This established gallery features contemporary artists and printmakers. In addition to the Pearl District location, there is also a location downtown.

Ⓐ 716 NW Davis St.
Ⓣ (503) 546-5056
Ⓗ Tu-F 11 a.m.-5:30 p.m., Sa 11 a.m.-5 p.m.
Ⓦ augengallery.com / Ⓜ p. 290-39

One Grand Gallery

Fine art and graphic design group and solo shows are the focus at this hip gallery near the Jupiter Hotel.

Ⓐ 1000 E Burnside St.
Ⓣ (971) 266-4919
Ⓗ W-Sa 12 p.m.-6 p.m.
Ⓦ onegrandgallery.com
Ⓜ p. 296-7

PDX Contemporary Art

Gallery owner Jane Beebe opened this impressive contemporary art gallery in 1996 in one of the oldest buildings in the Pearl District.

Ⓐ 925 NW Flanders St.
Ⓣ (503) 222-0063
Ⓗ Tu-Sa 11:00 a.m.-6 p.m.
Ⓦ pdxcontemporaryart.com / Ⓜ p. 290-24

Fourteen30 Contemporary

This contemporary art gallery opened in 2008 and features a wide selection of art from video to sculpture.

Ⓐ 1501 SW Market St.
Ⓣ (503) 236-1430
Ⓗ Sa-Su 11 a.m.-5 p.m.
Ⓦ fourteen30.com
Ⓜ p. 288-5

Eutectic Gallery

A hybrid ceramics art gallery and boutique store. This gallery exhibits ceramics exclusively.

Ⓐ 1930 NE Oregon St.
Ⓣ (503) 974-6518
Ⓗ M-Th 10 a.m.-5:30 p.m., F-Sa 10 a.m.-6 p.m.
Ⓦ eutecticgallery.com
Ⓜ p. 294-32

Newspace Center for Photography

In addition to exhibitions, this non-profit resource center is a vibrant photography hub offering classes and studio access.

Ⓐ 1632 SE 10th Ave.
Ⓣ (503) 963-1935
Ⓗ M-Th 10 a.m.-10:30 p.m., F-Su 10 a.m.-6 p.m.
Ⓦ newspacephoto.org / Ⓜ p. 296-69

Hap Gallery

Opened in 2013, this contemporary Pearl District art gallery launched HapWorks in 2016 with limited edition artwork. Check out their website for more info.

Ⓐ 916 NW Flanders St.
Ⓣ (503) 444-7101 / Ⓗ Tu-Sa 11 a.m.-6 p.m.
Ⓦ hapgallery.com / Ⓜ p. 290-25

Blue Sky Gallery

We highly recommend visiting this nonprofit photography gallery founded in 1975 by five young photographers.

Ⓐ 122 NW 8th Ave.
Ⓣ (503) 225-0210
Ⓗ Tu-Su 12 p.m.-5 p.m.
Ⓦ blueskygallery.org / Ⓜ p. 290-38

Get Inspired

Bullseye Projects

This gallery run by local glass-maker Bullseye Glass Co. features contemporary glass art as well as artist lectures.

Ⓐ 300 NW 13th Ave.
Ⓣ (503) 227-0222
Ⓗ Tu-Sa 10 a.m.-5 p.m.
Ⓦ bullseyeprojects.com / Ⓜ p. 290-20

Stark's Vacuum Museum

Located inside the showroom of this Stark's Vacuum store, this free museum has more than 100 antique vacuums on display.

Ⓐ 107 NE Grand Ave. / Ⓣ (503) 232-4101
Ⓗ M-F 8 a.m.-7 p.m., Sa 9 a.m.-6 p.m., Su 11 a.m.-5 p.m.
Ⓦ starks.com/vacuum-museum / Ⓜ p. 294-40

Portland Institute for Contemporary Art

This contemporary performance and visual arts organization, known as PICA puts on the annual, hugely popular Time-Based Art Festival.

Ⓐ 415 SW 10th Ave. Suite 300
Ⓣ (503) 242-1419
Ⓗ Tu-F 11 a.m.-6 p.m.
Ⓦ pica.org / Ⓜ p. 288-17

Oregon Museum of Science and Industry

Founded in 1944, this is one of the largest science museums in the world. Portlanders refer to it as OMSI.

Ⓐ 1945 SE Water Ave.
Ⓣ (503) 797-4000
Ⓗ 9:30 a.m.-5:30 p.m. daily
Ⓦ omsi.edu
Ⓜ p. 296-70

Hollywood Theatre

This nonprofit arthouse movie theater built in 1926 has strong ties to the local community and excellent programming.

Ⓐ 4122 NE Sandy Blvd.
Ⓣ (503) 493-1128
Ⓗ call for movie schedule
Ⓦ hollywoodtheatre.org
Ⓜ p. 294-28

Bagdad Theater & Pub

This movie theater has operated since 1927. Enjoy a slice of pizza and a beer during the show. If you sit in the balcony they'll even deliver it to you.

Ⓐ 3702 SE Hawthorne Blvd.
Ⓣ (503) 467-7521
Ⓗ Su-Th 11 a.m.-12 a.m., F-Sa 11 a.m.-1 a.m.
Ⓦ mcmenamins.com
Ⓜ p. 296-66

131

Get Inspired

An arty display at Little Axe Records. While it may have been a few years since you listened to a cassette tape, don't be surprised if you see more than a few Portlanders rocking a Walkman like it's 1985. Apparently, just like vinyl, there's a unique flavor you only get on magnetic tape.

EXILED RECORDS

CRYSTAL BALLROOM

RONTOMS

THE GHOST EASE

SATSUMA

GENDERS

LISTEN

MISSISSIPPI RECORDS

MISSISSIPPI STUDIOS AND BAR BAR

LILACS & CHAMPAGNE

PSYCHOMAGIC

MUSIC

LITTLE AXE RECORDS

WONDER BALLROOM

HOLOCENE

THE ARLENE SCHNITZER CONCERT HALL

DOUG FIR LOUNGE

BEACON SOUND

JACKPOT RECORDS

VALENTINES

Music is your friend

Portland's music scene has gained ground in recent years with hip new venues and radio stations, a resurgence of vinyl and vinyl lovers, several burgeoning on-the-pulse indie record labels, and all sorts of skillful DJs. As a result, these days more and more talented musicians from across the U.S. are relocating to Portland. Hit shows like *Portlandia* have also certainly shined a spotlight on Portland as a music hub. There's a sense in Portland that no matter how out there your audio tastes are, the local music scene will have something original to fit your preferences. With as little as $30 you can easily pick up a few records and see a band playing really great music that you've never heard before. Portland is a music lover's friend.

EVERYDAY

ROSELAND THEATER

MUSIC MILLENNIUM

MUSIC

TENDER LOVING EMPIRE

CLINTON STREET RECORD & STEREO

Little Axe Records

*Feel like you're at the house of a
friend who's really into vinyl*

Originally run out of a garage, its strong following
of core customers helped owners Jed Bindeman and
Warren Hill relocate to a new space just off Alberta
Street in 2012 and to its current NE Sandy location in
2016. Expect an eclectic selection of mostly used vinyl
and cassette tapes at Little Axe because Bindeman is
a lover of experimental and heavy metal, while Hill is
into world and folk music — but the selection goes well
beyond those genres. Hill has done a lot of work with
the Mississippi Records Label, and he and Bindeman
have their own label, Little Axe Records, so you can
also peruse all of those labels' offerings too. All records
can be sampled at a listening station if you want to listen
before you buy. The store is in the same building at the
Hollywood Theatre (p. 131)

Information

Ⓐ 4142 NE Sandy Blvd.
Ⓣ (503) 320-3656
Ⓗ 12 p.m.-7:30 p.m. daily
Ⓦ littleaxerecords.com
Ⓜ p. 294-29

A small space packed wall-to-wall with records and used audio equipment—you can't help but feel you're about to find some really great music, and there's no way you're walking out empty-handed.

Mississippi Records

A must-visit
Portland music institution

Eric Isaacson's North Portland Mississippi Records is one of Portland's most loved record shops, and it's a very important part of the fabric of Portland's music scene. If you're planning to stop at one record shop, this is the one. Mississippi started as a record label specializing in world, gospel, and other more idiosyncratic genres (now with more than 200 releases), plus blues, folk, and soul; and the shop is frequently named as the favorite record shop of DJs worldwide. Don't expect to find any CDs, because they only sell vinyl and cassettes. There's also a selection of vintage audio equipment. Look above the door as you walk in to catch a glimpse of the store's motto, "Always -- Love Over Gold." After thirteen years in business, it seems that showing customers a little love is paying off.

Information

(A) 5202 N Albina Ave.
(T) (503) 282-2990
(H) 12 p.m.-7 p.m. daily
(M) p. 292-11

L

Listen

The staff does a great job of keeping their selection fresh. Check out their excellent electronic music section. Artists on the Beacon label include Gabriel Mindel Saloman of the Yellow Swans and composer Peter Broderick.

Beacon Sound

A one-stop-shop for dance music

Information

Ⓐ 3636 N Mississippi Ave.
Ⓣ (503) 493-7202
Ⓗ Su-Th 12 p.m.-7 p.m., F-Sa 12 p.m.-late
Ⓦ wearebeaconsound.com
Ⓜ p. 292-29

This Mississippi Avenue record store and label sets itself apart from Portland's profusion of used record stores as the go-to shop for new releases from EDM and modern composition experimental music. Check out their website for a schedule of in-store shows.

Exiled Records

An idiosyncratic selection including tapes and vinyl

This is a great place to get your fix for eclectic music and a heavy dose of psychedelic and experimental sounds. Fans of the Seattle record label Sublime Frequencies will find plenty to love here. Co-owner Scott Simmons, plays in the punk band Eat Skull on the label Woodsist. If you're planning on hitting up multiple record stores while you're in town, go here first and pick up a copy of Simmons's annual *Portland Guide to Independent Record Stores* for an exhaustive list of all the stores in the area.

Information

Ⓐ 4628 SE Hawthorne Blvd.
Ⓣ (503) 232-0751
Ⓗ Tu-Sa 11 a.m.-7 p.m., Su 12 p.m.-5 p.m.
Ⓦ exiledrecords.com
Ⓜ p. 296-67

Exiled Records is so small you can flip through the entire selection in a couple hours.

Clinton Street Record & Stereo

Tested and approved by local musicians

Don't be fooled by its size—Clinton Street Record & Stereo is the local hub for DJs and music lovers. You can catch co-owner R. Jared White, a.k.a. DJ Maxx Bass, spinning records at venues like Dig a Pony and Holocene (p. 141). The stock at his shop is eclectic and ranges from hip-hop, DJ Maxx Bass's personal preference, to Italo house. Co-owner Aaron Heuberger can also be found working behind the counter at Mississippi Records (p. 136). You've got to love a city where working for the competition is no big deal.

Information

Ⓐ 2510 SE Clinton St.
Ⓣ (503) 235-5323
Ⓗ Tu-Su 1 p.m.-7 p.m.
Ⓦ clintonstreetrecordandstereo.com
Ⓜ p. 296-81

Mississippi Studios and Bar Bar

Heavenly acoustics in a former church

Located in what used to be a Baptist church, this beloved music venue and recording studio has fantastic sound no matter what you're checking out. Shows are intimate with balcony seating or standing up close at stage level. The cocktail and burger lounge Bar Bar is located on the "sunny" side of the venue. It's open daily from 11 a.m., so get to the show early and grab a meal or drink during happy hour.

Information

Ⓐ 3939 N Mississippi Ave.
Ⓣ (503) 288-3895
Ⓗ 11 a.m.-2 a.m. daily
Ⓦ mississippistudios.com
Ⓜ p. 292-21

L

Listen

Holocene

Home to some of Portland's hippest dance parties

This on-the-pulse industrial music and arts venue is especially popular for its dance parties, although you can also catch a wide variety of bands and solo acts. Regular dance parties such as the Snap! '90s Dance Party and the disco- and techno-focused Main Squeeze range from free to $5.

Information

Ⓐ 1001 SE Morrison St.
Ⓣ (503) 239-7639
Ⓗ call for live schedule
Ⓦ holocene.org
Ⓜ p. 296-38

Crystal Ballroom

Catch a show at this historic dance hall

The Crystal Ballroom, one of Portland's largest music venues, is located in a beautiful 1914 building with one of the country's last remaining "floating" dance floors. For most shows, the venue is split down the middle, with 21-and-over on the bar side and all ages on the other. Balcony seating is available on the second floor.

Information

Ⓐ 1332 W Burnside St.
Ⓣ (503) 225-0047
Ⓗ call for live schedule
Ⓦ crystalballroompdx.com
Ⓜ p. 288-6

Wonder Ballroom

Historic venue with Bunk Bar Wonder in the basement

The Wonder opened in 2004 in a historic Northeast Portland building that was once a cultural center for Irish immigrants, as well as a boxing school. This is a great Portland venue to catch up-and-coming as well as established artists. A fair amount of shows here are all ages. Stop by the Bunk Bar Wonder in the basement pre- or post-show for tasty drinks and sandwiches.

Information

Ⓐ 128 NE Russell St.
Ⓣ (503) 284-8686
Ⓗ call for live schedule
Ⓦ wonderballroom.com
Ⓜ p. 294-22

Doug Fir Lounge

Subterranean tunes at the Jupiter Hotel

Located next to Jupiter Hotel (p. 26), Doug Fir Lounge has a bar, patio, and dining area on the ground floor, and a stylish and beautifully designed live music venue in the basement. The sound system here is one of the best in Portland. The stage is relatively low to the ground, which adds to the intimacy.

Information

Ⓐ 830 E Burnside St.
Ⓣ (503) 231-9663
Ⓗ 7 a.m.-2:30 a.m. every day
Ⓦ dougfirlounge.com
Ⓜ p. 296-5

143

L

Listen

Tender Loving Empire

Get up to speed with Portland's indie music scene

Jared Mees, of the band Jared Mees & The Grown Children, and his wife and artist/musician, Brianne Mees, run this indie music label and local handmade art and goods store. Bands on their label include Y La Bamba, Typhoon, and Radiation City.Their downtown location is near the Powell's City of Books, but they also have shops on SE Hawthorne Boulevard and NW 23rd Avenue. If you're not sure which album to pick up, consider *Friends and Friends of Friends*. It's a compilation of Tender Loving Empire artists and other local indie bands. If vinyl is your thing, you can listen to all of their albums on the shop's custom record players built inside coffee tables.

144

L

Listen

Information

Ⓐ 3541 SE Hawthorne Blvd.
Ⓣ (503) 548-2927
Ⓗ 10 a.m.-7 p.m. daily
Ⓦ tenderlovingempire.com
Ⓜ p. 296-57

The Hawthorne Boulevard location is larger than the downtown location. All locations sell local artists' creations as well as Portland-themed items.

Kill Rock Stars

killrockstars.com

This kick-ass indie rock (and some comedy) label is best known as one of the original labels of Sleater-Kinney and the late, great Elliott Smith. Other Kill Rock Star musicians and comedians include Deerhoof, The Decemberists, Cameron Esposito, and Hari Kondabolu.

Party Damage

partydamagerecords.com

This Portland label was started in 2013 so that founders Ben Hubbird and Casey Jarman could release music by their favorite local bands. Bands on their tiny but mighty label include as Mascaras, Dragging An Ox Through Water, and Point Juncture Washington.

Dropping Gems

droppinggems.bandcamp.com

In case you thought Portland's music scene was just indie rock and experimental music, check out Natasha Kmeto and Devonwho on Dropping Gems for healthy doses of West Coast electronic and hip hop music.

Fresh Selects

freshselects.bandcamp.com

Started in 2013 by DJ Kenny Fresh, this label is diverse and features hip hop, alternative soul, and R&B. Releases from Knxwledge and Mndsgn helped boost the label's profile.

Lilacs & Champagne
lilacschampagne.bandcamp.com

©Eliza Sohn

This experimental/psychedelic sample-based band is the latest from Grails' Emil Amos and Alex Hall. Their sound is like a mixtape of world music and horror movie soundtracks. They have a few albums on the label Mexican Summer.

Psychomagic
psychomagic.bandcamp.com

©Todd Walberg

This five-piece band is one of Portland's more popular freak-psych groups. Their unique mixture of psychedelic and surf-punk found a home on the L.A. label Lolipop Records in late 2014.

Genders
gendersband.com

©Jim Leisy

This four-piece unit with an infectious dreamy indie rock sound was chosen by *Willamette Week* readers as one of 2013's best new bands.

Sama Dams
Samadamsbandcamp.com

©Todd Walberg

Coming conspicuously close to sharing a name with Portland's former mayor Sam Adams, this moody three-piece prog post-punk band has two albums.

The Ghost Ease
theghostease.com

©Shannon Wolff

This three-piece all-women band has been making waves since their debut self-release in 2013. They released a second album in 2015. Their low-fi pop/grunge sound is a must-listen for fans of Cat Power.

Satsuma
satsumasatsuma.bandcamp.com

©Rich Oakin

Formed in 2014, this dark wave dream pop band is deeply influenced by the music of the 4AD label. Check them out if you're a fan of TOPS. So far, they've released four tracks on cassette. They are definitely a band to watch.

BANDS TO WATCH

Crossroads Music

The inventory at this record store is organized by dealer rather than genre. Each of the more than 35 dealers maintain their own inventory on a consignment basis.

Ⓐ 3130 SE Hawthorne Blvd. / Ⓣ (503) 232-1767
Ⓗ M-Th 11 a.m.-6 p.m., F-Sa 11 a.m.-7 p.m.,
   Su 12 p.m.-6 p.m.
Ⓦ xro.com / Ⓜ p. 296-62

Music Millennium

One of the largest independent music stores in the U.S., and the oldest record store in the Northwest.

Ⓐ 3158 E Burnside St.
Ⓣ (503) 231-8926
Ⓗ M-Sa 10 a.m.-10 p.m., Su 11 a.m.-9 p.m.
Ⓦ musicmillennium.com
Ⓜ p. 296-13

Rontoms

With free shows every Sunday night, this bar is a great place to grab a drink and catch some local music.

Ⓐ 600 E Burnside St.
Ⓣ (503) 236-4536
Ⓗ M-F 11 a.m.-2:30 a.m., Sa-Su 2 p.m.-2:30 a.m.
Ⓦ rontoms.net
Ⓜ p. 296-2

Everyday Music

Just like the name says, they're open every day of the year. The stores (several locations) are typically split down the middle, with records on one side and CDs on the other.

Ⓐ 1313 W Burnside St. / Ⓣ (503) 274-0961
Ⓗ 10 a.m.-10 p.m. daily
Ⓦ everydaymusic.com / Ⓜ p. 290-30

Valentines

This small two-story bar is close to downtown's Voodoo Doughnut. Most nights there's a band or DJ, but sometimes you can catch readings or comedy here.

Ⓐ 232 SW Ankeny St. / Ⓣ (503) 248-1600
Ⓗ 5 p.m.-2:30 a.m. daily
Ⓦ valentinespdx.com / Ⓜ p. 288-41

The Arlene Schnitzer Concert Hall

This gorgeous, historic home of the Oregon Symphony is most easily recognized by the large lit up "Portland" marquee at the entrance. The Schnitzer has hosted big ticket shows by acts like Bob Dylan, Prince, and Madonna.

Ⓐ 1037 SW Broadway / Ⓣ (503) 248-4335
Ⓗ call for concert schedule
Ⓦ portland5.comarleneschnitzer-concert-hall
Ⓜ p. 288-58

Jackpot Records

In this record store, new items are marked in red and used items are marked in blue.

Ⓐ 3574 SE Hawthorne Blvd .
Ⓣ (503) 239-7561
Ⓗ M-Th 10 a.m.-7 p.m., F-Sa 10 a.m.-8 p.m.,
   Su 11 a.m.-6 p.m.
Ⓦ jackpotrecords.com / Ⓜ p. 296-64

Roseland Theater

Located in Old Town/Chinatown, this large 1,000-plus capacity music venue with a balcony specializes in rock, hip hop, rap, and blues.

Ⓐ 8 NW 6th Ave. / Ⓣ (971) 230-0033
Ⓗ call for live schedule
Ⓦ roselandpdx.com
Ⓜ p. 290-44

147

L

Listen

Listed

The Portland Music Scene

Jay Kogami
Music blogger, editor of *All Digital Music*, deputy editor of *Gizmodo Japan*, specializes in covering the latest musical trends, including music technology and services, that tend not to receive much attention in Japan. As well as penning articles for various websites and magazines, he also appears regularly on TV and radio. Jay grew up in Portland and is an avid collector of vinyl.
jaykogami.com

*An authentic musical experience
in the digital age*

Thanks to the spread of the internet and smartphones, we live in a time when you can enjoy music from all over the world wherever you are, but for many people the musical identity of Portland remains distinct.

The area is best known for a deep-rooted indie scene that has nurtured many fledgling artists. Minor labels like Kill Rock Stars, Hush, and Dropping Gems have played a key role in bringing the work of genre-spanning creators like Elliott Smith, Sleater-Kinney, and Esperanza Spalding to the world. Meanwhile, in-store gigs are one way in which local record stores have provided forums for artists to find fans.

Live venues, so ubiquitous in the city, provide a platform for all sorts of music. With a visit to Crystal Ballroom, Mississippi Studios, or the Roseland Theater, you can tap into the enthusiasm of local audiences and enjoy Portland's best. Although, over the past decade or so, the annual autumn festival MusicfestNW has built a national reputation, artists with links to Portland still play a central role in the festival's lineups. Portland's strong sense of community lets artists, labels, live spaces, and fans exist as part of a harmonious whole.

Another key factor contributing to Portland's fascinating scene is the city's unique and nonconformist music. If, as an example, we were to cast Seattle as a city that has spawned celebrity acts like Jimi Hendrix, Nirvana, and Macklemore and Ryan Lewis, Portland is a cradle for more offbeat talents.

For a music lover, this proximity creates an extremely appealing sense of hunting for genuine buried treasure. Jay Kogami uses his slot on KWVA, the college radio station of the University of Oregon, for this purpose. Through it he has met memorable DJs playing great music by Oregon artists who have made talking seem like a waste of airtime.

In the spotlight of the internet age it may be a simple task to discover new music. But Portland's music buffs eschew that well-trodden path, each individual freely seeking out sounds to fall in love with. It's a special Portland pleasure.

Listen

CAPITAL

OF

SPORTS

CULTURE

Outdoor exercise and sports are an integral part of daily life for people in Portland. Streets are filled with joggers and cyclists, and when the weekend rolls around, many people choose to spend their days exploring the great outdoors. Portland is a creative city, but it's also a city that loves to break a sweat.

NIKE DNA

What in NIKE's DNA has driven the evolution of sports?

Nike is Portland's best-known sporting brand and its world headquarters is located about thirty minutes outside of Portland on a huge plot of land in the suburb of Beaverton. With offices around the world, Nike employs over 60,000 workers.

Throughout its history, Nike has dedicated itself to helping athletes take their performance to the next level. But what keeps Nike at the top of its game? CEO Mark Parker describes Nike's philosophy like this: "We believe in potential, not limits. The four-minute mile was safe, until Roger Bannister beat it. Lou Gehrig's 2,130-straight-games-played record was safe, until Cal Ripken topped it. No one would ever clear twenty-nine feet in the long jump, until Bob Beamon did. Nobody would ever beat Bob Beamon's record, until Michael Powell. That's how it is with Nike. We believe."

Nike's game-changing waffle sole was the innovation that started it all. It made shoes like Nike Air, Nike Free, and Nike Flywire possible. Nike+ brought the technology of Silicon Valley to running, allowing athletes to accumulate statistical data about their running habits and share that data with an online community.

"To bring inspiration and innovation to every athlete in the world." All over Nike's campus you'll find employees playing sports. Here, it's not good enough to just think about exercise, you've got to get out there and do it. Inside the halls, the average employee is wearing a backpack, jeans, and a pair of sneakers. It can feel more like a college campus than a corporate headquarters. Portland seems to have inherited some of the DNA that defines Nike.

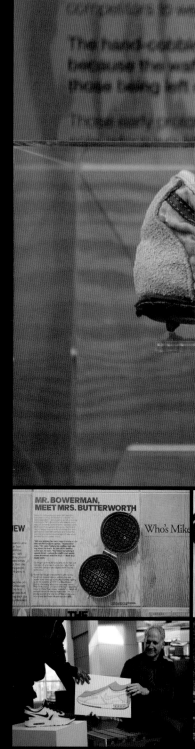

DYLAN RAASCH

Designer (NIKE)

Raasch moved to Portland seven years ago to work at Nike. Before that he was living in San Diego, where he worked at a skateboarding company. Extreme sports are pretty big in San Diego, and Raasch says it's a nice city, but it's basically situated in a desert. Portland's very different weather-wise, but he's glad he came here because of the amazing creative community and the nature surrounding the city.

Many people like Raasch see Portland as a city on the way to becoming one of America's great centers for art, design, food, and culture. It's hard to argue with this assessment when you factor in all the people moving to Portland from New York, San Francisco, and L.A. One thing's for sure: Portland is a top-notch environment for flexing creative muscles and passionate entrepreneurship. You can see this even at a huge company like Nike. Many of the talented and driven people working there go on to start their own businesses right down the road in Portland.

Raasch says that cultural collaboration is an important concept at Nike. The idea is to nurture collaboration between the cultures that emerge around various creative fields, including art and fashion design. Having all of these immensely talented people working close together generates amazing new opportunities. For Raasch, Nike is more than just a brand; it's a community that's constantly searching to redefine how it celebrates sports and lifestyles.

Raasch practices meditation as part of his creative process and some of his best ideas occur to him when meditating, whether it's a new design or an insight into consumer trends. Of course, if you live in Portland, nature is another major source of inspiration. Raasch goes hiking every two or three days and goes camping once a week in the summer, but he prefers not to say where.

Celebrating Culture

Bio

Director of design at Nike for NSW Running, NSW Football, NSW Tennis. Originator of the ever-popular Nike Roshe Run sneakers.

Columbia
Sportswear Company

156

Portland's global sportswear enterprise got its start more than seventy years ago when a German family bought a local hat firm. The Columbia Hat Company eventually grew into an enterprise offering gear for the outdoor enthusiast, but like the great river after which it was named, Columbia Sportswear Company went through twists and turns along the way.

Bio

Settled in Portland at age thirteen. After graduating from college, she and husband Neal went to work for the company that her parents had established. After her father and husband died, Boyle led Columbia to global success as chairperson.

158

Serendipity:
the secret to growth

In the 1930s, Paul Lamfrom was running a successful shirt factory in Germany. By 1938, the family had relocated to Portland, where Lamfrom bought a local hat company. In subsequent decades, his daughter Gert Boyle became the driving force behind the company's rise to global success as an outdoor clothing maker. Along the way she acquired a reputation for being "one tough mother," an epithet later adopted as the title of her autobiography. Boyle became a corporate icon, even starring in the company's TV commercials. Columbia's current CEO is her son Tim Boyle.

Columbia Sportswear Company has experienced its fair share of drama over the decades. A few years after founder Paul Lamfrom died so did his successor and son-in-law Neal Boyle, Gert's husband. Gert took the helm, but banks weren't eager to lend a helping hand to a teetering enterprise. When it became clear no buyer would be willing to shoulder the struggling firm's debts, a decision was made to rebuild Columbia from the inside. When this challenge began, Gert Boyle was forty-six and her son Tim was a senior in college.

GERT BOYLE

Chairwoman of the Board (Columbia Sportswear Company)

BIO

Began supporting his mother's efforts at Columbia in 1971 while still attending the University of Oregon. Became CEO in 1989.

The "Tough Mother" behind the rise of a global sportswear company

These days Columbia is a globally re-nowned brand. Tim Boyle says serendipity has played a part in that success. He points in particular to a quiet but relentless commitment to learn, an unanticipated consequence of being pushed to the brink. As a result, Columbia has maintained a steady, no-frills focus on high-quality goods. This is an approach that from a Portland perspective may seem ortho-dox to the point of being super conventional. If weird is the word for Portland, then Columbia is "weird" for being normal.

Energetic employees add to a healthy corporate environment. Tim reports that the company gym is busy during the lunch hour, and he speaks with pride of the company's beach volleyball team. He himself loves run-ning, skiing, and yachting, and enthuses over Oregon's outdoor activities.

He also notes that a fair number of em-ployees enjoy making their own beer and getting together to sample brews.

And how is the great woman herself? Gert is ninety-three now, and Tim says she's still reporting for duty. One tough mother indeed.

159

TIM BOYLE

Chief Executive Officer, Director (Columbia Sportswear Company)

Icebreaker

JEREMY MOON

Chairman / Creative Director (Icebreaker)

Portland is the Silicon Valley for outdoor sports

Nature, creativity, and sports are among the words that spring to mind when you think about Portland, and a company from New Zealand has embraced all of that: Icebreaker.

When New Zealander Jeremy Moon was twenty-four years old, his life changed after a man showed him a prototype fabric made from merino wool. Moon was so impressed with the fabric's potential that he quit his job at a research firm to found Icebreaker. Within twenty years, the company was known to outdoor sports enthusiasts the world over.

Icebreaker is especially renowned for underwear. Merino feels great, absorbs moisture,

helps to regulate warmth, and stays odor free. Above all, Icebreaker is a brand that pays close attention to the environment, something that greatly concerns many outdoor enthusiasts. Merino wool is closely associated with the natural processes by which it is manufactured. "We know where the product comes from. We know the people who raise the sheep. And we talk about that story as we do design," says Mark Koppes, vice president of product, noting a clear link to the natural goodness of merino that's hard to match when discussing other manufactured fabrics. Merino output is limited, but Koppes says he enjoys the process

In *A Day with Icebreaker*, a 2015 concept book that's viewable online, you can see for yourself how the company's products reflect Jeremy Moon's vision.

of seeking creative solutions that harness the power of nature, an important theme for the entire company.

Choosing Portland as Icebreaker's U.S. headquarters draws attention to what so many people value in this city. Portland's great access to nature is important to the sporty types who work at Icebreaker. Engaging with nature feeds back into their every-day work. With key Nike and Adidas offices nearby, many active lifestyle companies big and small are based in, and emerge from, Portland. "The heart of outdoor culture in the U.S. is in Portland," says Moon, noting that the city is an excellent place to

encounter outstanding talent with shared interests. Jeremy goes so far as to describe Portland as the "Silicon Valley for outdoor sports." The whole city is a wellspring of disruptive creativity, a pacesetter in the race to the next great idea.

Bio

Chairman / Creative Director, Icebreaker. Icebreaker currently employs about six hundred people and is sold in more than three thousand shops in thirty-seven countries.

The trail up Mount Hood is accessible by ▮▮▮▮ downtown
in about an ▮▮▮▮ a half.

ABRAHAM FIXES BIKES

COLUMBIA RIVER GORGE

SNOW PEAK

NIKE PORTLAND

EVERYBODY'S BIKE RENTALS & TOURS

PORTLAND TRAIL BLAZERS

REI PORTLAND

ADIDAS TIMBERS TEAM STORE

MOUNT HOOD

RUN

PORTLAND TIMBERS

FOREST PARK

THE CIRCUIT

ANGEL'SREST TRAIL

NEXT

KEEN GARAGE

VELO CULT

RIVER CITY BICYCLES

Sports culture nurtured by the proximity of nature

With the mighty Willamette Valley and its many mountain-fed rivers at its feet and the sprawling West Hills rolling in from the Northwest, it's no wonder that Portland is home to so many nature lovers. Running, biking, yoga, and gym workouts are all popular physical activities during the week, but come Saturday, many Portlanders prefer hiking close-in trails, or taking a day trip to the coast, Mt. Hood, or the Columbia River Gorge. Portland is perfectly positioned for maximum enjoyment of life in the city and in the great outdoors. Are you going for a bike ride, kayaking on one of the rivers, taking to the slopes for skiing? Whatever you do, just get out there and move.

FLEET FEET SPORTS PDX

ADVENTURE

CHRIS KING

FAT TIRE FARM

ICEBREAKER PORTLAND

OREGON COAST TRAIL

U.S. OUTDOOR STORE

CASCADE LOCKS

THE POLER FLAGSHIP STORE

PACIFIC CREST TRAIL

The Pacific Crest Trail runs from Mexico up through California, Oregon, and Washington, and all the way up to Canada. Clocking in at 2,650 miles, it's one of the longest hiking trails in the U.S. In Oregon the trail boasts some spectacular views near Mt. Hood. And best of all, it's easily accessible by car from downtown. In addition to the Pacific Crest Trail, the region also has plenty of urban and coastal trails. No matter what your pace, Portland is a fantastic place to get in touch with nature.

Oregon's natural beauty: to each their own, and at their own pace

TRAIL SPOTS OF OREGON

PCT in OREGON

It's possible for accomplished hikers to walk the entire length of the PCT in one season, though most people who attempt the 2,650-mile hike take five or six months. Many hikers walk upwards of twenty miles a day. The trail takes you along volcanic formations and crystal clear lakes as you travel through some of the highest portions of the Sierra Nevada and Cascade mountain ranges. By the time you reach the trail's midpoint, you'll find yourself facing the volcanic peaks of North Sister, Jefferson, and Mt. Hood. Past them it's on to the banks of the Columbia River, the lowest point of the trail at only a few feet above sea level.

165

R

Run

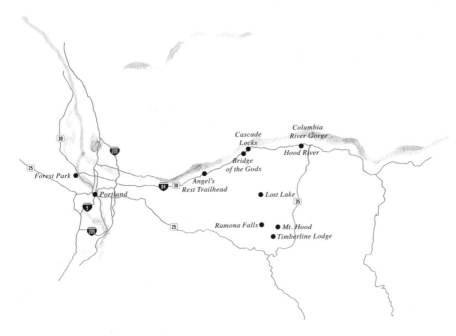

Columbia River Gorge
Cascade Locks
Hood River
Bridge of the Gods
Forest Park
Angel's Rest Trailhead
Portland
Lost Lake
Ramona Falls
Mt. Hood
Timberline Lodge

Forest Park is a favorite for runners and hikers, and because it's so close many people prefer its trails to a walk around city streets.

Forest Park

Get wild and rugged in this enormous Portland forest with trails

Forest Park is one of the largest urban forests in the U.S. with over 5,100 acres of canopy. The 112 species of birds and 62 species of mammals that call Forest Park home can be observed from more than 70 miles of park trails used for walking, running, hiking, cycling, and occasionally horseback riding. The 30-mile Wildwood Trail is one of the parks most popular and it winds through Forest Park as well as nearby Washington Park. If hiking isn't your thing, this park is also great for grabbing a sketchbook and drawing, snapping some trailside photos, birdwatching, or enjoying a good book. One of the park's best features: It's easily accessible from downtown by foot, bus, or the MAX.

Information

Ⓐ NW 29th Ave. & Upshur Street to Newberry Rd.
Ⓦ portlandoregon.gov/parks

Angel's Rest Trail

A view worthy of the climb

Angel's Rest is a large bluff that lies on the western end of the Columbia River Gorge. The long, rocky, popular trail passes by waterfalls that lead to an amazing view that's nearly 360 degrees across the Columbia and beyond. The relatively moderate-difficult, often steep, cliff-side trail extends only 2.4 miles (nearly 5 miles round trip), making it a good choice for day trips. Angel's Rest is accessible by car in about thirty-five minutes from downtown Portland, and it's an especially popular trail during the warmer summer months. Many long-distance backpackers take a detour through this area while on longer hikes.

Information

Ⓐ The trailhead is only thirty-five minutes by car from downtown by way of I-84.

Cascade Locks

A bridge forged by the gods from Oregon to Washington

Cascade Locks is a small town forty miles east of Portland, located in the middle of the Columbia River Gorge National Scenic Area with the Pacific Crest Trail passing through it. The name of the steel toll-bridge that crosses the Columbia River — Bridge of the Gods — was inspired by a Native American legend about a natural formation that once blocked the river's flow. The Cascade Range is a great place for a bike ride, day hike, overnight backpacking or camping trip, or picnic. The Columbia Gorge Sternwheeler operates out of Cascade Locks and offers fun sightseeing cruises down the Columbia River. You can even grab brunch or dinner on board.

Information

Ⓐ Cascade Locks is about fifty minutes from Portland by car via I-84.

Bridge of the Gods spans the Columbia River linking Oregon and Washington. The name comes from a Native American legend that says the bridge was created by Manito, the Great Spirit, so people could cross the Columbia. Today hikers can walk across the man-made bridge to get to Washington.

Columbia River Gorge

Nature's majesty and the power of the Columbia River

Information

Ⓐ A great way to experience the gorge is driving along the Historic Columbia River Highway off exit 17.

The Columbia River Gorge is a designated National Scenic Area. The eighty-mile-long gorge runs along the Columbia River and is easily accessible from downtown Portland. The Cascade Range separates the lush forests to the west from the high desert to the east. It's a popular destination for hikers and boasts many waterfalls, including Oregon's largest and most famous, the spectacular 620-foot Multnomah Falls.

Oregon Coast Trail

Oregon's coast is rich with biodiversity

This 382-mile trail runs along the Pacific Coast from Astoria at the mouth of the Columbia River south to Brookings, just north of the California border. It passes along the bluffs of Oregon's sandy coastline and through untouched evergreen forests further inland. The trail is widely varied and includes hiking along beaches, streets, trails, and dirt roads. Easy access from Portland, connection to multiple state parks, and picturesque lighthouses all make it the OCT an excellent way to enjoy Oregon's natural splendor.

Information

Ⓐ Astoria, at the northern tip of the Oregon coast, is about two hours northwest of Portland on Route 30.

Mount Hood

Oregon's mountain of choice

Mt. Hood is more than 11,200 feet tall and only an hour and a half from downtown Portland. It's the tallest peak in Oregon and the fourth tallest in the Cascade Range. The peak is snowcapped year-round and surrounded by an evergreen forest. For skiers, climbers, and hikers, there is the magestic Timberline Lodge, which operates year-round. It was completed in 1937 and is a National Historic Landmark, though it's probably most recognizable as an exterior filming location for Stanley Kubrick's 1980 film *The Shining*. Five ski resorts operate on Mt. Hood, including North America's largest night skiing area, the Mt. Hood Skibowl. From spring to fall, when the snow recedes, Mt. Hood is a popular destination for hiking and camping as well. If you're looking for a mountain hike, the Crescent Trail and many others traverse Mt. Hood.

Information

Ⓐ Accessible from Portland
by car in about an hour and a half.

Mt. Hood Skibowl

Ⓐ 87000 E Highway 26,
    Government Camp, Oregon
Ⓣ (503) 222-2695
Ⓦ skibowl.com

Timberline Lodge

Ⓐ 27500 W Leg Rd.
Ⓣ (503) 272-3311
Ⓦ timberlinelodge.com

173

R

Run

A hiker spots a Pacific Crest Trail marker on a tree.

Camping beneath Mount Hood's permanently snowcapped peak.

Lost Lake is located at the base of Mt. Hood. On a clear day, Mt. Hood reflects perfectly on its surface.

The Timberline Lodge was built by local artisans during the Great Depression. It was dedicated by Franklin D. Roosevelt upon completion.

The "Bargain Basement" has great deals on used gear. Pop in and you just might find something you didn't even know you were looking for.

Next Adventure

Portland's favorite new and used outdoor store

Information

(A) 426 SE Grand Ave.
(T) (503) 233-0706
(H) M-F 10 a.m.-7 p.m., Sa 10 a.m.-6 p.m.,
   Su 11 a.m.-5 p.m.
(W) nextadventure.net / (M) p. 296-21

Longtime friends Deek Heykamp and Bryan Knudsen opened Next Adventure in 1997 fueled by their shared passion for the outdoors. Whether you're into kayaking, mountaineering, hiking, camping, skiing, snowboarding, or simply like going on picnics, this place has you covered. This one-stop-outdoor-gear-shop has all sorts of high-quality new and used gear at reasonable rates. Keep in mind that Next Adventure also rents out gear for skiing, snowboarding, climbing, and kayaking if you're just looking to try something out for a day. Regular shop visitors are rewarded with a constantly rotating stock, top-notch customer service, and even kayaking classes if you're interested.

One of the country's best and largest outdoor brands

Columbia Sportswear Flagship Store

Information

Ⓐ 911 SW Broadway
Ⓣ (503) 226-6800
Ⓗ M-Sa 9:30 a.m.-7 p.m., Su 11 a.m.-6 p.m.
Ⓦ columbia.com
Ⓜ p. 288-56

Columbia Sportswear was founded in Portland in 1938. Their flagship store opened in 1996 in downtown's historic United Carriage Building a couple blocks away from Pioneer Square and it's become a Portland landmark. If you're looking for expertly designed, well-made outdoor apparel or gear for fishing, mountaineering, skiing, snowboarding, and other active outdoor pursuits, you should plan a visit here.

Keen Garage

Outdoor and casual footwear

Keen's first sandal, the Newport, was born from the simple question: Is it possible to design a sandal that protects your toes? Apparently it is. Since 2003, Keen has been designing and manufacturing footwear, bags, and socks that express their concept HybridLife, which is all about balancing work, play, and giving back to the community. In addition to their online shop and shelf space in stores across the country, they also have two Keen-only retail stores called Keen Garages in Portland and Palo Alto, California.

Information

Ⓐ 505 NW 13th Ave.
Ⓣ (971) 200-4040
Ⓗ M-Sa 10 a.m.-7 p.m., Su 11 a.m.-5 p.m.
Ⓦ keenfootwear.com
Ⓜ p. 290-14

The Poler Flagship Store

Smart designs for outdoor and urban clothing and gear

Outdoor and urban clothing and gear brand Poler was founded in Portland in 2010 by photographer Benji Wagner and filmmaker Kharma Vella. In 2014 they moved to a larger spot and opened their flagship store. There's plenty of floor space to test tents, try out bags, and peruse their great selection of colorful, smartly designed gear.

Information

Ⓐ 413 SW 10th Ave.
Ⓣ (503) 432-8120
Ⓗ M-Sa 11 a.m.-7 p.m., Su 11 a.m.-6 p.m.
Ⓦ polerstuff.com
Ⓜ p. 288-18

Icebreaker Portland

Outdoor wear made from high-quality merino wool

This outdoor clothing brand stands apart from the flock with its line of natural apparel layering system made from superior New Zealand merino wool. Founded in 1994, Icebreaker started using natural wool in its garments at a time when artificial fabrics dominated the market. The company is based in New Zealand, but Portland's status as a hub for outdoor wear makes it the perfect location for their stylish product design HQ, which opened in 2007.

Information

Ⓐ 1109 W Burnside St.
Ⓣ (503) 241-8300
Ⓗ M-Sa 10 a.m.-7 p.m., Su 11 a.m.-6 p.m.
Ⓦ icebreaker.com
Ⓜ p. 290-33

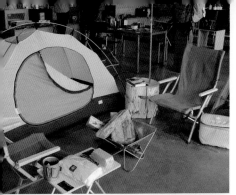

Snow Peak

Made in Japan, loved worldwide

This outdoor goods company specializing in "exceptional natural lifestyle products" was founded in 1958 in Niigata Prefecture, Japan. Unhappy with the quality of hiking goods available at the time, Yukio Yamai took a risk and started his own brand. This location is the first U.S. retail store. In addition to their stylish, high-quality gear, they launched an apparel line in 2015.

Information

Ⓐ 410 NW 14th Ave.
Ⓣ (503) 697-3330
Ⓗ M-Sa 11 a.m.-7 p.m., Su 11 a.m.-6 p.m.
Ⓦ snowpeak.com/portland
Ⓜ p. 290-18

REI Portland

The first U.S. retail store to receive LEED® Gold Certification

REI was founded in Seattle in 1938, and its first Portland location opened in 1976. The Pearl District store was the first retail store in the U.S. to achieve LEED® Gold Certification. Whether it's gear for mountaineering, hiking, camping, cycling, skiing, or something entirely different, the knowledgeable staff here will help you find what you need.

Information

Ⓐ 1405 NW Johnson St.
Ⓣ (503) 221-1938
Ⓗ M-Sa 10 a.m.-9 p.m., Su 10 a.m.-7 p.m.
Ⓦ rei.com/stores/portland.html
Ⓜ p. 290-11

Portland Outdoor Store

Nearly a century of western wear and outdoor clothing

Founded in 1919, this family-run western gear and outdoor store specializes in a great lineup of cowboy hats and boots from a range of brands. The giant old green and red neon sign that hangs alongside the three-story building is a Portland landmark.

Information

Ⓐ 304 SW 3rd Ave.
Ⓣ (503) 222-1051
Ⓗ M-Sa 9:30 a.m.-5:30 p.m.,
  Su 11 a.m.-4 p.m.
Ⓦ portlandoutdoorstore.us
Ⓜ p. 288-44

R

Run

U.S. Outdoor Store

Outdoor goods since 1957

Information

Ⓐ 219 SW Broadway
Ⓣ (503) 223-5937
Ⓗ M-F 9 a.m.-8 p.m., Sa 10 a.m.-6 p.m.,
  Su 11 a.m.-5 p.m.
Ⓦ usoutdoor.com
Ⓜ p. 288-30

Downtown's U.S Outdoor Store has been serving the Portland area since 1957. In addition to their sportswear and outdoor wear, they have a great selection of gear for surfing, skiing, snowboarding, and skateboarding. They also carry a wide selection of travel goods such as backpacks, carry-on bags, neck pillows, and adapters.

Nike Portland

Sneaker holy land
in downtown Portland

Welcome to the holy land of sneakers and sport gear. We don't need to tell you that Nike hits the sweet spot between high-tech design and old-school nostalgia. This enormous store's layout feels more like an art gallery for sneakers, clothing, and sporting goods than a retail space. Don't miss the Bowerman Wall, a giant video installation that celebrates Nike's history. The shop is located downtown in the Kress Building, which was granted LEED® Platinum Certification. We recommend the Nike Run Club, which has weekly events and is open to all. Check the Nike website for more information.

Information

Ⓐ 638 SW 5th Ave.
Ⓣ (503) 221-6453
Ⓗ M-Sa 10 a.m.-8 p.m., Su 11 a.m.-6 p.m.
Ⓦ nike.com / Ⓜ p. 288-61

Adidas Timbers Team Store

Get ready for match day

Information

Ⓐ 1844 SW Morrison St.
Ⓣ (503) 553-5519
Ⓗ M-Sa 10 a.m.-9 p.m., Su 10 a.m.-7 p.m.
Ⓦ timbers.com/adidas-timbers-team-store
Ⓜ p. 288-1

The German brand Adidas has their U.S. headquarters in Portland. Located in a renovated hospital complex called The Village, each building is named after a former Olympic host city such as Rome and Athens. Adidas is also the official kit provider for the Portland Timbers, and there's a team store located in the Timbers' home stadium, Providence Park.

Portland Timbers

Portland's adored Major League Soccer team

Portland's Major League Soccer team since 2011, the Timbers won the league championship in 2015. Soccer season runs from March to December and the main group of supporters chanting and cheering at every game is called the Timbers Army. Providence Park seats over 20,000, and games sometimes sell out. Whenever the team scores a goal, the official mascot, Timber Joey, cuts a round from a large log with a chainsaw.

Craig Mitchelldyer / Portland Timbers

Information

Ⓦ timbers.com

R

Run

Portland Trail Blazers

Portland's NBA championship-winning team

Information

Ⓦ nba.com/blazers

The beloved Blazers, whose home stadium is the Moda Center, play in the NBA's Western Conference Northwest Division. They have reached the NBA play-offs 31 times, including a streak of 21 straight playoff appearances from 1983 through 2003. Despite making it to the playoffs finals in 2014, 2015, and 2016, their one NBA championship was in 1977.

*Tradition and modernity meet
in Portland's premiere athletic club*

Multnomah Athletic Club
(MAC)

Information

Ⓐ 1849 SW Salmon St.
Ⓣ (503) 223-6251
Ⓗ M-F 5 a.m.-11 p.m., Sa-Su 6 a.m.-11 p.m.
Ⓦ themac.com
Ⓜ p. 288-3

The Multnomah Athletic Club (known by locals as the MAC Club) was founded in 1891 by local football and cricket players to meet demand for an athletic club in the area. The exclusive club is a nonprofit, and you must be a member or a member's guest to use the facilities. In addition to top-notch exercise equipment, they also have a well-regarded restaurant and lounge. The eighth floor of the clubhouse has a great view of Providence Park. Currently the MAC has over 17,000 members and an extremely long, multiple-year waitlist.

The Circuit Bouldering Gym

Expansive climbing gym for all experience levels with three locations

This bouldering gym with three locations feels less like a gym and more a community for local bouldering enthusiasts. There are walls for all experience levels, more than 300 climbing routes, and neither ropes nor harnesses on site. Don't worry, the walls are fairly short and the floor is padded. One-day admission is $14 for adults and $12 for students, and only $7 for first-time visitors. Every Saturday night after 5 p.m. is discounted beginners' night. This kid-friendly gym can be booked for birthday parties, and they also run a summer camp.

Information

Ⓐ 410 NE 17th Ave.
Ⓣ (503) 719-7041
Ⓗ M 9 a.m.-11 p.m., Tu 7 a.m.-11 p.m.,
  W 9 a.m.-11 p.m., Th 7 a.m.-11 p.m.,
  F 9 a.m.-11 p.m., Sa-Su 8 a.m.-11 p.m.
Ⓦ thecircuitgym.com
Ⓜ p. 294-38

R

Run

Velo Cult

Grab a beer, talk bikes, even catch a show

This bike shop is not only a place to pop in for repairs or an upgrade, it's also a bar and coffee shop serving craft beer, wine, tea, and locally roasted coffee. If that's not enough, there's also regular live music and comedy shows. Portlanders' love of cycling is reflected in Velo Cult's wide range of customers, from families to solo beer and bike lovers. Check out the Nintendo-inspired mural on the wall out back.

Information

Ⓐ 1969 NE 42nd Ave.
Ⓣ (503) 922-2012
Ⓗ Tu-Sa 10 a.m.–10 p.m., Su-M 11 a.m.-7 p.m.
Ⓦ velocult.com
Ⓜ p. 294-27

As you walk in the front door, the maintenance area is on your right and the bar on your left. The ceiling and walls are decorated with vintage bicycles. The display case-style tables in the middle are filled with, you guessed it, bicycle parts.

Chris King

This bike manufacturer pays attention to the environmental impact of each and every part that goes into making a bicycle. Their super-precise, durable headset is a work of true craftsmanship. Join one of their Gourmet Century rides through the most beautiful parts of the U.S. and Japan for adventure, exercise, and great food.

Information

Ⓦ chrisking.com

River City Bicycles

River City is one of the largest bike shops in Portland and they carry everything from high-end rides and city bikes to a huge selection of riding wear. Check out their free maintenance classes and weekly group rides. There's also an outlet store two blocks away.

Information

Ⓐ 706 SE Martin Luther King Jr. Blvd
Ⓣ (503) 233-5973
Ⓗ M-F 10 a.m.-7 p.m., Sa 10 a.m.-6 p.m., Su 12 p.m.-6 p.m.
Ⓦ rivercitybicycles.com / Ⓜ p. 296-31

185

R

Run

Community Cycling Center

Since 1994 this nonprofit cycling center and bike shop has been broadening access to bicycling and serving the community, particularly low-income youth and adults. Profits and donations go toward community events such as the annual summer Bike Camp and the Holiday Bike Drive.

Information

Ⓐ 1700 NE Alberta St. / Ⓣ (503) 287-8786
Ⓗ 10 a.m.-7 p.m. daily
Ⓦ communitycyclingcenter.org / Ⓜ p. 294-16

Fat Tire Farm

From twenty-nine-inch tires and fat bikes to downhill and cross-country tires, this is one of Portland's best shops for mountain biking. The diverse staff is friendly and a great resource for anyone looking to take advantage of Oregon's amazing mountain biking trails.

Information

Ⓐ 2714 NW Thurman St.
Ⓣ (503) 222-3276
Ⓗ Tu-F 11 a.m.-7 p.m., Sa 10 a.m.-6 p.m.
Ⓦ fattirefarm.com / Ⓜ p. 290-1

Portland Design Works

Simplicity and functionality are an art form for this bicycle gear manufacturer. Bird-shaped water bottle cages and leather "whiskey" handlebar grips are just a few of the playful and expertly crafted items that they make.

Information

Ⓦ ridepdw.com

Sugar Wheel Works

Jude Gerace is owner of this environmentally-conscious custom bicycle wheel business. She believes that getting to know her customers is an important step in creating perfect handmade wheels. The relaxed shop interior feels more like a cafe than a bike shop. Sugar Wheel also offers classes on wheel-building basics.

Information

Ⓐ 3808 N Williams Ave. Suite 134
Ⓣ (503) 236-8511
Ⓗ Tu-F 10 a.m.-6:30 p.m., Sa 11 a.m.-5 p.m.
Ⓦ sugarwheelworks.com / Ⓜ p. 292-26

R

Run

Abraham Fixes Bikes

This North Portland shop handles everything from changing tires to tuning and repairing every part of your bicycle. Their love for bicycles and their technical skills will help you get the most out of your ride.

Information

Ⓐ 3508 N Williams Ave.
Ⓣ (503) 281-6394
Ⓗ M-Th 10 a.m.-7 p.m., F 10 a.m.-6 p.m., Sa 10 a.m.-5 p.m.
Ⓦ abrahamfixesbikes.com
Ⓜ p. 292-31

Everybody's Bike Rentals & Tours

Rent one of more than 100 city and vintage road bikes by the hour or for $25-$45 a day. The shop also organizes different part-day bike tours around Portland catered to beer, coffee, and legal cannabis lovers.

Information

Ⓐ 305 NE Wygant St.
Ⓣ (503) 358-0152
Ⓗ 10 a.m.-5 p.m. daily
Ⓦ pdxbikerentals.com
Ⓜ p. 292-14

North St. Bags

Portland is rainy, so bike bags have to be waterproof and tough. From start to finish, North St. manufactures its edgy, durable bags in their SE Portland showroom location, and most materials are U.S. made. North St. bags also does custom design bike bag and basket work.

Information

Ⓐ 2716 SE 23rd Ave.
Ⓣ (503) 419-6230
Ⓗ 11 a.m.-6 p.m. daily
Ⓦ northstbags.com
Ⓜ p. 296-83

The Athletic

This sportswear brand and retail shop got its start making socks with the same pattern as the carpets in PDX International Airport. Today their lineup includes running, cycling, and casual wear with a colorful, youthful look that goes great with a pair of sneakers.

Information

Ⓐ 925 NW 19th Ave., Suite A
Ⓗ M-F 12 p.m.-6 p.m., Sa-Su 11 p.m.-6 p.m.
Ⓦ theathleticcommunity.com
Ⓜ p. 290-9

187

R

Run

Fleet Feet Sports PDX

Try on all sorts of running and walking shoes and apparel, then give them a whirl on this flagship shop's mini track. The shop also hosts the First Thursday Urban Adventure Run, a fun scavenger hunt that goes from April through September.

Information

Ⓐ 2258 NW Raleigh St.
Ⓣ (503) 525-2122
Ⓗ M-F 10 a.m.-7 p.m., Sa 10 a.m.-6 p.m., Su 12 p.m.-5 p.m.
Ⓦ fleetfeetpdx.com / Ⓜ p. 290-5

Stay Wild Magazine

This free seasonal magazine is dedicated to the modern adventures of traveling, playing sports, and spending time outdoors. Each issue is also available online. Check out the Stay Wild Adventure Festival in the summer.

Information

Ⓦ staywildmagazine.com

United Bicycle
Institute Portland

Information

Ⓐ 3961 N Williams Ave., Suite 100
Ⓣ (541) 488-1121
Ⓦ bikeschool.com
Ⓜ p. 292-22

A school for bicycle maintenance and frame building

Most people don't consider making their own bicycle frame. Even if you have the tools and the space, who's going to teach you how to do it? UBI brings together two defining aspects of Portland: DIY culture and bicycles. Most students are regular folks who simply love riding bicycles and want to take that love to the next (potentially professional) level. The school attracts students from all walks of life and from all over the world. There are ten different bicycle maintenance and frame building classes available from the school's experienced faculty.

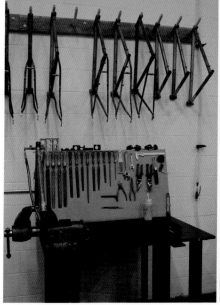

189

R

Run

Running Trails in Oregon

Commentary by

Gregory Gourdet
The trendsetting executive chef at Portland's popular pan-Asian restaurant Departure. Gourdet trained and worked at Jean-Georges restaurant in New York. Later, as chef de cuisine at modern Chinese eatery Restaurant 66, Gourdet cultivated an affinity for the Asian cuisines and flavors for which he is known at Departure. Gourdet loves to bring the bold flavors and unique ingredients of Asian cuisine to the table. He's also a part-time ultrarunner.

The Gorge is filled with amazing trails

Wildwood Trail, Forest Park

Forest Park is one of the largest urban forests in the United States. Just two miles from downtown Portland, it stretches for more than 5,000 acres. This is a lush forest full of green and year-round runnable trails. Wildwood Trail is one of the best to run here. It stretches for thirty miles of grand Douglas-firs, cedar trees, and wildflowers. Wildwood Trail is relatively flat with a few nice hills so you can run it fast and get a good leg workout. The trail winds and has a few entrances and scenic points including Pittock Mansion and Lower Macleay Park.

Eagle Creek to Wahtum Lake, The Columbia River Gorge

The Gorge is filled with amazing trails and this twenty-six-mile loop is one of them. With great views of waterfalls, steep cliffs, rainforests, and an almost secret lake as a turnaround point, Eagle Creek to Wahtum Lake is the quintessential Pacific Northwest trail run. This run has 5,000 feet of elevation gain and is very scenic. Highlights on the run are Punchbowl Falls, Vertigo Mile, Tunnel Falls, and peaceful Wahtum Lake. Feeling adventurous? Go two more miles and climb to the

top of Mt. Chinidere for a truly spectacular mountain view of the Gorge. You overlook lake vistas and feel eye-to-eye with snowcapped Mount Hood across the way.

Biking
In Portland

Commentary by

Chris Tang
Born and raised in Portland. Thirty-nine years old. I love my family and friends. I love riding bikes and the outdoors. I love Portland, Oregon. I've been mountain biking for almost twenty-five years. I try to ride any chance I get. Living in the Pacific Northwest, we are blessed with some of the best mountain biking in the country. Riding a bike will change your life for the better.
Apothecanna.com / Mahalls20Lanes.com / N0-Titles.com

*Two great rides for both beginner
and advanced mountain bikers near PDX*

Timberline to Town Trail
—90 minutes from Portland

One of those rides where you get a little of everything. It is technical, it's smooth, and it has beautiful scenery from beginning to end. The ride starts at Timberline Lodge near the summit of Mount Hood in Government Camp and takes you all the way down the mountain to the town of Rhododendron, Oregon. The ride is about fifteen miles long. From the Timberline Lodge parking lot, start at Timberline to Town Trail next to the Magic Mile chairlift and follow it down to Crosstown Trail (Trail #755). From Crosstown Trail, connect to Pioneer Bridle Trail (Trail #795) to finish the ride.

Sandy Ridge Trail System
—55 minutes from Portland

Sandy Ridge is one of the most popular trails in the country for mountain bikers. What makes this trail unique is that it was built and is maintained by mountain bikers who volunteer their time. So it is quite well-designed and maintained. Multiple trails totaling approximately fifteen miles can be found in the Sandy Ridge Trail System. A very fun trail to ride.

This is the kind of hands-on appeal The Good Mod offers just a few steps from the shop space.

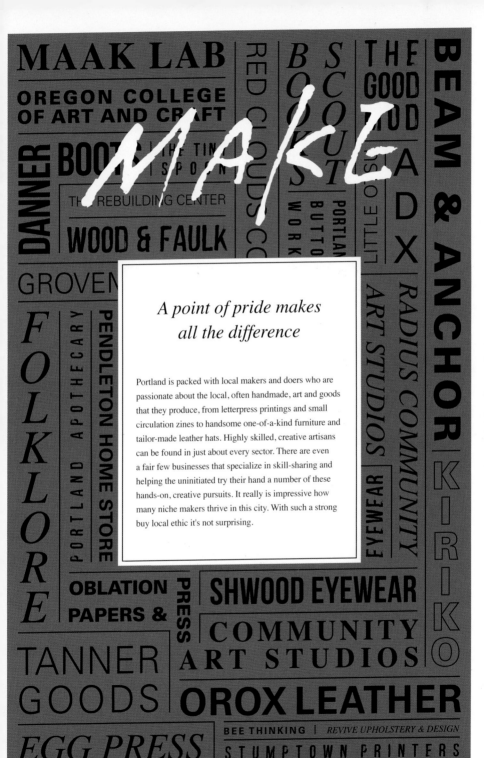

MAKE

MAAK LAB

OREGON COLLEGE OF ART AND CRAFT

DANNER

BOOT

THE TINY SPOON

THE REBUILDING CENTER

WOOD & FAULK

GROVEN

FOLKLORE

PORTLAND APOTHECARY

PENDLETON HOME STORE

RED CLOUDS CO

BSCOUKU

PORTLAND BUTTON WORK

THE GOOD MOD

LITTLE O

ART STUDIOS

RADIUS COMMUNITY

EYEWEAR

BEAM & ANCHOR

ADX

KIRIKO

A point of pride makes all the difference

Portland is packed with local makers and doers who are passionate about the local, often handmade, art and goods that they produce, from letterpress printings and small circulation zines to handsome one-of-a-kind furniture and tailor-made leather hats. Highly skilled, creative artisans can be found in just about every sector. There are even a fair few businesses that specialize in skill-sharing and helping the uninitiated try their hand a number of these hands-on, creative pursuits. It really is impressive how many niche makers thrive in this city. With such a strong buy local ethic it's not surprising.

OBLATION PAPERS & PRESS

SHWOOD EYEWEAR

COMMUNITY ART STUDIOS

TANNER GOODS

OROX LEATHER

EGG PRESS

BEE THINKING | REVIVE UPHOLSTERY & DESIGN

STUMPTOWN PRINTERS

The Good Mod

Mid-century Danish design furniture with custom restoration and design

Information

Ⓐ 1313 W Burnside St. 4th Floor.
Ⓣ (503) 206-6919
Ⓗ 11 a.m.-6 p.m. daily
Ⓦ thegoodmod.com
Ⓜ p. 290-29

"Is this really the entrance to a store?" you may wonder as you tentatively open the doors. But follow the signs down a corridor to the ancient elevator at the back, ride it up to the fourth floor, and step out into a whole new world filled with an elegant jumble of furnishings with the sublime patina of temps perdu. Mid-century Danish design junkies will be happy here. The huge loft is filled with custom-restored Scandinavian, European, and American furniture, as well as pieces of head-scratchingly inscrutable origin. The store also designs and builds furniture to order, mainly for Portland stores and offices. If you enjoy furniture auctions, check out their latest projects online.

The in-store displays change regularly, always with an eclectic, museum-like selection of sofas, chairs, tables, lamps, and artwork.

Why the zine-button combo? Because it's Portland. At Portland Button Works you can get handmade, custom, artful gifts for you and those you love.

Portland Button Works

Custom pinback buttons, magnets, and bottle openers

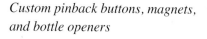

At Portland Button Works there are walls of zines and a table topped with a strange contraption. Shop owner Alex Wrekk stands at this machine, intently making . . . something. Is this a movie? It feels like it. Wrekk is making pinback buttons—custom buttons that she or customers have designed. Buy the 2pac and Biggie set or the Michael Jackson, Prince, Madonna set, each for $5. Although Portland Button Works, open since 2012, no longer has regular shop hours you can still schedule an appointment or order custom buttons, magnets, and bottle openers online to pick up at the shop. Wrekk also stocks a lot of independently published zines, books, and comics.

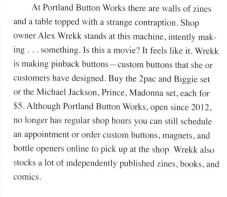

Information

Ⓐ 1505 N Bryant St.
Ⓣ (503) -922-2684
Ⓗ open by appointment only
Ⓦ portlandbuttonworks.com
Ⓜ p. 292-5

Beam & Anchor

Portland craftmanship and beautiful design

Jocelyn and Robert Rahm's selection of beautifully designed vintage furniture, home decor, kitchen goods, and accessories is on the first floor of this 7,000-foot North Portland old warehouse space, while the second floor is a workshop. Many of the handmade goods produced and restored upstairs are sold downstairs. You can't buy any more local than that.

Information

Ⓐ 2710 N Interstate Ave.
Ⓣ (503)367-3230
Ⓗ M-Sa 11a.m.-6 p.m., Su 12 p.m.-5 p.m.
Ⓦ beamandanchor.com
Ⓜ p. 292-33

M | *Make*

Maak Lab

Small batch, handmade soaps, candles, and salves

Information

Ⓐ 916 W Burnside St.
Ⓣ (503) 893-9933
Ⓗ Tu-Su 11 a.m.-6 p.m.
Ⓦ maaklab.com
Ⓜ p. 288-21

This brand of 100% natural handmade soaps and candles was launched in 2011 by Anoria Gilbert and Taylor Ahlmark. They often scent their soaps, salves, and candles with the oils of plants from the Pacific Coast of North America as well as from Portland products such as local honey and Stumptown Coffee. There are no synthetic additives in their beautiful scented handmade, small-batch products. Follow your nose around the store to find whichever ones delight you the most. Nearly half of Maak's wholesale business these days is in Japan.

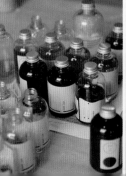

Tanner Goods

The value of timeless durability

One of the wonderful things about fine leather goods is that they gain character over time. If you purchase a handmade belt, bag, or wallet at Tanner Goods, it should last you the rest of your life and improve with age. This North Portland location is Tanner's flagship store, with the full lineup of leather goods as well as homewares, furniture, stationery, and more. Pick up a one-of-a-kind lifelong leather companion here and visit The Wayback bar/cafe at the back of the shop while you're at it.

Information

Ⓐ 4719 N Albina Ave.
Ⓣ (503) 222-2774
Ⓗ 11 a.m.-8 p.m. daily
Ⓦ tannergoods.com
Ⓜ p. 292-15

198

M

Make

This is Folklore

Handsome bespoke hats and other leather goods

Information

Ⓐ 2926 NE Killingsworth St.
Ⓣ (906) 281-6961
Ⓗ open by appointment only
Ⓦ thisisfolklore.com
Ⓜ p. 294-6

If you are seeking a beautiful, tailor-made, one-of-a-kind hat, wallet, or other leather good, schedule an appointment with This is Folklore owner John Fish or stop by his Northeast Portland studio and shop. He'll design and craft a handsome, unique hat that you'll treasure for life. The small shop also carries an impressive collection of antique Americana.

Vintage Japanese fabric with a Portland twist

Kiriko

Information

(A) 325 NW Couch St.
(T) (503) 222-0335
(H) M-F 10 a.m.-6 p.m., Sa-Su 12 p.m.-6 p.m.
(W) kirikomade.com
(M) p. 290-48

Kiriko specializes in products made from vintage Japanese fabrics, mostly woven by hand and made with natural pigment dyes. These shibori, kasuri, katazome, aizome and other traditional hand-dyed, woven fabrics are given a Portland design twist when made into stunning scarves, pocket squares, shirts, ties, and more. Kiriko actively collaborates with other makers, and J. Crew has been selling their goods since 2014. Kiriko has a showroom/studio in Old Town and also carries select merchandise from local brands like Beam & Anchor (p. 197).

199

M

Make

Portland Apothecary

Wildcrafted and handmade body-care products

Owners Kristen Dilley and Elie Barausky's line of handcrafted, wellness-supporting soaps, herbal teas, balms, and other body-care products are plant-based and inspired by their garden and fueled by local wildcrafting. A few spritzes of their Ritual Master blend of aromatherapy oils makes any room inviting and soothing. Portland Apothecary also runs a CSH (community supported herbalism), shipping an assortment of their salves, elixirs, and other herbal products seasonally.

Information

(W) portlandapothecary.com

Stumptown Printers

Portland's punk rock printing press

Two punk rock-loving brothers from Ohio gravitated to Portland for the music scene and started Stumptown Printers with a friend in 1999. Committed to letterpress printing (offset is available too), this now cooperatively owned business prints high-quality album covers and unique music packaging. Beyond music, they print custom book covers, cards, and more. There's a small shop at the entrance to their print production shop that carries postcards, posters, and other printed goods. If you come at the right time, you might get a peek at printing in action.

Information

Ⓐ 2293 N Interstate Ave.
Ⓣ (503) 233-7478
Ⓗ Tu-F 9 a.m.-6 p.m.
Ⓦ stumptownprinters.com
Ⓜ p. 292-39

At the back of the store, the smell of ink grows stronger and the space opens up into the print shop jammed with machinery. There's something very soothing about the rhythmic clunking of a printing press.

Oblation Papers & Press

In-house paper-making and letterpress printing

Oblation is a papermaking shop and letterpress printer that uses traditional rag paper (cotton paper) methods as well as a letterpress printer to craft the shop's products as well as custom-designed business cards, wedding and party invitations, and so much more. The shop's own line of cards is colorful, creative, and fun. We recommend chatting with the smart and friendly staff as you browse for gifts and souvenirs.

Information

Ⓐ 516 NW 12th Ave.
Ⓣ (503) 223 -1093
Ⓗ M-Sa 10 a.m.-6 p.m., Su 12 p.m.-5 p.m.
Ⓦ oblationpapers.com
Ⓜ p. 290 -15

Scout Books

Custom notebooks and books made with recycled paper

Scout Books produces a line of notebooks designed in-house, plus they make custom books and notebooks. All their of products are handmade in Southeast Portland using 100% recycled paper and vegetable-based inks. Renewable energy powers all of the printing, binding, and packaging machinery. Scout also has a line of other artist-designed goods available from their online shop. If you want to visit, call or email the company and schedule an appointment.

Information

Ⓐ 2130 SE 10th Ave.
Ⓣ (503) 238-4514
Ⓗ M-F 9 a.m.-5 p.m.
Ⓦ scoutbooks.com
Ⓜ p. 296-71

M

Make

Fortress Letterpress

Artistic letterpress prints by PNCA grad

Bruce Collin Paulson, who studied printmaking at PNCA (p. 231), runs this letterpress shop with a century-old press out of his garage. More and more Portland stores are bringing him work these days, and he also prints custom business cards, postcards, art prints, and more. Most of his work is inspired by geometric motifs found in nature. Schedule an appointment to visit.

Information

Ⓐ 10901 NE Eugene St.
Ⓦ fortressletterpress.com

Nothing says Portland like someplace where you can make your own stuff. From a petite objet d'art to a whole wooden boat, people come to ADX to turn ideas into actual things.

ADX

Kelley Roy's rad DIY hub with member workspaces and classes

This 14,000-square-foot shared DIY hub was founded by Kelley Roy in 2011. It is crammed with equipment for woodworking, welding, 3D printing, and more. Along with material-specific shops, individuals and companies can lease dedicated workspace. There are various memberships that give you access to tools, shared shops, and discounts on classes ranging from introduction to woodworking or screen printing to tailoring your own wool coat. If you have that maker itch, this is an awesome Portland place to scratch it.

Information

Ⓐ 417 SE 11th Ave.
Ⓣ (503) 915-4342
Ⓗ M-F 9 a.m.-10 p.m., Sa-Su 9 a.m.-9 p.m.
Ⓦ adxportland.com
Ⓜ p. 296-25

Oregon College of Art and Craft

A beautiful campus and leading arts college for artists, writers, and makers

It's a twenty-minute bus ride from downtown to the quiet, wooded OCAC campus. It's the perfect environment in which to focus on mastering media ranging from ceramics and book arts to textiles and jewelry making. With only 180 full-time students, OCAC classes are small and professors are accessible. There are also typically about 2,500 people enrolled in extension programs, some of which are multi-day intensive workshops. The campus includes many studios supporting hands-on learning, a gallery, shop, and cafe. More than 80% of OCAC's alumni are employed in the arts.

Information

Ⓐ 8245 SW Barnes Rd.
Ⓣ (503) 297-5544
Ⓦ ocac.edu

Programs for OCAC students include book arts, ceramics, drawing, painting, metal arts, photography, woodworking, and more. Here you have good access to the heart of the city as well as a quiet, forested campus. It's a wonderful place to hone your talents in art and craft.

Radius Community Art Studios

*Community art studio
with art workshops and classes*

Information

Ⓐ 322 SE Morrison St.
Ⓦ radiusstudio.org
Ⓜ p. 296-39

Radius was founded by artists and art-educators Kim McKenna and Mark Brandau in 2002. What got its start as evening drawing classes in a cramped apartment has evolved into a large collaborative space with private and shared studios, art classes, and workshops. Novice and seasoned artists use the facilities to make art, and study ceramics, painting, printing, and more. Visitors can take a tour of Radius and get a sneak peek into what the 50-plus members are working on.

Shared and solo studio space for all sorts of artists.

The ReBuilding Center

This fabulous nonprofit puts salvaged building materials to good use. It's a really fun North Portland spot to visit even if you don't have a DIY project you're shopping for.

Information

(A) 3625 N Mississippi Ave.
(T) (503) 331-9291
(H) M-F 10 a.m.-6 p.m., Sa 9 a.m.-5 p.m.,
    Su 10 a.m.-5 p.m.
(W) rebuildingcenter.org / (M) p. 292-28

Pendleton Home Store

With a company history dating back more than 150 years, this flagship store is known for its high-quality wool products, including blankets, throws, and home furnishings. Native American blankets are a specialty.

Information

(A) 220 NW Broadway
(T) (503) 535-5444
(H) M-Sa 10 a.m.-5:30 p.m.
(W) pendleton-usa.com
(M) p. 290-40

M

Make

Egg Press

This letterpress print shop specializes in greeting cards, business communication products, and other customized print products. Care is taken not to generate waste in the production process, and local resources are used whenever possible.

Information

(A) 2181 NW Nicolai St.
(T) (503) 234-4233
(H) M-F 9 a.m.-5 p.m. (customer service)
(W) eggpress.com / (M) p. 292-42

Little Otsu

Little Ostu publishes artistic illustrated books, calendars, notebooks, cards, and other paper goods made from recycled paper. It got its start as Otsu in San Francisco in 2002. Portland is now home base.

Information

(A) 3225 SE Division St.
(T) (503) 236.8673
(H) W-M 11 a.m.-7 p.m.
(W) littleotsu.com
(M) p. 296-73

Wood & Faulk

Born from founder/designer/builder Matt Pierce's personal blog featuring DIY projects, Wood & Faulk crafts handmade travel bags, accessories, and then some.

ⓣ (971) 295-1105
ⓦ woodandfaulk.com

Revive Upholstery & Design

Since 2011, Leland Duck has tackled custom redesign projects that turn vintage furniture into one-of-a-kind pieces, shaped by conversations with clients.

Ⓐ 2030 N Willis St. / ⓣ (971) 678-8593
Ⓗ Sa-Su 11 a.m.-5 p.m.
ⓦ revivepdx.com / Ⓜ p. 292-1

Shwood Eyewear

Handcrafted wood-frame sunglasses are this company's most popular product made from premium wood selected for its sustainability and beauty.

ⓣ (503) 893-4277
ⓦ shwoodshop.com

Grovemade

Grovemade's good looking iPhone cases and desk accessories are handcrafted from wood, leather, and metal, combining function and sleek design.

ⓣ (971) 229-0528
ⓦ grovemade.com

Bee Thinking

Are you a newbie backyard beekeeper? Find hives and everything else you need here, along with honey and bee-derived products such as candles and waxes.

Ⓐ 1744 SE Hawthorne Blvd.
ⓣ (877) 325-2221
Ⓗ Su-W 10 a.m.-6 p.m., Th-Sa 10 a.m.-8 p.m.
ⓦ beethinking.com / Ⓜ p. 296-91

Red Clouds Collective

Red Clouds is all about high-quality lifestyle accessories such as leather wallets, durable waxed canvas bags, and aprons with perfectly placed pockets—all crafted with American-made materials.

Ⓐ 727 SE Morrison St.
Ⓗ M-F 10 a.m.-6 p.m., Sa 12 p.m.-5 p.m.
ⓦ redcloudscollective.com / Ⓜ p. 296-36

Orox Leather Co.

This family-run brand with ties to Mexico and Japan fuses long-lasting leather with eco-friendly materials. Watch design and fabrication at their store.

Ⓐ 450 NW Couch St. / ⓣ (503) 954-2593
Ⓗ M-Th 10 a.m.-5p.m., F-Sa 10 a.m.-7 p.m., Su 12 p.m.-5 p.m.
ⓦ oroxleather.com / Ⓜ p. 290-45

The Tiny Spoon

Perry Pfister values when a graphic can evoke feelings in people, without having to spell it out in words. You can see his rad custom neon work at many Portland establishments.

Ⓐ 2925 NE Glisan St. / ⓣ (504) 344-2357
Ⓗ appointment required
ⓦ thetinyspoon.com / Ⓜ p. 294-36

Danner Boots

Quality craftsmanship has been behind this company's sturdy handmade boots since 1932. You can find quality boots, apparel, and leather-care products here.

Ⓐ 1022 W Burnside St.
ⓣ (503) 262-0331
Ⓗ M-Sa 11 a.m.-7 p.m., Su 11 a.m.-6 p.m.
ⓦ danner.com / Ⓜ p. 288-14

Make | **M** | 208

Richard Darbonne

The Good Flock's inviting space inspires making. There's a wall of neatly hung tools, huge tables with enough room to build almost anything, and vintage sewing machines all in a soothing white space.

The Good Flock

Information

Ⓐ 1801 NW Irving #300
Ⓦ thegoodflock.com
Ⓜ p. 290-10

Handcrafted products that solve life's everyday challenges

How the Good Flock started

The brand was founded by Marco Murillo, an eight-year veteran of Nike, after he came to a realization while working in the firm's Amsterdam office: despite the excitement of doing business on a vast global scale, the longer he stayed with a mass-production brand, the more he was losing touch with what it really means to make something. So he set out to create products that, rather than being designed for consumers to covet, would be designed to meet real human needs and solve various little problems of every-day life, and be made in small quantities from sustainable materials by local craftspeople.

Tackling the little things that get to you

Traveling always entails various kinds of small annoyances. Murillo jetted around the world for his previous job. He honed his approach to traveling efficiently, but one thing he could never fix was that his favorite electric toothbrush from home wouldn't fit in his toiletries bag. It's a perfect example of a commonplace annoyance needing a solution. Which is how The Good Flock's DOPP KIT--long enough to fit electric tooth-brushes—was born.

Products that prove their worth

Murillo believes in products you can use in many different contexts of life: at work, at play, and at home. He asks, "How should the product be made, by whom, and from what materials, in order to be useful in every sphere?" That's why the Good Flock's products are made from materials that Mother Nature will break down without harming the environment.

From product to workshops

Murillo recognizes the current desire for products that palpably exhibit the process by which they were made. To fulfill that yearning for a sense of connection, not just for a finished object, the Good Flock offers workshops for groups to actually try their hand at fabrication. Creating products and services that enhance enjoyment of life by providing an extra dose of meaning that today's discerning buyers are looking for: this is the ongoing mission he has set for the company.

M

Make

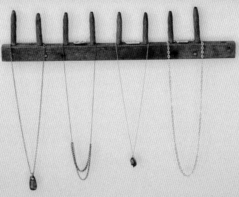

This display at Lowell embodies
the artful affection for the
object that can be found in so
many Portland stores.

DIG

Embark on a shopping expedition

Portland is home to all sorts of fiercely independent stores specializing in everything from vintage and antique wares to cool modern products from around the block or around the world. There are also plenty of shops selling items that are just plain weird. Setting off on a shopping expedition through Portland's lush retail jungle will definitely fan your treasure-hunting fire. We think you'll find some hidden gems.

WEST END SELECT SHOP

Beautiful store where each item is specially "selected" for you

Information

Ⓐ 927 SW Oak St.
Ⓣ (503) 477-6221
Ⓗ M, W-Sa 11 a.m.-6 p.m., Su 12 p.m.-5 p.m.
Ⓦ westendselectshop.com
Ⓜ p. 288-22

Interview with

ANDI BAKOS *Owner*

Please tell me about your store and the name "SELECT SHOP specifically?"

"Select Shop" is a Japanese retail term meaning a multi-brand store, which is unique in Asia where you find mostly mono-brand stores. We don't use the term "Select Shop" in the States so in a way it's kind of a secret code to those who know the phrase. "West End" simply refers to the West End corner of downtown Portland. It's a bustling area with lots of great shops, restaurants, cafes, bars, and food carts. It's where all the life is happening in downtown Portland. So, West End Select Shop refers to places that are important to me personally and that drive the creative inspiration behind the store.

I always feel that your store is very different from others in Portland. What makes it so unique?

My store is unique because it comes from me, and I am unique (like everyone else). I was born in Portland and I love the city deeply, BUT I have never quite fit the mold. Many of the things that define Portland are just not for me. I am the daughter of European immigrants who are avid travelers and have instilled those values in me. I have lived in both Europe and Asia and feel curious and excited by other cultures, which is how I buy for the shop. Although I love working with Portland makers, I don't limit my search to just American-made goods. I like to utilize

the whole globe for inspiration.

Portland is changing and growing rapidly, what do you think about it?

At first I mourned the Portland I once knew. Though I felt it was small and dingy, it was cool and it was mine! As I grew, the city did too, and it grew and grew and grew. Now when I look around I hardly remember the city as it once was. I miss old Portland but the new Portland is beautiful too. People have taken care to preserve many of the things that made old Portland great! Small businesses can thrive here, creative communities are supported and nurtured here. The crafters and makers have only gotten better and more skilled. New Portland is cool too. Just not the traffic!

What's your plan for next few years for WEST END SELECT SHOP?

We plan to continue to engage with our local community, we have a lot of great ideas for events in our near future. We are trying to expand our online reach with our website. Also, I would love to do more product collaborations, soon we have an incense coming out which is a collaboration with a Japanese incense maker called "Kuumba."

Do you have any recommendations of newly-opened restaurants, bars, or stores in Portland?

I just had the best lunch the other day at Poke Mon, they opened recently on SE Hawthorne Blvd and do Hawaiian style Poke bowls. I'm still dreaming of that lunch! I go to the new Pine Street Market (p. 38) often and there's something for everyone. Solabee (p. 223) is a plant shop opened recently. It's beautiful and you must see it!

213

D

Dig

Lowell

Inventive handicrafts from local artists

Information

(A) 819 N Russell St.
(T) (503) 753-3608
(H) W-Su 12 p.m.-7 p.m.
(W) lowellportland.com
(M) p. 292-34

Not far from an industrial area, this little shop's red door is eye-catching. Once inside, owner Maya Rose greets you with smile. The Lowell shelves and racks are stocked with handmade and Lowell-made vintage and contemporary furniture, clothing, and art. A hefty percentage of the merchandise is made by local artists and the owner's friends and can only be purchased here. Lowell is named after Rose's father, and that etymology suits the atmosphere well. Customers often feel like family when they come to browse.

MadeHere PDX

Mecca for made-in-Portland gifts and souvenirs

This large Pearl District store, which opened in November 2014, carries the work of talented designers, artisans, and makers based in Portland. Portland, of course, has a dense concentration of creators of world-class stuff, so expect to find products from local roasters, local clothing designers, and local furniture makers all side-by-side. If you are seeking a full-spectrum view of the diversity and creativity of Portland-produced cool stuff, this is the spot. What's a better gift for the folks back home than something made in Portland?

Information

Ⓐ 40 NW 10th Ave.
Ⓣ (503) 224-0122
Ⓗ M-W 11 a.m.-6 p.m., Th 11 a.m.-7 p.m.,
  F 11 a.m.-6 p.m., Sa 10 a.m.-7 p.m., Su 11 a.m.-6 p.m.
Ⓦ madeherepdx.com
Ⓜ p. 290-36

D

Dig

Canoe

*Beautiful functional goods
that you'll love forever*

Canoe offers a wide range of one-of-a-kind, carefully-curated home, office, and life goods collected from all over the world by shop owners Craig Olson and Sean Igo. A large part of the shop is devoted to beautiful, functional, lasting goods from Japan, Scandinavia, Europe, and local makers. Take advantage of the generous complimentary gift wrapping.

Information

Ⓐ 1233 SW 10th Ave.
Ⓣ (503) 889-8545
Ⓗ Tu-Sa 10 a.m.-6 p.m., Su 11 a.m.-5 p.m.
Ⓦ canoeonline.net
Ⓜ p. 288-66

Milk Milk Lemonade

Take a whiff of "Eau de Portland"

Information

Ⓐ 1407 SE Belmont St.
Ⓣ (503) 970-1173
Ⓗ Th-Sa 11 a.m.-6 p.m.
Ⓦ milkmilklemonade.virb.com
Ⓜ p. 296-43

Milk Milk Lemonade, opened in July 2014, is the showroom and work studio of OLO Fragrance. The interior is minimalist yet inviting, with a full line of OLO products as well as a select assortment of home accessories and personal-care items. Owner Heather Sielaff has a background in aromatherapy and is a self-taught parfumier. Her handmade perfumes contain no alcohol and are made with a coconut-oil base.

North of West

Not just a designer crafts collection,
a crafts connection

In this light-flooded downtown space you'll find homewares, jewelry, and more from forty-plus brands. The store's primary focus, however, is on its three core brands: Nell & Mary (homewares, totes, and backpacks), Make It Good (women and men's apparel), and Pigeon Toe (ceramic goods). Not only does North of West stock a slew of handmade products under one roof, it is a window into Portland's dynamic craft culture.

Information

Ⓐ 203 SW 9th Ave.
Ⓣ (503) 208-3080
Ⓗ M-Sa 11 a.m.-7 p.m., Su 12 p.m.-6 p.m.
Ⓦ shopnorthofwest.com
Ⓜ p. 288-25

Alder & Co.

They went, they saw, they bought

Information

Ⓐ 616 SW 12 th Ave.
Ⓣ (503) 224-1647
Ⓗ M-Sa 11 a.m.-6 p.m., Su 11 a.m.-4 p.m.
Ⓦ alderandcoshop.com
Ⓜ p. 288-47

Following a simple rule—would I want this in my own life?—this store's buyers have travelled across America and to the far corners of the world to find daily essentials such as kitchenware and apparel as well as jewelry and art, for this large downtown Portland shop. Every item has been carefully chosen to liven up everyday life with its timeless beauty and functionality. You can also pick up fresh flowers from Hilary Horvath Flowers inside the shop.

Palace

Curated clothing from vintage to modern

Owner Charlotte Reich opened Palace in 2010. On its adorable racks, arranged by color, are a rainbow of vintage dresses from the 1920s, Italian wool sweaters from the 1950s, South American textiles, and Navajo accessories. Vintage threads are racked alongside modern brands such as Fog Linen, Hansel from Basel, Made on the Moon, and Fjällräven.

Information

Ⓐ 2205 E Burnside St.
Ⓣ (503) 517-0123
Ⓗ 11 a.m.-7 p.m. daily
Ⓦ palacestore.com
Ⓜ p. 294-44

betsy & iya

A jeweler's venture turned lifestyle boutique

betsy & iya started as a handcrafted jewelry line and is now a lifestyle boutique carrying fragrances, fashion, and gifts created in house as well as by independent artists and designers. The shop is located in a historic building that housed a movie theater from 1912 to 1954 and is now also home to the betsy & iya studio where jewelry makers design and craft jewelry marked by intricate geometric designs and vintage gold.

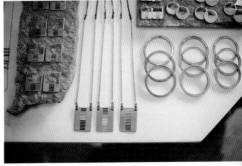

Information

Ⓐ 2403 NW Thurman St.
Ⓣ (503) 227-5482
Ⓗ 10 a.m.-6 p.m. daily
Ⓦ betsyandiya.com/brick-and-mortar/
Ⓜ p. 290-2

D | *Dig*

Compound Gallery

Street fashion and art emporium

Information

Ⓐ 107 NW 5th Ave.
Ⓣ (503) 796-2733
Ⓗ M-Sa 11 a.m.-7 p.m., Su 12 p.m.-6 p.m.
Ⓦ compoundgallery.com
Ⓜ p. 290-43

The first floor of Katsu Tanaka's Compound is an exclusive sneaker and streetwear fashion shop, while the second floor houses an on-the-pulse art gallery and shop showcasing brands Stussy and Undefeated. This Old Town shop also stocks trendy Japanese toys and a large selection of urban backpacks.

Vintalier

High-quality vintage and new women's apparel

Information

Ⓐ 412 NW 13th Ave.
Ⓣ (503) 222-0148
Ⓗ M-Sa 11 a.m.-6 p.m., Su 11 a.m.-5 p.m.
Ⓦ vintalier.com
Ⓜ p. 290-19

Much of the clothing for sale at this Pearl District women's boutique is vintage and in great condition, although Vintalier also carries new designer threads. Owner Ellen Hsu also stocks her store with well-designed shoes, bags, and accessories, all neatly organized in a charming way. If you are lucky, you may even get to meet shop dog, Kenji!

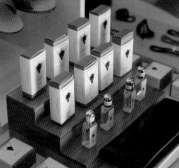

San Johnny

Mexican household items and mid-century furniture

As you step into this Old Town/Chinatown store, you are met with an array of beautiful Mexican arts and crafts, household items, ceramics and porcelain goods, as well as mid-century furniture. If you are interested in adding few well-designed handmade accents to your home, we highly recommend visiting this store.

Information

Ⓐ 217 NW Couch St.
Ⓣ (503) 344-4830
Ⓗ Tu-F 12 p.m.-6 p.m., Sa 12 p.m.-4 p.m.
   or by appointment
Ⓦ sanjohnny.com
Ⓜ p. 290-51

WM Goods

A highly-refined women's boutique

Information

Ⓐ 1136 SW Alder St.
Ⓣ (503) 954-3398
Ⓗ 11 a.m.-5 p.m. daily
Ⓦ shopwmgoods.com
Ⓜ p. 288-46

Portland native Whitney Goodman's spacious shop is home to many beautiful items including designer women's clothing, natural skin care products, jewelry, and furniture. It's a gorgeous space that will make you feel as if you were visiting the house of a friend with exceptionally good taste.

Hoodoo Antiques & Design

Vintage and antique items close to Portland Saturday Market

Founded in Portland in 1994, this treasure trove is blocks away from both Voodoo Doughnut (p. 70) and Portland Saturday Market. The shop specializes in vintage and antique art, furniture, and home decor from around the world. Soak up the unique atmosphere and all the funky stuff on display.

Information

Ⓐ 122 NW Couch St.
Ⓣ (503) 360-3409
Ⓗ F-Su 11 a.m.-5 p.m.
Ⓦ hoodooantiques.com
Ⓜ p. 290-52

Pistils Nursery

One of Portland's favorite neighborhood nurseries

Gardening culture is deep-rooted in the Rose City, and Mississippi Avenue's Pistils is a hub for it. The nursery/shop is filled with indoor and outdoor plants from local growers along with gardening supplies and living art. There are free-range chickens, potted plants, and seedlings out back. Pistils is a charming spot, well worth a visit, that helps Portlanders elevate gardening to urban farming.

Information

Ⓐ 3811 N Mississippi Ave.
Ⓣ (503) 288-4889
Ⓗ M-F 11 a.m.-7 p.m., Sa-Su 10 a.m.-7 p.m.
Ⓦ pistilsnursery.com
Ⓜ p. 292-24

Solabee Flowers & Botanicals

One of Martha Stewart's favorite floral studios and plant shops

Stepping into this full-service floral studio and plant shop is like stumbling upon a secret garden. The breathtakingly wide variety of beautiful and unusual plants feels like a scaled down botanical garden. Martha Stewart chose the shop as one of her favorite florists in the nation in 2015. Solabee also offers floral delivery, so it's the perfect place to get a little something to add some color to your hotel room.

Information

Ⓐ 801 N Killingsworth St.
Ⓣ (503) 307-2758
Ⓗ M-F 11 a.m.-6 p.m., Sa-Su 10 a.m.-6 p.m.
Ⓦ solabeeflowers.com
Ⓜ p. 292-9

Portland Knife House

The best in retail knives, knife sharpening, and repair

This knife shop caters to culinary professionals (but welcomes home cooks) with its 400-plus high-quality, primarily Oregon and Japan artisan-made knives. Plus you'll find chef gear like kitchen clogs, knife rolls, and aprons. As soon as the doors open, in pour cooks and chefs looking for just the right knife for their culinary endeavors, or hoping to consult with the in-store knife pros and get their knives sharpened (on a Japanese-style whetstone from $6 or on a grinder from $3). The knife inventory includes Portland-based Bridgetown Forge knives, made by Arnon Kartmazov who mastered Western knife-making techniques and then spent twelve years apprenticing in Japan. Knife House is in many ways an outpost of Japan's lauded artisan knife culture.

Information

Ⓐ 2637 SE Belmont St.
Ⓣ (503) 234-6397
Ⓗ M-Th 10 a.m.-6 p.m., Su 10 a.m.-3 p.m.
Ⓦ portlandknifehouse.com
Ⓜ p. 296-44

Station Knives (left middle photo) are the work of an artisan who studied sculpture in college and include gorgeously made blocks with each knife. The store also carries Japanese straight razors.

Schoolhouse Electric

Go here for reproductions of vintage lighting fixtures, Portland-made furniture, and homewares.

Ⓐ 2181 NW Nicolai St.
Ⓣ (503) 230-7113
Ⓗ 9 a.m.-6 p.m. daily
Ⓦ schoolhouseelectric.com
Ⓜ p. 292-43

Hand-Eye Supply

This cool downtown shop is run by the two founders of the industrial design blog Core77. They sell tools, work clothes, and more.

Ⓐ 427 NW Broadway
Ⓣ (503) 575-9769
Ⓗ 11 a.m.-6 p.m. daily
Ⓦ handeyesupply.com / Ⓜ p. 290-26

Hippo Hardware & Trading Co.

Hippo Hardware has been open since 1976. The first two floors carry doorknobs, faucets, toilets etc., and the third floor features vintage lighting.

Ⓐ 1040 E Burnside St.
Ⓣ (503) 231-1444 / Ⓗ M-Th 10 a.m.-5 p.m., F-Sa 10 a.m.-6 p.m., Su 12 p.m.-5 p.m.
Ⓦ hippohardware.com / Ⓜ p. 296-8

Lodekka

This hip dress store lives in a 1960s double-decker bus from Liverpool.

Ⓐ Tidbit Food Farm & Garden
 2880 SE Division St.
Ⓣ (503) 704-1754
Ⓗ Th-Su 12 p.m.-6 p.m.
Ⓦ lodekka.com
Ⓜ p. 296-77

Wildfang

Get your tomboy fashion here, ranging from button-down shirts to overalls, including a house line and select brands.

Ⓐ 1230 SE Grand Ave.
Ⓣ (503) 208-3631
Ⓗ Su-Th 11 a.m.-8 p.m., F-Sa 10 a.m.-8 p.m.
Ⓦ wildfang.com / Ⓜ p. 296-49

Grand Marketplace

This huge mall-like space houses a curated stock of antiques brought in by collectors.

Ⓐ 1005 SE Grand Ave.
Ⓣ (503) 208-2580
Ⓗ 12 p.m.-6 p.m. daily
Ⓦ grandmarketplacepdx.com
Ⓜ p. 296-45

225

D

Dig

Artemisia

Terrariums, succulents, and air plants growing in glass containers are the draw here.

Ⓐ 110 SE 28th Ave.
Ⓣ (503) 232-8224
Ⓗ 10:30 a.m.-6 p.m. daily
Ⓦ collagewithnature.com
Ⓜ p. 296-17

Hawthorne Vintage Modern

There are 7,000 square feet of mid-century modern used furniture, homewares, and lighting here.

Ⓐ 4722 SE Hawthorne Blvd.
Ⓣ (503) 230-2620
Ⓗ 11 a.m.-6 p.m. daily
Ⓜ p. 296-68

Crafty Wonderland

What started as an event has evolved into a store showcasing the handicrafts of 200-plus local artists.

Ⓐ 808 SW 10th Ave.
Ⓣ (503) 224-9097
Ⓗ M-Sa 10 a.m.-6 p.m., Su 11 a.m.-6 p.m.
Ⓦ craftywonderland.com
Ⓜ p. 288-53

Boys Fort

Here you'll find furniture, jewelry, and leather goods geared toward men—all from local artists and artisans.

Ⓐ 902 SW Morrison St.
Ⓣ (503) 567-1015
Ⓗ Su-M 12 p.m.-5 p.m., Tu-Sa 11 a.m.-6 p.m.
Ⓦ boysfort.com
Ⓜ p. 288-52

Portland Flea + Food

This flea market is held on the last Sunday of every month in Southeast between Rejuvenation and Jacobsen Salt Co.

Ⓐ Intersection of SE 6th Ave. and SE Salmon St.
Ⓗ Last Su 11 a.m.-4 p.m.
Ⓦ pdxflea.com
Ⓜ p. 296-48

Una

Carefully curated women's clothing, jewelry, and homewares from across the globe. There's a fun, slightly off-beat fashion sense here.

Ⓐ 922 SE Ankeny St.
Ⓣ (503) 235-2326
Ⓗ M-Sa 11 a.m.-6 p.m., Su 12 p.m.-6 p.m.
Ⓦ unanegozio.com / Ⓜ p. 294-49

House of Vintage

Hawthorne Boulevard boasts a cluster of vintage stores, and this is the granddaddy of them all.

Ⓐ 3315 SE Hawthorne Blvd.
Ⓣ (503) 236-1991
Ⓗ 11 a.m.-7 p.m. daily
Ⓦ houseofvintageportland.com
Ⓜ p. 296-56

Woonwinkel

Women-run shop with a colorful selection of work from independent West Coast designers.

Ⓐ 935 SW Washington St.
Ⓣ (503) 334-2088
Ⓗ Su-W 11 a.m.-6 p.m., Th-Sa 10 a.m.-7 p.m.
Ⓦ woonwinkelhome.com
Ⓜ p. 288-27

Animal Traffic

This shop's three locations feature new and used Northwest outdoorsy styles for men and women.

Ⓐ 4000 N Mississippi Ave.
Ⓣ (503) 249-4000
Ⓗ M-Th 11 a.m.-6 p.m., F-Sa 11 a.m.-8 p.m., Su 11 a.m.-7 p.m.
Ⓦ animaltrafficpdx.com / Ⓜ p. 292-20

Spruce Apothecary

Spruce Apothecary in Union Way offers the best in contemporary and European unisex grooming products such as fragrances, hair care, and skin care made with carefully selected ingredients.

Ⓐ 1022 W Burnside St., Unit K / Ⓣ (503)206-4022
Ⓗ M-Sa 11 a.m.-6 p.m., Su 11 a.m.-5 p.m.
Ⓦ spruceapothecary.com / Ⓜ p. 288-12

Machus

Machus is an up-market purveyor of contemporary menswear from international designers.

Ⓐ 542 E Burnside St.
Ⓣ (503) 206-8626
Ⓗ M-F 12 p.m.-7 p.m., Sa 11 a.m.-7 p.m., Su 12 p.m.-5 p.m.
Ⓦ machusonline.com / Ⓜ p. 296-1

Worn Path

Check out the select outdoor apparel and gear for daily life at this North Portland shop.

Ⓐ 4007 N Mississippi Ave.
Ⓣ (971) 331-8747
Ⓗ M-Tu 11 a.m.-7 p.m., Th-Sa 11 a.m.-7 p.m., Su 11 a.m.-6 p.m.
Ⓦ worn-path.com / Ⓜ p. 292-19

Revival Drum Shop

This vintage and custom drum store is great for novice and veteran players.

Ⓐ 2045 SE Ankeny St., Suite R
Ⓣ (503) 719-6533
Ⓗ 11 a.m.-6 p.m. daily
Ⓦ revivaldrumshop.com
Ⓜ p. 296-10

Elements Vape

This lounge-like supplier of vaping gear and goods even has a vape bar.

Ⓐ 3340 SE Hawthorne Blvd.
Ⓣ (971) 373 -8192
Ⓗ Su-Th 12 p.m.-8 p.m., F-Sa 12 p.m.-9 p.m.
Ⓦ elementsvape.com
Ⓜ p. 296-63

Blue Moon Camera and Machine

Peruse ultra-compact to large-format film cameras, accessories, and supplies, and a lot of typewriters. We love Blue Moon!

Ⓐ 8417 N Lombard St.
Ⓣ (503) 978-0333
Ⓗ M-F 9 a.m.-6 p.m., Sa 9 a.m.-5 p.m.
Ⓦ bluemooncamera.com

Paxton Gate

Where else can you buy taxidermy, fossils, and other wildlife specimens? Paxton also has workshops that teach how to stuff and mount a squirrel.

Ⓐ 4204 N Mississippi Ave.
Ⓣ (503) 719-4508
Ⓗ 11 a.m.-7 p.m. daily
Ⓦ paxtongate.com / Ⓜ p. 292-18

Hattie's Vintage Clothing

Jamie French / travelportland.com

Spanning 1900 to 1980, this inventory of vintage dresses, hats, shoes, and boots always yields unique finds.

Ⓐ 729 E Burnside St., Suite 101
Ⓣ (503) 238-1938
Ⓗ M-Th 11 a.m.-6:30 p.m., F-Su 11 a.m.-7 p.m.
Ⓦ hattiesvintageclothing.com
Ⓜ p. 294-42

Andy and Bax

Open since 1945, this is Portland's oldest military surplus store. They also carry rafting and camping equipment.

Ⓐ 324 SE Grand Ave.
Ⓣ (503) 234-7538
Ⓗ M-Th 9 a.m.-6 p.m., F 9 a.m.-9 p.m.
Sa 9 a.m.-6 p.m.
Ⓦ andyandbax.com / Ⓜ p. 296-20

227

D

Dig

Bridge & Burn

This classic, practical Northwest men's and women's apparel brand was founded in 2009.

Ⓐ 1122 SW Morrison St.
Ⓣ (971) 279-4077
Ⓗ Su-Th 11 a.m.-6 p.m., F-Sa 11 a.m.-7 p.m.
Ⓦ bridgeandburn.com
Ⓜ p. 288-50

Much of the $34 million investment in renovations for the new Pacific Northwest College of Art campus came from local donors. This is a testament to the belief in this institution's role as a vibrant and creative hub for Portland art and learning.

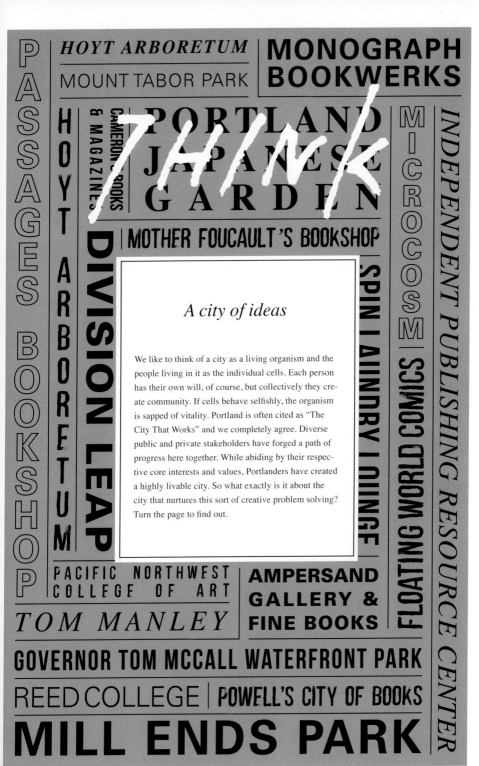

HOYT ARBORETUM

MONOGRAPH BOOKWERKS

MOUNT TABOR PARK

PASSAGES BOOKSHOP

HOYT ARBORETUM

CAMERON'S BOOKS & MAGAZINES

DIVISION LEAP

PORTLAND JAPANESE GARDEN

THINk

MOTHER FOUCAULT'S BOOKSHOP

MICROCOSM

INDEPENDENT PUBLISHING RESOURCE CENTER

SPIN LAUNDRY LOUNGE

FLOATING WORLD COMICS

A city of ideas

We like to think of a city as a living organism and the people living in it as the individual cells. Each person has their own will, of course, but collectively they create community. If cells behave selfishly, the organism is sapped of vitality. Portland is often cited as "The City That Works" and we completely agree. Diverse public and private stakeholders have forged a path of progress here together. While abiding by their respective core interests and values, Portlanders have created a highly livable city. So what exactly is it about the city that nurtures this sort of creative problem solving? Turn the page to find out.

PACIFIC NORTHWEST COLLEGE OF ART

AMPERSAND GALLERY & FINE BOOKS

TOM MANLEY

GOVERNOR TOM MCCALL WATERFRONT PARK

REED COLLEGE | POWELL'S CITY OF BOOKS

MILL ENDS PARK

T

Think

Pacific Northwest College of Art

New PNCA campus propels Portland art scene

Founded in 1909 as part of the Portland Art Museum, PNCA attracts talented students from around the world. It was one of the first schools to establish graduate courses in fine arts and crafts, among which is a unique MFA in Applied Craft and Design. Tom Manley, the school's president from 2003 until 2015, said that creative thinking is the key to solving many of the world's problems, and he described PNCA's mission as the training of artists with the creativity and entrepreneurial spirit that equips them to become influential.

Manley led the recent campus expansion that moved the school into a renovated historic post office building in the North Park Blocks, now dubbed the Arlene and Harold Schnitzer Center for Art and Design. The architect was Brad Cloepfil of Portland-based Allied Works Architecture. With ample experience in art-related buildings, he designed the new campus so that it retains historic details and incorporates new spaces such as a theater and gallery serving the public as an interface between the school and the city. The new campus is expected to strengthen PNCA's role as an engine of Portland's creative economy and a launch pad for art and culture in the city.

Information

Ⓐ 511 NW Broadway
Ⓣ (503) 226-4391
Ⓦ pnca.edu
Ⓜ p. 290-16

TOM MANLEY

Former President (Pacific Northwest Collage of Art)

*PNCA is a platform
for the creativity that
can change the world*

Ask Tom Manley, and he will tell you that the importance of creativity is increasing in today's world, and it needs to be taught. Not just the kind of purely artistic creativity expressed in painting or designing furniture, but a broader sense of creativity as the whole process of creating new things.

In Manley's worldview, though the state of things can appear grim or even hopeless, creativity is key to unlocking solutions. Human civilization is a product of humanity's creative powers, and with civilization in big trouble creativity holds the key to renewing and regenerating it. Which is why he envisioned making Portland a platform for developing world-class creativity that can change the world. Manley sees Portland as a new model of the city, transcending the dichotomy between rural and urban.

That's why he led the effort to relocate PNCA to a new campus in a renovated historic building in central Portland: to create a base from which to cultivate in students the type of creativity that can improve the world.

Why is Portland such a wellspring of creativity? According to Manley, just as Portland is located geographically at the confluence of the Willamette and Columbia rivers, it is also where different streams of culture converge. That makes Portland ideally situated for the challenge of the twenty-first century: the need to overcome clashes of values and aesthetic sensibilities, and in overcoming them bring forth new and creative things. Manley helped establish the Lemelson Innovation Studio at PNCA to inculcate the forward-looking, innovative thinking needed to address that challenge.

Bio

Served as PNCA President from 2003–2015. Previously had a long career at Claremont McKenna College, one of California's most respected liberal arts schools. Hailed as Portland's creative strategist for raising PNCA's profile as an art school. Studies poetry and identifies as a foodie.

Portland Japanese Garden

Visit Japan
without leaving Portland

Information

Ⓐ 611 SW Kingston Ave.
Ⓣ (503) 223-1321
Ⓗ Summer Public Hours (March 13-September 30)
M 12 p.m.-7 p.m., Tu-Su 10 a.m.-7 p.m.
Winter Public Hours (October 1-March 12)
M 12 p.m.-4 p.m., Tu-Su 10 a.m.-4 p.m.
Members of the garden have special access from
Tu-Su 8 a.m. - 10 a.m.
Ⓦ japanesegarden.com

In 1958, a new sister-city relationship between Portland and Sapporo, Japan, spurred the founding of a nonprofit called the Japanese Garden Society of Oregon. Takuma Tono designed the garden in 1963 and it was opened to the public in 1967. It consists of five subgardens dotted with attractions such as a waterfall with koi pond, a rock garden, and a teahouse.

Portland's Japanese Garden has been hailed as the most beautiful and authentically Japanese of the 300 or so public Japanese gardens in the U.S. Many of the materials used in building it were shipped from Japan. Since the garden opened, it has been operated under a nonprofit with close supervision by Japanese garden designers. New buildings and landscape design are currently underway by architect Kengo Kuma. This jewel of a garden exhibits Japan's respect for the beauty of the passing seasons so convincingly that you might forget which side of the Pacific you're on.

Powell's City of Books

The world's largest independent bookstore and a Portland institution

Powell's is a Portland institution and cultural pillar. This largest new and used independent bookstore in the world occupies an entire city block with four floors of books. The store's roots, however, are in Chicago, where bibliophile grad student Michael Powell opened his first bookstore in 1970. When he wanted to take some much-needed time off one summer, Michael asked his retired father Walter to mind the store. Walter enjoyed the experience of running his son's bookstore so much that he opened Powell's Books back home in Portland in 1971.

In 1979, Michael returned to join him in the venture, and the rest is history. Michael's daughter Emily is now Powell's president. The store's unique policy of shelving new and used books together was, "my father's idea," says Michael. "He had no experience in the bookstore business and people thought it was crazy, but it proved to be surprisingly advantageous to all parties." The enormous building's split-level floors, color-coded by subject, house more than a million books. Powell's also sells a wide selection of gifts and has a cafe into which you can take books for perusal before purchase. Allow plenty of time for a City of Books visit and try to catch an author reading. It's only natural to lose track of time soaking in this fountain of Portland bibliophilia.

Information

Ⓐ 1005 W Burnside St.
Ⓣ (800) 878-7323
Ⓗ 9 a.m.-11 p.m. daily
Ⓦ powells.com
Ⓜ p. 290-34

Powell's City of Books is located in a huge space that was a former car dealership. Current Powell's CEO Miriam Sontz notes that expertise in a subject area is not enough to get a job there; only passionate book lovers need apply.

Monograph Bookwerks

Incredible art bookstore with well-curated paintings and prints

Information

Ⓐ 5005 NE 27th Ave.
Ⓣ (503) 284-5005
Ⓗ W-Su 11 a.m.-7 p.m.
Ⓦ monographbookwerks.com
Ⓜ p. 294-13

Artists John Brodie and Blair Saxon-Hill opened this art-focused bookstore just off of Alberta Street in 2010. It is home to a wide selection of new, used, and rare books about everything from modern architecture, graphic design, photography, and fashion to art criticism, theory, and counterculture. Beyond books, Monograph also sells mid-century ceramics, vintage art, and office supplies and showcases a meticulously curated selection of art, paintings, and prints. Owners Brodie and Saxon-Hill wanted to create a store where Portland artists and art lovers could purchase world-class books about modern art that would contribute to the growth of the local art and design scene. They certainly succeeded.

As you browse art books and magazines, don't forget to check out all of the art decorating the store.

239

T

Think

Make your own zine
and become your own publisher

Independent Publishing Resource Center

Printing press? Typesetting? Copiers? Check, check, check. The nonprofit IPRC is outfitted with everything you need to produce a book, zine, comic, or other printed work or website, and the space and equipment are available through tiered membership fees. The mission since IPRC's founding in 1998 is to support creative expression and community by providing access to the tools needed to create independently published art and media. Even if you don't become a member it's a great place to visit. Check out the library and its 9,000-plus zines.

Information

Ⓦ iprc.org
Planning to move to the new location in 2017.
Read more on the website.

Think

Ampersand Gallery & Fine Books

Found photography, art books, and monthly art exhibits

Opened in 2008 by Myles Haselhorst, Ampersand deals in new and used art, design, and photography books. The NE Alberta Street store also doubles as a gallery space with monthly exhibits. One of the specialties here is Ampersand's large photo collection of found photography and artists' work for sale. Seeing the art and browsing the books is sure to give you a flash of inspiration.

Information

Ⓐ 2916 NE Alberta St., Suite B
Ⓣ (503) 805-5458
Ⓗ W-Sa 12 p.m.-7 p.m., Su 10 a.m.-5 p.m.
Ⓦ ampersandgallerypdx.com
Ⓜ p. 294-19

Floating World Comics

All you could hope for in comics and vinyl

Information

Ⓐ 400 NW Couch St.
Ⓣ (503) 241-0227
Ⓗ 11 a.m.-7 p.m. daily
Ⓦ floatingworldcomics.com
Ⓜ p. 290-46

The comic book scene is alive and well in Portland and this is one of our favorite comic stores in the city. The shelves are arranged by author, publisher, and genre, and if you want a regular dose of shop-picked comics join the subscription box service. There's a substantial selection of art books here as well. Floating World shares its space with Landfill Rescue Unit, a new and rare vinyl shop with an emphasis on punk, metal, funk, and soul.

Passages Bookshop & Gallery

Top-notch rare and out-of-print books

Passages Bookshop & Gallery specializes in unusual, fine, and rare books and graphic art, focusing on poetry, modern art and literature, fine printing and artist's books, and related material. In December 2015, Passages relocated to a storefront on NE Martin Luther King Jr. Boulevard, just two blocks north of the Oregon Convention Center, where they host regular changing exhibitions and frequent literary and art-related events. Proprietor David Abel, a poet and editor, has been a bookseller for thirty years, since the days of his Bridge Bookshop in New York City's East Village in the late 1980s.

Information

Ⓐ 1223 NE Martin Luther King Jr Blvd.
Ⓣ (503) 388-7665
Ⓗ Th-Sa 12 p.m.-6 p.m.
Ⓦ passagesbookshop.com
Ⓜ p. 294-30

Spin Laundry Lounge

Laundry doesn't have to be a boring chore

This retro mod establishment is a coin laundry bar and cafe. The high-ceilinged space features rows of state-of-the-art washing machines that run so efficiently you can wash and dry a load in just forty-five minutes and you get a text message when your load is complete. Spin is a green operation with eco-friendly detergent (you don't have to bring your own) and supplies. The café/bar serves tasty, locally-sourced fare so you can kick back with coffee and food while your clothes get clean. You can even get some work done here, thanks to the free WiFi, or play some retro arcade games. Spin Laundry magically makes doing your laundry fun.

242

T

Think

Information

Ⓐ 750 N Fremont St.
Ⓣ (503) 477-5382
Ⓗ 8 a.m.-12 a.m. daily
Ⓦ spinlaundrylounge.com
Ⓜ p. 292-32

Spin opened in 2014. Wash-and-fold service is available if you don't feel like hanging out.

Reed students are renowned as both intellectual and countercultural, and they are expected to be self-starters and independent thinkers. The campus is accessible to the public, and we recommend a stroll around Reed's beautiful premises and Tudor Gothic brick buildings.

Reed College

Famed liberal arts college is a cradle for critical thinkers

A young Steve Jobs famously attended this private liberal arts college for a short time before dropping out, but he continued to attend calligraphy, dance, and literature classes here for another year and a half (without paying tuition), an experience that laid the groundwork for Apple Computer's adoption of its elegant fonts. Founded in 1908, Reed's credo is to cultivate "the life of the mind." The similarity to the Ivy League schools of the East Coast ends at the park-like campus: Reed is more freewheeling with a counter-culture West Coast vibe. Reed is not easy to get into, and the college refuses to provide data about admitted students to college ranking publications, stating that it doesn't want to be judged on selectivity numbers but prefers to attract students who are in tune with the college's ideals.

Information

Ⓐ 3203 SE Woodstock Blvd.
Ⓣ (503) 771-1112
Ⓦ reed.edu

Cameron's Books & Magazines

Visit one of Portland's oldest bookstores, open since 1938, and peruse the vintage magazines and used books.

Ⓐ 336 SW 3rd Ave.
Ⓣ (503) 228-2391
Ⓗ M-Sa 11 a.m.-6 p.m., Su 11 a.m.-4 p.m.
Ⓦ cameronsbooks.com
Ⓜ p. 288-45

Hoyt Arboretum

Hoyt Arboretum is home to diverse plants from around the world, including 1,100 tree species. It's a great hiking destination with twelve miles of forested trails.

Ⓐ 4000 SW Fairview Blvd. / Ⓣ (503) 865-8733
Ⓗ M-F 9 a.m.-4 p.m., Sa-Su 11 a.m.-3 p.m.
Ⓦ hoytarboretum.org

Mill Ends Park

The world's smallest government-administered public park got its start in 1948 when a reporter for the Oregon Journal planted flowers in a hole dug for a streetlamp.

Ⓐ SW Naito Pkwy. & Taylor St.
Ⓜ p. 288-63

Mount Tabor Park

The summit of this 630-foot hill in Southeast Portland, the cinder cone of an ancient volcano, offers fantastic views of downtown and Mt. Hood.

Ⓐ SE 60th Ave. & Salmon St.
Ⓦ portlandoregon.gov/parks

Governor Tom McCall Waterfront Park

This large recreational space downtown along the Willamette River is named for a former Oregon governor.

Ⓐ 1020 SW Naito Pkwy.
Ⓦ portlandoregon.gov/parks
Ⓜ p. 288-64

Division Leap

Out-of-print books, rare art books, periodicals, and zines headline this downtown Portland bookstore's fiercely independent stock.

Ⓣ (503) 206-7291
Ⓗ Reservation required
Ⓦ divisionleap.com / Ⓜ p. 288-38

Mother Foucault's Bookshop

Mother Foucault's feels like someone's wonderful secret private library filled with literature, philosophy, literary criticism, and foreign language books.

Ⓐ 523 SE Morrison St. / Ⓣ (503) 236-2665
Ⓗ M 11 a.m.-3 p.m., Tu-W 11 a.m.-6 p.m.,
  Th-F 11 a.m.-7 p.m., Sa 11 a.m.-6 p.m.,
  Su 1 p.m.-4 p.m. / Ⓜ p. 296-33

Microcosm

This independent, empowering book and zine publisher uses only recycled paper and animal-product-free inks.

Ⓐ 2752 N Williams Ave.
Ⓣ (503) 232-3666
Ⓗ M-Sa 11 a.m.-7 p.m.
Ⓦ microcosmpublishing.com
Ⓜ p. 292-37

244

Think

TOM MANLEY

Creativity works here.

And to work, creativity needs places where people can study art, design, and information.
That's why PNCA moved from the Pearl District to an edgier neighborhood.

Creative Management

I'd like to see art college graduates running companies, running for president.
Don't we need people with creativity nurtured by studying at an art college among our business
and political leaders, instead of just people with economics degrees and MBAs?

Design as Contemporary Craft

In Portland, the concept of "craft" is applied to everything. Craft beer, craft food, you name it.
What does it mean to be labeled "craft"? It means something made by hand with care,
somehow more enlightened, more human. And that is reflected in contemporary design trends.

Interior of Icon Tattoo.
Not your stereotypical tattoo
parlor look. Icon projects a new,
more woman-friendly image for
the tattoo industry.

LOVE

COMMONWEALTH SKATEBOARDING

ODDBALL STUDIOS TATTOO

ACROPOLIS

SUNKEN HEAD SKATEBOARDS

SILVER

EAGLE PORTLAND

SCAPEGOAT TATTOO

SEA TRAMP TATTOO CO.

TATTOO STU

DIRTY SKATE

SKELETON

SCANDALS | MARY'S CLUB

PIER PARK

DARCELLE XV

CC SLAUGHTERS

GABRIEL PARK

ANATOMY TATTOO

ROBOT PIERCING & TATTOO | SASSY'S BAR & GRILL

CAL SKATE SKATEBOARDS

INFINITY TATTOO

CRUSH

CASA DIABLO

TATTOO HISTORIC

ATLAS TATTOO

DEVILS POINT

ED BENEDICT SKATEPARK

From Portland with love

When you love someone or something, it's natural to want other people to appreciate that person or thing too. But even if they don't, they can love your passion for whatever or whoever you love and be happy for you. We might love different stuff, but that diversity is exciting. Here are some more only-in-Portland treasures that we wholeheartedly love.

Tattoo

Portland has a thriving and diverse tattoo culture

Tattoos are so common in Portland that they have become a fixture of the urban landscape. The Portland Art Museum has even held exhibitions on tattoo art. A large tattoo-loving population requires plenty of tattoo parlors to keep the ink flowing. Icon Tattoo Studio (owned by Melanie Nead, who has plenty of ink herself, much of it self-applied from her original designs) is one of Portland's most notable with its female staff. The light-filled, inviting space suggests a hair salon. In Portland, tattoo parlors typically don't fit the stereotype of dark dens for rough-around-the-edges folks (primarily men) that prevails in many other parts of the country. At Icon, starting at $100, you can get a tattoo in a wide range of styles.

Icon's high-ceilinged, sunny space is charming. Just down the road is the shop Lowell (p. 214). This district is probably the next in Portland's parade of emerging hot neighborhoods.

Icon Tattoo Studio

Information

Ⓐ 813 N Russell St.
Ⓣ (503) 477-7157
Ⓗ Tu-Sa 11 a.m.-6 p.m.
Ⓦ icontattoostudio.com
Ⓜ p. 292-35

Atlas Tattoo

Information

Ⓐ 4543 N Albina Ave.
Ⓣ (503) 281-7499
Ⓗ 12 p.m.-7 p.m. daily
Ⓦ atlastattoo.com
Ⓜ p. 292-17

Historic Tattoo

Information

Ⓐ 2001 SE 50th Ave.
Ⓣ (503) 236-3440
Ⓗ 11 a.m.-7 p.m. daily
Ⓦ historictattoo.com
Ⓜ p. 296-72

Oddball Studios Tattoo

Information

Ⓐ 2716 SE 21st Ave.
Ⓣ (503) 231-1344
Ⓗ 1 p.m.-7 p.m. daily
Ⓦ oddballstudios.com
Ⓜ p. 296-82

Tattoo Shop List

Infinity Tattoo

Ⓐ 3316 N Lombard St.
Ⓣ (503) 231-4777
Ⓗ M-W 11 a.m.-8 p.m., Th Appointment only,
    F-Sa 11 a.m.-8 p.m., Su 12 p.m.-6 p.m.
Ⓦ infinitytattoo.com
Ⓜ p. 292-3

Anatomy Tattoo

Ⓐ 2820 NE Sandy Blvd.
Ⓣ (503) 231-1199
Ⓗ 12 p.m.-8 p.m. daily
Ⓦ anatomytattoo.com
Ⓜ p. 294-35

Robot Piercing
& Tattoo

Ⓐ 2330 NW Westover Rd.
Ⓣ (503) 224-9916
Ⓗ M-Th 11 a.m.-6 p.m., F-Sa 11 a.m.-7 p.m.,
    Su 12 p.m.-5 p.m.
Ⓦ mega-robot.com
Ⓜ p. 290-17

Scapegoat Tattoo

Ⓐ 1223 SE Stark St.
Ⓣ (503) 232-4628
Ⓗ 12 p.m.-8 p.m. daily
Ⓦ scapegoattattoo.com
Ⓜ p. 296-26

Adorn Tattoos
Piercing & Jewelry

Ⓐ 3941 SE Hawthorne Blvd.
Ⓣ (503) 232-6222
Ⓗ 12 p.m.-8 p.m. daily
Ⓦ adornbodyart.com
Ⓜ p. 296-59

Skeleton Key Tattoo

Ⓐ 1729 SE Hawthorne Blvd.
Ⓣ (503) 233-4292
Ⓗ Tu-W 11 a.m.-8 p.m., Th-F 11 a.m.-10 p.m.,
    Sa 11 a.m.-8 p.m., Su 12 p.m.-8 p.m.
Ⓦ skeletonkeytattooportland.com
Ⓜ p. 296-53

ThoughtCrime Tattoo

Ⓐ 420 SW Washington St., Suite. 601
Ⓣ (503) 265-8157
Ⓗ Tu-Sa 2 p.m.-8 p.m.
Ⓦ thoughtcrimetattoo.com
Ⓜ p. 288-39

Imperial Tattoo

Ⓐ 5504 E Burnside St.
Ⓣ (503) 223-1181
Ⓗ 12 p.m.-8 p.m. daily
Ⓦ imperialtattoopdx.com

Sea Tramp Tattoo Co.

Ⓐ 523 SE Stark St.
Ⓣ (503) 224-4668
Ⓗ 4 p.m.-12 a.m. daily
Ⓦ seatramptattoo.com
Ⓜ p. 296-22

Skate Culture

Skating for the people

Located in a converted warehouse, Commonwealth is Portland's only concrete indoor skatepark, and it was built by local firm Evergreen Skateparks in 2011. The on-site skate shop sells skate gear as well as sneakers and apparel. Saturday mornings are kids-only, and Sunday mornings are girls-only, but other than that, it's open to all ages and skill levels. Individual lessons are available (reservations required). If you're new to skating, we recommend taking the plunge here in Portland, a city with a very proud skate culture. Use fee is $7 for two hours or $10 for the day.

Commonwealth
Skateboarding

Information

Ⓐ 1425 SE 20th Ave.
Ⓣ (503) 208-2080
Ⓗ M 2 p.m.-10 p.m., Tu-Th 2 p.m.–8 p.m.,
   F 2 p.m.-10 p.m., Sa 10 a.m.-8 p.m., Su 12 p.m.-8 p.m.
Ⓦ commonwealthskateboarding.com
Ⓜ p. 296-54

Burnside Skatepark

*Don't ask, just do it
world-renowned skatepark*

Information

Ⓐ SE 2nd Ave. Under Burnside Bridge
Ⓜ p. 294-39

In the late 1980s, skaters who wanted to skate even during Portland's rainy winters found a spot under the Burnside Bridge and without asking for permission, poured the concrete ramps and bowls that came to be known as Burnside Skatepark. To win the approval of local residents, the skaters promised to keep the area around the skate park clean and tidy. This began a dialogue between the city and its skaters that blossomed into a productive relationship that has even given skaters a voice in urban planning. Portland is now one of the nation's most skater-friendly cities, with marked skate routes downtown, skater-friendly bike lanes, and several city-approved skateparks. Burnside was a DIY skate park trailblazer and is now a pilgrimage site for skaters from around the world.

Cal's Pharmacy

Got a bad case of "Skate or Die"? Fill your prescription here

Information

Ⓐ 1400 E Burnside St.
Ⓣ (503) 233-1237
Ⓗ M-F 11 a.m.-6 p.m., Sa 11 a.m.-7 p.m.,
Su 11 a.m.-5 p.m.
Ⓦ calspharmacy.com
Ⓜ p. 296-9

Cal's was originally an actual pharmacy that opened in the 1980s on lower Burnside. When the owner's son became a fanatical skater, a section of the store gave way to skateboard decks, and eventually the whole place morphed into a skate shop. After being closed for a long time, Cal's reopened in 2013. Loved by locals since its pharmacy days, Cal's is now hailed as Portland's friendliest skate shop. The employees are happy to recommend skating spots around the city.

Skate Spot & Shop List

Ed Benedict Park
Ⓐ SE 100th Ave. & Powell Blvd.

Glenhaven Park
Ⓐ NE 82nd Ave. & NE Siskiyou St.

Daddies Board Shop
Ⓐ 5909 NE 80th Ave.
Ⓣ (503) 281-5123
Ⓗ M-F 12 p.m.-8 p.m., Sa 11 a.m.-7 p.m.,
Su 11 a.m.-6 p.m.
Ⓦ daddiesboardshop.com

Gabriel Park
Ⓐ SW 45th Ave. & Vermont St.

Shrunken Head Skateboards
Ⓐ 531 SE Morrison St.
Ⓣ (503) 232-4323
Ⓗ M-F 12 p.m.-7 p.m., Sa 10 a.m.-6 p.m.,
Su 12 p.m.–5 p.m.
Ⓦ shrunkenheadskateboards.com
Ⓜ p. 296-34

Pier Park
Ⓐ N Lombard St. & Bruce Ave.

Cal Skate Skateboards
Ⓐ 210 NW 6th Ave.
Ⓣ (503) 248-0495
Ⓗ M-F 11 a.m.-6 p.m.,
Sa 10 a.m.-6 p.m., Su 11 a.m.-5 p.m.
Ⓦ calsk8.com
Ⓜ p. 291-42

LGBTQ

A friendly, welcoming city for all

Portland has long been an LGBTQ-friendly city and you can see that in the many businesses that proudly hang the rainbow flag and support great community organizations like Basic Rights Oregon. The city is a welcoming, thriving place for residents and visitors of all sexual orientations.

Top Spots

CC Slaughters

This gay club located in Old Town/ Chinatown has DJs nightly and a drag show every Sunday night.

Ⓐ 219 NW Davis St.
Ⓣ (503) 248-9135
Ⓗ 3 p.m.-2:30 a.m. daily
Ⓦ ccslaughterspdx.com
Ⓜ p. 290-49

The Embers Avenue

Catch drag shows Wednesday through Saturday and karaoke on Sundays at this forty-plus year old show, bar, and dance club.

Ⓐ 110 NW Broadway
Ⓣ (503) 222-3082
Ⓗ 11 a.m.-2:30 a.m daily
Ⓦ facebook.com/embersavenue
Ⓜ p. 290-41

Darcelle XV

At eighty-seven years old, Darcelle is Portland's most famous, and probably most senior, drag queen, and this is her cabaret revue and venue.

Ⓐ 208 NW 3rd Ave.
Ⓣ (503) 222-5338
Ⓗ W-Th 6 p.m.-11 p.m. F-Sa 6 p.m.-2:30 a.m.
Ⓦ darcellexv.com
Ⓜ p. 290-50

Silverado

Portland has its fair share of strip clubs, but not many have only male dancers as this one does.

Ⓐ 318 SW 3rd Ave.
Ⓣ (503) 224-4493
Ⓗ 9 a.m.-2:30 a.m. daily
Ⓦ silveradopdx.com
Ⓜ p. 288-43

Scandals

This gay club has been going strong since 1979, when the area was known as the "pink triangle."

Ⓐ 1125 SW Stark St.
Ⓣ (503) 227-5887
Ⓗ 12 p.m.-2:30 a.m. daily
Ⓦ scandalspdx.com
Ⓜ p. 288-10

Crush

This bar and restaurant has dance parties and a burlesque show. It's a fun place for anyone.

Ⓐ 1400 SE Morrison St.
Ⓣ (503) 235-8150
Ⓗ M–F 12 p.m.-2 a.m., Sa 11 a.m.-2 a.m.,
    Su 11 a.m.-12 a.m.
Ⓦ crushbar.com
Ⓜ p. 296-42

Eagle Portland

A masculine gay bar known equally for its wild parties and fundraising events. They also have lesbian nights.

Ⓐ 835 N Lombard St.
Ⓣ (503) 283-9734
Ⓗ 2 p.m.-2:30 a.m. daily
Ⓦ eagleportland.com
Ⓜ p. 292-4

STRIP CLUB

Shower the people you love with money

Portland's funky reputation might not immediately conjure up the image of strip clubs, but Portland has the highest number of strip clubs per capita of any city in the U.S. Because there are so many of them, Portland strip clubs work hard for claims to fame here. There's a vegan strip club, a steakhouse strip club, an all-male strip club, and even Stripparaoke—karaoke with strippers.

Top Spots

Casa Diablo

Check out the world's first strip club with a vegan menu.

Ⓐ 2839 NW St Helens Rd.
Ⓣ (503) 222-6600
Ⓗ 11 a.m.-2:30 a.m. daily
Ⓦ casadiablo.com

Mary's Club

This is Portland's oldest strip club, located downtown.

Ⓐ 129 SW Broadway
Ⓣ (503) 227-3023
Ⓗ M-Sa 11 a.m.-2:30 a.m.,
Su 11:30 a.m.-2:30 a.m.
Ⓦ marysclub.com / Ⓜ p. 288-28

Sassy's Bar & Grill

This hipster-friendly club is located across the street from Holocene. (p. 141)

Ⓐ 927 SE Morrison St.
Ⓣ (503) 231-1606
Ⓗ 10:30 a.m.-2:30 a.m. daily
Ⓦ sassysbar.com
Ⓜ p. 296-37

Devils Point

Sunday nights are Stripparaoke night here. Stripping plus karaoke!

Ⓐ 5305 SE Foster Rd.
Ⓣ (503) 774-4513
Ⓗ 11 a.m.-2:30 a.m. daily
Ⓦ devilspoint.net

Acropolis

Here you get a great beer, cheap steak, and strippers.

Ⓐ 8325 SE McLoughlin Blvd.
Ⓣ (503) 231-9611
Ⓗ M-Sa 7 a.m.-2 a.m., Su 11 a.m.-2 a.m.
Ⓦ acropolispdx.com

Union Jacks Club

One of Portland's more established strip clubs in the fun Lower Burnside area.

Ⓐ 938 E Burnside St.
Ⓣ (503) 236-1125
Ⓗ 2:30 p.m.-2:30 a.m. daily
Ⓦ unionjacksclub.com
Ⓜ p. 296-6

Lucky Devil Lounge

This club's interior is an homage to classic Playboy Clubs.

Ⓐ 633 SE Powell Blvd.
Ⓣ (503) 206-7350
Ⓗ 11 a.m.-2:30 a.m. daily
Ⓦ luckydevillounge.com
Ⓜ p. 296-84

St. Johns

Commentary by

Christine Dong
Fueled by '90s R&B and noodle soups, Christine Dong is a photographer and an amateur basketball player living in Portland, Oregon. She is an Oregon native with an obsession with identifying dog breeds and singing karaoke. Find more of her work at christinedong.com

Beautiful bridge, Cathedral Park, and hidden gems

St. Johns is a quaint neighborhood located in North Portland. It's most well known for its bridge—the only suspension bridge in the Willamette Valley, and the tallest bridge in Portland. The gorgeous Cathedral Park underneath the St. Johns Bridge provides walking trails, picnic benches, and a floating dock that extends into the Willamette River. Closer into the core of St. Johns, you'll find boutique shops and restaurants. My personal favorite shop and restaurant is Tienda Santa Cruz, located on Lombard Street—a bustling Mexican joint with a sea of colorful piñatas, an array of hot sauces, and hidden in the back, the best tacos in town. My favored summer memories consist of food to-go at Tienda Santa Cruz and biking down to the dock to grub. St. Johns is a lovely place to escape the mayhem of the city.

Information

Tienda Santa Cruz
Ⓐ 8630 N Lombard St.
Ⓣ (503) 289-2005
Ⓗ 7 a.m.-10 p.m. daily
Ⓦ tiendasantacruz.com

L

ITINERARY

48 HOURS in PORTLAND

261

*Insider guides to forty-eight hours
in Portland*

When you're new to a place, insider recommendations can be invaluable—assuming that you are on the same wavelength. In an effort to match up insider expertise and reader diversity, we sought out several perspectives on how to spend forty-eight hours in Portland. As it turned out, these people's recommendations—reflecting different experiences, lifestyles, and preferences—generated a pretty great assortment of fun things to see and do in town. Each of these itineraries is a personal, heartfelt eye into Portland. We're pretty sure you're going to find some new things to add to your ever-growing Portland to-do list. We hope so.

Fashion - only the good stuff

I want to help visitors find the BEST places to shop from a local point-of-view.

ANDI BAKOS

West End Select Shop

Owner + Everything of West End Select Shop
Portland-Native, Wife + Mother, Fashion Obsessed

DAY 1

8:30 AM **Tasty n Alder** [1]

Start out from the Ace Hotel, let's say this is where you're staying! Walk around the corner to Tasty n Alder for brunch. If you get there after 9 a.m. the wait will be long, and you don't have that kind of time.

10:00 AM **Shopping**

After brunch, walk off that full tummy and check out some of the neighboring stores, like Alder & Co. (p. 218), WM Goods (p. 221)—great places to find gifts for your friends back home.

10:45 AM **Shopping**

Go back down 12th, where you came from, passing Tasty n Alder, and check out Odessa [2]. A small but wonderful shop with lots of fascinating designers like Vetements, Sophie D'Hoor, and Isabel Marant. From there walk to SW 10th & Washington and check out the big, grand Frances May [3] store—it's full of great clothes from big-name designers. After that, hop across the street to the adorable and cheerful Woonwinkel (p. 226), a modern gift/housewares store where you will want to buy everything for your home. While you're in the hood don't miss Backtalk [4], Poler (p. 178), Wildfang (p. 225), and Animal Traffic (p. 226).

1:00 PM **Food Carts**

You're probably a bit hungry by now! Why not grab a bite from one of the food carts ? Personally I recommend getting a boba tea from the boba tea cart and then a lamb and rice dish from the Mediterranean cart Aybla. Winning combo.

2:00 PM **Stand Up Comedy** [5]

OK, let's get back on track. Next stop is Stand Up Comedy on SW Broadway. It's a funny store with strange and wonderful clothing, I think you will really like it.

2:30 PM **The Fresh Pot** [6]

Maybe it's time for a coffee? Go into Morgan's Alley, where Stand Up Comedy is, and find Fresh Pot. Have a coffee and a salted chocolate chip cookie—YUMMMM!

3:00 PM **Milk Milk Lemonade** (p. 217)

Get a taxi, we're on the move! Your next stop is Milk Milk Lemonade on SE 14th & Belmont. It's a small beauty and jewelry shop run by my friend Heather, who makes the most wonderful fragrances called OLO. You can try all the scents there and pick your favorite. Mine is called Lightning Paw, and it's my most complimented scent. The store is spacious and there are lots of nice things to touch and smell. The studio where they make the perfume is in the back. Take a peek and see where all the magic happens.

3:30 PM **House of Vintage** (p. 226)

Head down to SE Hawthorne. We're about to dig into some vintage here. Are you ready? You're heading to House of Vintage. It's a huge warehouse space with hundreds of vintage dealers selling clothing, household items, and accessories. Usually I like to wear headphones and listen to music and shop all the booths. There are so many treasures! I often leave with a pile of clothes.

4:20 PM **The Perfume House** [7]

Across the street is an old Perfume House called... Perfume House. They have EVERY perfume ever made (almost). They are perfume experts and have been in business since 1985. Have a smell!

4:50 PM The Red Light [8]

Keep walking up Hawthorne and check out Red Light—another large vintage shop that's been around for a long long time. Get lost in here for a while. Maybe try on a crazy outfit and take your photo in it.

5:20 PM Shopping

Come back to Earth; you have one more vintage shop in this hood before you go. Are you feeling tired? Get a healthy juice at Harlow (p. 46) up the street, something with ginger in it. Feel better? Now find Buffalo Exchange. This is your last stop of the day, so enjoy the racks of treasures, both old and new.

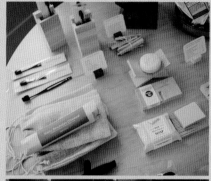

6:00 PM Drop off your bags and fix your make-up

You deserve a treat! Head back to your hotel and drop off your bags and fix your make-up. Don't sit for too long or you may not get up. Keep moving!

7:30 PM Kask [9]

Next stop is Kask for a cocktail or glass of wine. You earned it today, good job! Try a cocktail with smoke in it. They light some wood and capture it in the glass. It's stinky and delicious at the same time. While you're there, put your name down for a table at SuperBite, next door. That's where you'll have dinner!

9:00 PM SuperBite [10]

Enjoy small, artfully arranged tasting plates with inventive foods.

10:30 PM Ruby Jewel [11]

On your way home, swing by Ruby Jewel ice cream shop and have a scoop of the salted vanilla ice cream. Or buy an ice cream sandwich takeout, go back to your hotel, and eat it in your bed!

DAY2

9:00 AM Blue Star Donuts (p. 70)

Sleep in a little today; yesterday was so tiring! When you're ready, walk to Blue Star Donuts and eat one of each donut and drink lots of coffee.

9:30 AM Powell's City of Books (p. 236)

Now that you're high on sugar and caffeine, spend some time at Powell's and look for fashion books from the nineties, they're the best. (You can find them in the Pearl section of the store.)

11:00 AM Shopping

Walk one block to see my shop, West End Select Shop (p. 212). You should also visit my neighbors at Maak Lab (p. 197), Billy Galaxy Vintage Toys [12], North of West (p. 217), and Courier Coffee (p. 100).

12:00 PM Måurice (p. 48)

Eat a nice lunch at Måurice. I recommend the quiche, lemon tart, and a nice tea. You should take pictures of their food because it's so beautiful! At this point, you may want to run back to your hotel to drop off your shopping bags—I would!

1:30 PM Shopping

Get a taxi and go to 811 East Burnside. There is a cluster of shops to explore, including Six/Seven and Seven Sisters[13], OKO[14]. After you're done there, if you're in the mood for some vintage, check out Hattie's Vintage Clothing (p. 227). Cross the street and head to Machus (p. 226) to get futuristic men's fashions and meet the store's pet—a tiny dog named Moose. Definitely get your photo taken with Moose. There's one more stop in this neighborhood, Una (p. 226). From Machus walk a few blocks to Una and shop the lovely finds of my friend Giovanna. Her store is wonderful; you will totally love it.

3:30 PM Nong's Khao Man Gai (p. 81)

Are you hungry? Maybe you should have a little snack? Go back toward Machus and find Nong's Khao Man Gai and split a chicken and rice dish with your friends. You want to save room for dinner.

4:30 PM Palace (p. 218)

Keep going up Burnside to 22nd (long walk or short drive) and you will find Palace. They have vintage clothing, new clothing from local designers, and beauty products. Everything has a very natural feel and smells good.

5:00 PM Heart Roasters (p. 113)

Maybe it's time for coffee? Go to Heart, right next to Palace

and order a latte or an Americano, try a cookie too if you have room for it.

7:00 PM Angel Face (p. 115)

I think you're done shopping for the day, don't you? You deserve a cocktail! Head to Angel Face, where beautiful people drink beautiful cocktails with a backdrop of beautiful hand-painted wallpaper. Don't forget to take a photo against the wallpaper!

8:00 PM Navarre [15]

You must be SO hungry (if you didn't eat too much at Nong's). Time for dinner. Head next door to Navarre and settle in for a nice, long, wine-soaked dinner. The plates are small so you can try many things and share with others. This is a comfortable and warm restaurant and the favorite of many of my friends.

10:30 PM Pix Patisserie [16]

How do you feel? Maybe one last drink before you go to bed? Go to Pix Patisserie back where Palace was and have some dessert wine, a macaroon, or a yummy jelly candy.

12:00 PM Hotel

Time for bed. You leave tomorrow. I miss you already.

Love, Andi

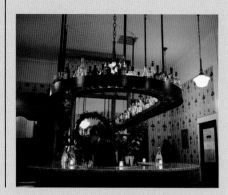

48 HOURS in PORTLAND

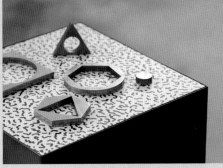

Shop Information

[1] Tasty n Alder
Ⓐ 580 SW 12th Ave.　Ⓣ (503) 621-9251
Ⓗ Su-Th 9 a.m.-2 p.m., 5:30 p.m.-10 p.m.,
　F-Sa 9 a.m.-2 p.m., 5:30 p.m.- 11 p.m.
Ⓦ tastynalder.com

[2] Odessa
Ⓐ 410 SW 13th Ave.　Ⓣ (503) 223-1998
Ⓗ M-Sa 11 a.m.-7 p.m., Su 12 p.m.-6 p.m.
Ⓦ odessaportland.com

[3] Frances May
Ⓐ 1003 SW Washington St.　Ⓣ (503) 227-3402
Ⓗ M-Sa 11 a.m.-7 p.m., Su 12 p.m.-6 p.m.
Ⓦ francesmay.com

[4] Backtalk
Ⓐ 421 SW 10th Ave.　Ⓣ (503) 477-7144
Ⓗ 11 a.m.-6 p.m. daily
Ⓦ backtalkpdx.com

[5] Stand Up Comedy
Ⓐ 511 SW Broadway　Ⓣ (503) 233-3382
Ⓗ M-Sa 11 a.m.-6 p.m.
Ⓦ standupcomedytoo.com

[6] The Fresh Pot
Ⓐ 724 SW Washington St.　Ⓣ (503) 780-4504
Ⓗ M-F 6:30 a.m.-5 p.m., Sa 7 a.m.-4 p.m.
Ⓦ thefreshpot.com

[7] The Perfume House
Ⓐ 3328 SE Hawthorne Blvd.　Ⓣ (503) 234-5375
Ⓗ Tu-Sa 10 a.m.-5 p.m.
Ⓦ theperfumehouse.com

[8] The Red Light
Ⓐ 3590 SE Hawthorne Blvd.　Ⓣ (503) 963-8888
Ⓗ M-Th 11 a.m.-8 p.m., F-Sa 11 a.m.-9 p.m.,
　Su 12 p.m.-7 p.m.
Ⓦ redlightclothingexchange.com

[9] Kask
Ⓐ 1215 SW Alder St.　Ⓣ (503) 241-7163
Ⓗ Tu-Th 5 p.m.-10 p.m., F-Sa 5 p.m.-11 p.m.,
　Su 5 p.m.-10 p.m.
Ⓦ superbitepdx.com/kask/

[10] SuperBite
Ⓐ 527 SW 12th Ave.　Ⓣ (503) 222-0979
Ⓗ Tu-Th, Su 5 p.m.-10 p.m., F-Sa 5 p.m.-11 p.m.
Ⓦ superbitepdx.com

[11] Ruby Jewel
Ⓐ 3713 N Mississippi Ave.　Ⓣ (503) 954-1345
Ⓗ 12 p.m.-11 p.m. daily
Ⓦ rubyjewel.com

[12] Billy Galaxy Vintage Toys
Ⓐ 912 W Burnside St.　Ⓣ (503) 227-8253
Ⓗ M-Sa 11 a.m.-6 p.m.
Ⓦ billygalaxy.com

[13] Seven Sisters
Ⓐ 811 E Burnside St., Suite112　Ⓣ (503) 877-5486
Ⓗ Sa-M 12 p.m.-5 p.m.
Ⓦ sevensisterspdx.com

[14] OKO
Ⓐ 811 East Burnside St. Suite 113　Ⓣ (503) 867-0968
Ⓗ Su-M 12 p.m.-4 p.m., W-Sa 12 p.m.-6 p.m.
Ⓦ okoportland.com

[15] Navarre
Ⓐ 10 NE 28th Ave.　Ⓣ (503) 232-3555
Ⓗ M-Th 4:30 p.m.-10:30 p.m., F 4:30 p.m.-11:30 p.m.,
　Sa 9:30 a.m.-11:30 p.m., Su 9:30 a.m.-10:30 p.m.
Ⓦ navarreportland.com

[16] Pix Patisserie
Ⓐ 2225 E Burnside St.　Ⓣ (971) 271-7166
Ⓗ M-F 4 p.m.-12 a.m.,
　Sa-Su 2 p.m.-12 a.m.
Ⓦ pixpatisserie.com

48 HOURS in PORTLAND

My weird Portland

I can pretty much guarantee you're going to have a great time in the Portland since everyone in here is nice, and you won't feel weird asking for directions if you're lost or need a recommendation.

JARRETT REYNOLDS

Designer

Designer, Shibori Nerd, Professor of Hip Hop

DAY 1

8:30 AM **Ace Hotel** (p. 24)

Wake up! I'll assume you're staying at the Ace Hotel because you're super cool, so get dressed and head downstairs.

9:00 AM **Stumptown Coffee in the Ace Hotel**

I'm sure you can get Stumptown Coffee wherever you live, but it wouldn't be a trip to Portland without stopping here.

9:30 AM **Kure Juice Bar** [1]

Now that you're caffeinated, walk two blocks to Kure Juice Bar for a healthy breakfast. I think you should order a Bowl of The Gods which is delicious even though it's made out of healthy stuff like almond milk, goji berries, and hemp-seed granola.

12:00 PM **The Circuit Gym** (p. 183)

I know you're on vacation and just want to chill out in Portland and watch bearded guys in tight jeans make coffee, but maybe it would be a good idea to go to The Circuit Gym and work off some of those calories by climbing in this indoor rock wall gym.

1:00 PM **Pollo Norte** [2]

I bet you're hungry, so get in a cab and head to Pollo Norte in Northeast for some Mexican rotisserie chicken. Their menu is as close as you can get to a Mexican In 'N' Out. No pork. No beef. Just chicken, a couple sides, and delicious handmade tortillas.

2:00 PM **West End Select Shop** (p. 212)

To start off your Portland shopping experience, head over to my wife Andi's shop West End Select Shop. If I was a girl this is where I would shop.

4:00 PM **Tailor Blade and Co.** [3]

Sorry ladies, this next spot is mostly for the guys. Head over to Tailor Blade and Co. to get a tight fade from Denario at my favorite barber shop in Portland. Text Denario for an appointment at (503) 516-1597.

7:00 PM **Teote Restaurant** [4]

Dinnertime! My dinner choice for you is Teote, which serves Latin American food in a fun atmosphere. If I were you I would order the Teote plate and a Michelada, and head upstairs to sit outside.

10:00 PM **Lovecraft Bar** [5]

If H.R. Giger and Trent Reznor joined forces to open a horror themed dance bar, it would be Lovecraft Bar. This place is a melting pot of steampunks, adult ravers, goths, and hipsters who all come together to dance to music by Skinny Puppy and Nine Inch Nails.

DAY 2

10:00 AM **Navarre** [6]

If it's a weekend, this is the only place you should be thinking about having brunch at. Damn Navarre is good.

12:00 AM **MadeHere PDX** (p. 215)

I know you're going to go to Powell's to buy some obscure books and postcards, so why not stop at Made Here PDX right across the street first. Everything they sell is locally made from hot sauce, leather wallets, backpacks, and varsity jackets.

1:00 PM **Tea Bar** (p. 102)

You could order a peppermint or Earl Grey tea at Tea Bar, but that's kinda lame. You should order the matcha boba tea instead cause its delicious (and not lame).

2:00 PM **Bike Gallery** [7]

I hate to say it, but you're walking really slowly. Head over to Bike Gallery to rent a bike so you can cover more ground faster.

7:00 PM **Pine Street Market** (p. 38)

Pine Street Market is basically Portland's version of a mall food court, except replace all the gross food with awesome food from places like Pollo Bravo, Marukin Ramen. Don't eat too much food though...you need to save room for dessert. Every few years there seems to be a citywide trend in desserts. First it was donuts, then it was cupcakes, and then it went back to donuts for some reason. Right now I'd say we're firmly in the ice cream era. What's next? This is going to sound very Portland, but I'd bet my money on artisanal frozen yogurt. Don't believe me? Try the Salted, Malted Chocolate Chip Cookie Dough Concrete (their version of a DQ Blizzard) at Wiz Bang Bar.

10:00 PM **The Toffee Club** (p. 113)

End your night drinking a Stella at the only English Football Pub outside of England worth visiting. If you're not too full, get a Scotch egg!

Shop Information

[1] **Kure Juice Bar**
Ⓐ 408 SW 12th Ave. Ⓣ (855) 777-5873
Ⓗ M-F 8 a.m.-6 p.m., Sa-Su 9 a.m.-6 p.m.
Ⓦ kurejuicebar.com

[2] **Pollo Norte**
Ⓐ 5427 NE 42nd Ave. Ⓣ (503) 287-0669
Ⓗ M-Su 11 a.m.-9 p.m. Ⓦ pollonorte.com

[3] **Tailor Blade and Co.**
Ⓐ 7100 NE Martin Luther King Blvd.
Ⓣ (503)-516-1597 Ⓗ only by an appointment

[4] **Teote Restaurant**
Ⓐ 1615 SE 12th Ave. Ⓣ (971) 888-5281
Ⓗ Su-Th 11 a.m.-10 p.m., F-Sa 11 a.m.-11 p.m.
Ⓦ teotepdx.com

[5] **Lovecraft Bar**
Ⓐ 421 SE Grand Ave.
Ⓗ S-Th 8 p.m.-2 a.m., F-Sa 4 p.m.-2 a.m.
Ⓦ thelovecraftbar.com

[6] **Navarre**
Ⓐ 10 NE 28th St. Ⓣ (503) 232-3555
Ⓗ M-Th 4:30 p.m.-10:30 p.m., F 4:30 p.m.-11:30 p.m.,
Sa 9:30 a.m.-11:30 p.m., Su 9:30 a.m.-10:30 p.m.
Ⓦ navarreportland.com

[7] **Bike Gallery**
Ⓐ 1001 SW 10th Ave. Ⓣ (503) 222-3821
Ⓗ M-F 9:30 a.m.-6 p.m., Sa 10 a.m.- 6 p.m.,
Su 12 p.m.-5 p.m. Ⓦ bikegallery.com

Walk and seek!

Welcome to Portland. This city is filled with all kinds of hidden treasures. If you are the type of traveler that enjoys on-foot exploration, then follows these steps.

CASSONDRA PITTZ

Odessa Boutique

Originally from Wisconsin, she studied fashion marketing and sustainability at The Art Institute of Portland. She styles and creates photo shoots and other art for personal projects and small shops here in Portland.

DAY 1

Explore the West Side!

9:00 AM Courier Coffee Roasters (p. 100)

Start with coffee. There are many options here for a caffeine fix but you can't go wrong with Courier Coffee Roasters. No matter what you order, you'll make a friend with a barista or one of the regulars. Make sure to try one of their pastries and head next door to Mâurice for breakfast.

11:00 AM Breakfast and Shopping

Mâurice (p. 48) keeps good company. Two doors down is one of my favorite shops, West End Select Shop (p. 212) and around the corner is sensory oasis, Maak Lab (p. 197). Grab some soaps or magazines and be sure to ask them about Cafe Nyleta.

1:00 PM Shopping

Keep up the local shopping with visits to Stand Up Comedy [1], Odessa [2], and Alder & Co. (p. 218). Of course, no Portland trip would be complete without getting lost in Powell's City of Books (p. 236). Grab a map at the door and find the rare books room.

3:00 PM Afternoon snacks and Tea

Afternoon snacks should include a trip to the food carts on SW 10th & SW Washington. Stroll around the block and try a few. Unwind with a walk to Northwest and enjoy some tea at T Project [3].

7:00 PM Dinner

On the west side, I would head over to Little Bird Bistro (try their burger!, p. 66) or Lúc Lác Vietnamese Kitchen (p. 82). I recommend these two places because they are in perfect walking distance for a night cap at Huber's.

10:00 PM Huber's Cafe [4]

Huber's! Founded in 1879, Huber's cafe and restaurant is an absolute must on your list. Hang out at their cozy bar and order their signature Spanish coffee. Then order another.

DAY 2

Explore the East Side!

9:00 AM Coffee

Again, start with coffee. Sip your way up East Burnside and try Ristretto Roasters [5], Heart Roasters (p. 113), or Kopi Coffee House (I'm a fan of their Kopi Jahe) [6].

10:00 AM Breakfast or Brunch

Canteen's (p. 81) juices, smoothies and bowls are great for a quick and healthy breakfast. If you feel like relaxing and enjoying some savory rice bowls, try Kopi Coffee House. However, if you're around on the weekend, try Navarre [7] for brunch!

12:00 PM Shopping

Shopping takes priority on my list of recommendations. Una (p. 226), Nationale (p. 124), and Palace (p. 218) are very unique local shops. For vintage, or secondhand, check out Hattie's Vintage (p. 227), Red Light [8], House of Vintage (p. 226), Ray's Ragtime Hollywood [9], and the Antique Alley [10].

3:00 PM Take a Break

If you need a break from shopping, stroll through Laurelhurst Park [11]. Sit on the benches near the pond and people watch. If you exit south from the park, stop by Avalon Theater [12] and play. Play all the games and win all the prizes. You deserve them. If you exit north from the park, go relax at the Everett House [13]. Their cozy spa will clear your mind just in time for happy hour.

48 Hours in Portland

heart

5:00 PM Happy Hours

NE 28th Ave. has plenty of happy hours and restaurants to keep you feeling good throughout the evening. Stammtisch [14] is a good place to start. Head south down to Beuahland [15] for something special, Angel Face (p. 115) for a custom cocktail, or Holman's [16] for some friendly faces.

8:00 PM Dinner

Enjoy a cozy dinner at Navarre or Luce (p. 82). If you're feeling a bit casual, go to Slow Burger [17] and get the 'Jack and Dill' or Guero's [18] for one of their tortas. After dinner, you can make your way to whichever bar you missed on the way or catch a movie at Laurelhurst Theater (p. 129).

Shop Information

[1] Stand Up Comedy
Ⓐ 511 SW Broadway Ⓣ (503) 233-3382
Ⓗ M-Sa 11 a.m.-6 p.m.
Ⓦ standupcomedytoo.com

[2] Odessa
Ⓐ 410 SW 13th Ave. Ⓣ (503) 223-1998
Ⓗ M-Sa 11 a.m.-7 p.m., Su 12 p.m.-6 p.m.
Ⓦ odessaportland.com

[3] T Project
Ⓐ 723 NW 18th Ave. Ⓣ (503) 327-3110
Ⓗ Th-Sa 11 a.m.-5 p.m. Ⓦ tprojectshop.com

[4] Huber's Cafe
Ⓐ 411 SW 3rd Ave. Ⓣ (503) 228-5686
Ⓗ M-Th 11:30 a.m.-12 a.m., F 11:30 a.m.-1 a.m.,
  Sa 11:00 a.m.-1 a.m., Su 4 p.m.-10 p.m.
Ⓦ hubers.com

[5] Ristretto Roasters
Ⓐ 555 NE Couch St. Ⓣ (503) 284-6767
Ⓗ M-Sa 6:30 a.m.-7 p.m., Su 7 a.m.-6 p.m.
Ⓦ rrpdx.com

[6] Kopi Coffee House
Ⓐ 2327 E Burnside St. Ⓣ (503) 234-8610
Ⓗ M-F 7 a.m.-5 p.m., Sa-Su 8 a.m.-5 p.m.

[7] Navarre
Ⓐ 10 NE 28th Ave. Ⓣ (503) 232-3555
Ⓗ M-Th 4:30 p.m.-10:30 p.m., F 4:30 p.m.-11:30 p.m.,
  Sa 9:30 a.m.-11:30 p.m., Su 9:30 a.m.-10:30 p.m.
Ⓦ navarreportland.com

[8] The Red Light
Ⓐ 3590 SE Hawthorne Blvd. Ⓣ (503) 963-8888
Ⓗ M-Th 11 a.m.-8 p.m., F-Sa 11 a.m.-9 p.m.,
  Su 12 p.m.-7 p.m. Ⓦ redlightclothingexchange.com

[9] Ray's Ragtime Hollywood
Ⓐ 4059 NE Sandy Blvd. Ⓣ (503) 226-2616
Ⓗ M-Sa 12 p.m.-8 p.m., Su 1 p.m.-6 p.m.

[10] Antique Alley
Ⓐ 2000 NE 42nd Ave. Ⓣ (503) 287-9848
Ⓗ M-F 10 a.m.-6 p.m., Sa 10 a.m.-5:30 p.m.,
  Su 12p.m.-5 p.m. Ⓦ antiquealleypdx.com

[11] Laurelhurst Park
Ⓐ SE Cesar E Chavez Blvd. & Stark St.

[12] Avalon Theater
Ⓐ 3451 SE Belmont St. Ⓣ (503) 238-1617 Ⓦ wunder-
landgames.com/avalontheatre.asp

[13] Everett House
Ⓐ 2917 & 2927 NE Everett St. Ⓣ (503) 232-6161
Ⓗ M 1 p.m.-11 p.m., Tu-Sa 11 a.m.-11 p.m.,
  Su 1 p.m.-9 p.m.(Women only 1 p.m.-3 p.m.)
Ⓦ everetthousehealingcenter.com

[14] Stammtisch
Ⓐ 401 NE 28th Ave. Ⓣ (503)206-7983
Ⓗ M-F 3 p.m.-1:30 a.m., Sa-Su 11 a.m.-1:30 a.m.
Ⓦ stammtischpdx.com

[15] Beuahland
Ⓐ 118 NE 28th Ave. Ⓣ (503) 235-2794
Ⓗ M-W 9 a.m.-12 a.m., Th-Su 9 a.m.-2 a.m.
Ⓦ beulahlandpdx.com

[16] Holman's
Ⓐ 15 SE 28th Ave. Ⓣ (503) 231-1093
Ⓗ 8 a.m.-2:30 a.m. daily
Ⓦ holmanspdx.com

[17] Slow Burger
Ⓐ 2329 NE Glisan St. Ⓣ (503) 477-5779
Ⓗ 11 a.m.-10 p.m. daily (Summer Hours),
  11 a.m.-9 p.m. daily (Winter Hours)
Ⓦ slowburger.net

[18] Guero's
Ⓐ 200 NE 28th Ave. Ⓣ (503) 887-9258
Ⓗ Su-Th 11:30 a.m.-8 p.m., F-Sa 11:30 a.m.-9 p.m.
Ⓦ gueropdx.com

A dérive through Portland

Portland is home to an abundance of charm. A visit through the richly green outdoors to residential neighborhood hangouts and creative urban spaces can invigorate and inspire.

JOHNNY LE

Curator and Marketing Art Director

Johnny Le is a Los Angeles-based curator raised in Portland, Oregon. Johnny is the founder and curator of Galerie Hideout, an ephemeral exhibition series and marketing art director at HUF Worldwide. He contributes to *Highsnobiety* and *Purple Fashion Magazine.*

DAY 1

7:30 AM Tryon Creek State Natural Area [1]

About a fifteen minute car ride southwest of downtown is the Tryon Creek State Natural Area. Lush Pacific Northwest trees, wildflowers, and wildlife inhabit 658 acres of forest. The trails offer a variety of hiking options (all skill levels welcome), paved bicycle paths and horse ride trails.

9:00 AM Byways Cafe [2]

Since 1999, The Byways Cafe diner is a Pearl District mainstay. Against retro-style Americana decoration, experience an intimate, old-fashioned diner atmosphere with wonderfully made-from-scratch classic American comfort food and desserts. Start with a freshly squeezed orange juice and ask for the The Redwood Omelet.

11:00 AM Rich's Cigar Store [3]

Rich's Cigar Store is a hidden gem in the West End. While the store offers cigars and smoking tobacco, an alluring selection of over 2,500 periodicals are the main draw.

12:00 PM Mâurice (p. 48)

The daylight brightens the Mâurice pastry luncheonette and its white-colored decor shine beautifully. The Nordic-French café is owned and run by top Portland dessert chef Kristen D. Murray. During lunch, begin savory with a glass of wine and Nora's Lefse w/tarragon & grapefruit kissed Gravlax then carry over into something sweet with a Fika pastry.

1:00 PM Lumber Room [4]

First off, make sure to check Lumberroom.com to look up the current exhibition and gallery hours. Upon arriving to Lumber Room on NW Ninth Avenue between Flanders

and Glisan, look for the blue-grey exterior door and dial the buzzer to be let in. Owned and run by art patron and collector Sarah Miller Meigs, the private loft residence functions as a multi-faceted exhibition space hosting dynamic exhibitions, lectures, and artist residencies inviting notable cultural figures and renowned artists worldwide.

5:00 PM Cal's Pharmacy (p. 255)

Formerly a merchandised wall of skate products inside a pharmaceutical store in the 1980s, Cal's Pharmacy has since become a culturally respected core skateboard specialty retailer in Portland. You'll either see manager Kyle Reynolds, filmmaker Kurt Hayashi, or skateboarder Dane Brady when you visit. If a chance permits itself, ask Kyle how he met Mark Gonzales.

8:00 PM Cassidy's [5]

Since 1979, Cassidy's Restaurant and Bar is Portland's best kept secret. This long-running establishment welcomes all comers. Cozy up over a nice date, or drinks with pals, and enjoy American fare and cocktails.

DAY2

10:30 AM **An Xuyen Bakery** [6]

An Xuyen Bakery is a French-Vietnamese bakery serving sweet and savory delights since 1995. Help yourself to a Pork Sausage Banh Mi sandwich, Pâté Chaud, and Vietnamese iced coffee.

12:30 PM **Nong's Khao Man Gai** (p. 81)

Nong's Khao Man Gai is a must stop for any visitor. Starting as a food cart in 2009, owner and chef Nong Poonsukwattana has since expanded her restaurant into several locations including a brick and mortar space in the inner SE industrial neighborhood. While her menu continues to experiment and expand, her signature Chinese-influenced Thai poached-chicken dish: Khao Man Gai is a staple and is as good as it gets.

1:30 PM **Galleries**

These galleries contribute distinctive perspectives and programming of international and regional artists to the Portland arts community: S1 [7], Yale Union (p. 126), Fourteen30 (p. 130), Adams and Ollman (p. 126)

5:00 PM **The Good Mod** (p. 194)

The Good Mod is a mid-century, Danish furniture store and design workshop located on the top floor of a parking garage building downtown. Founded by furniture maker and sculptor Spencer Staley, with support of a multidisciplinary team of builders, makers and designers, the shop invents, repairs, and sculpts.

7:00 PM **Phở Lê** [8]

Phở Lê is a family run Vietnamese restaurant serving the Portland-Metropolitan area since 1991. Located in the Fisher's Landing Market Place, the unassuming restaurant serves some of the best Vietnamese beef noodle soup. A highly recommended meal is the Chả Giò spring rolls, Phở Đặc Biệt soup bowl and Cafe Sữa Đá iced coffee.

9:00 PM **Expatriate** (p. 115)

The Expatriate cocktail lounge has an atmosphere both sophisticated and embellished with thoughtful design. Upon walking in the dimly lit lounge, a giant golden Chinese-American restaurant arch is in bold view. Plush low profile booths against internationally sourced decor are evocative to spark good conversations among friends and neighboring patrons. Co-owner and mixologist Kyle Linden Webster merges experimental cocktails with Southeast Asian and Burmese inspired drinking food in close collaboration with wife and chef-co-owner Naomi Pomeroy. A DJ sound system has Kyle on vinyl record selections that sonically enrich the senses. Share bites such as Hot and Sour Indian Spiced Fries, Crispy Brussels Sprouts, and Korean Fried Game Hen, and order yourself a After A Fashion cocktail drink.

Shop Information

[1] Tryon Creek State Natural Area
Ⓐ 11321 SW Terwilliger Blvd. Ⓣ (503) 636-4398
Ⓦ oregonstateparks.org

[2] Byways Cafe
Ⓐ 1212 NW Glisan St. Ⓣ (503) 221-0011
Ⓗ M-F 7 a.m.-3 p.m., Sa-Su 7:30 a.m.-2 p.m.
Ⓦ bywayscafe.com

[3] Rich's Cigar Club
Ⓐ 820 SW Alder St. Ⓣ (503) 228-1700
Ⓗ M-F 9 a.m.-7 p.m.
Ⓦ richscigarstore.com

[4] Lumber Room
Ⓐ 419 NW 9th Ave. Ⓦ lumberroom.com

[5] Cassidy's
Ⓐ 1331 SW Washington St. Ⓣ (503) 223-0054
Ⓗ 4 p.m.-2 a.m. daily
Ⓦ cassidysrestaurant.com

[6] An Xuyen Bakery
Ⓐ 5345 SE Foster Rd. Ⓣ (503) 788-0866
Ⓗ Tu-Sa 7 a.m.-6 p.m., Su 7 a.m.-3 p.m.

[7] S1
Ⓐ 4148 NE Hancock St. Ⓦ s1portland.com

[8] Phở Lê (in Vancouver)
Ⓐ 2100 SE 164th Ave. Ⓣ (360) 892-8484
Ⓗ M-Th 11 a.m.-8:30 p.m., F-Sa 11 a.m.-9 p.m.,
  Su 11 a.m.- 8 p.m. Ⓦ pho-le.com

For the love of music

Music makes Portland go 'round! We have a thriving scene of local artists and musicians who collectively shape the culture of our city.

ASHLEY VAUGHAN

Lead Buyer at Tender Loving Empire

Ashley grew up between the swamps of North Florida and the Colorado Rockies, but calls Portland home.

DAY 1

8:00 AM   **Ace Hotel** (p. 24)

Wake up, put a record on, and get ready. We've got a big day ahead!

9:00 AM   **Stumptown Coffee Roasters**

Grab coffee and breakfast downstairs in the Ace-adjacent Stumptown Coffee Roasters. Their big front windows make for great people watching, or head back to the hotel lobby. It's OK to bring your coffee and breakfast over and eat on the big comfy couches. Snap a photobooth portrait on your way out the door.

10:00 AM   **Know Your City Walking DIY PDX Tour** [1]

Know Your City offers awesome two-hour tours of Portland. The DIY PDX tour touches on Portland's burgeoning independent music and literary scenes, offering visitors a glimpse into the true grassroots culture of Portland.

12:00 PM   **Powell's City of Books** (p. 236)

Powell's City of Books is a must see. They have an awesome selection of new and used music-related titles, among everything else you can imagine. Spend a while browsing the titles and then head across the river into charming Southeast Portland.

1:00 PM   **Spielman Bagels** (p. 80)

Grab lunch at Spielman Bagels on Division St. They have the best bagels in town, and Raf Spielman, of local band the Woolen Men, is head cook and chief roaster. The soundtrack to Spielman's is Raf's awesome cassette collection. As founder of Portland tape label Eggy Records, he has some good ones. Browse the collection and jot down your faves.

2:00 PM   **Clinton Street Record & Stereo** (p. 140)

Walk a few blocks to Clinton St. for some record shopping. Also check out the vintage stereo goodies.

3:00 PM   **Tender Loving Empire** (p. 144)

Head over to Hawthorne Blvd. to Tender Loving Empire, the storefront of the local record label of the same name. The store has an awesome collection of local music, a killer vinyl and digital listening station, and the best selection of handmade goods in town. They also host performances in-store, so be sure to ask if any events are coming up. The staff are super knowledgeable about all things Portland and all things music.

4:00 PM   **House of Vintage** (p. 226)

Pop down the block to House of Vintage for some incredible vintage shopping. They have everything from clothes to furniture to old music equipment to records. You'll find something you want to take home, guaranteed.

5:00 PM   **Revival Drum Shop** (p. 227)

Head to Revival Drum Shop, Portland's best place to check out vintage and custom drums, hang out, and talk gear with some of Portland's most dedicated drum experts.

6:00 PM   **Laurelhurst Park** [2]

Beautiful Laurelhurst Park is a great place to lie back and listen to some music. Stream your fave discoveries of the day and relax, you've earned it!

7:00 PM   **Doug Fir Lounge** (p. 143)

The Doug Fir Lounge is one of Portland's most beloved music venues, and it also has a great restaurant and bar. Grab dinner and check out the show schedule. The bar is open until late, and be sure to check out the bathroom. It was voted one of Portland's "best places to pee."

48 HOURS in PORTLAND

DAY 2

9:00 AM Broadway Bridge

Get up and head over the Broadway Bridge from downtown and into North Portland.

10:00 AM Sweedeedee (p.42)

Start out your day at the best brunch spot in town. Everything on the menu is delicious, the staff are lovely, and they are always setting the mood by playing great music.

12:00 AM Mississippi Records (p. 136)

Pop next door for the best selection of new and used hard-to-find vinyl for cheap. The in-house label releases obscure titles from around the world—treasures for both collectors and casual listeners. The staff are both knowledgeable and approachable. Cash only.

1:00 PM Portland Museum of Modern Art (p. 127)

The Portland Museum of Modern Art is set in the basement of the Mississippi Studios building. With a commitment to diverse and interesting contemporary art, you'll see shows in this small gallery you won't see anywhere else.

2:00 PM ¿Por Qué No? (p. 67)

Grab lunch at ¿Por Qué No? on Mississippi Ave. Tacos or the Brian's Bowl are what to get, along with a midday pomegranate margarita!

3:00 PM Mississippi Ave. Shopping

Spend a few hours shopping on Mississippi Ave. Be sure to check out Beacon Sound (p. 138), which has a small,

but well-curated selection of vinyl. They also have shows regularly.

5:00 PM Lowell (p. 214)

Equal parts gallery, museum, and shop, Lowell is one of the most beautiful stores in town. Pore over every treasure and chat up Maya, the owner and expert curator of the space. At Lowell, find vintage housewares and textiles, jewelry, art shows on rotation, and even a few zines and cassette tapes.

6:00 PM Sunset at the Bluffs

Watching a sunset at the Bluffs will make you feel like a true local. Bring a blanket and snacks and take in the view.

8:00 PM Mississippi Studios and Bar Bar (p. 141)

Catch a show at Mississippi Studios, an intimate venue in Portland's historic Mississippi Neighborhood. The venue is built, owned, and run by and for musicians. It hosts a wide range of local, national, and international acts covering almost every music genre. Bar Bar, the bar next door, has an awesome burger.

11:00 PM Karaoke

Close out the night by singing your favorite karaoke tunes at the Alibi Tiki Lounge[3] or Baby Ketten Karaoke [4] . The Alibi has karaoke, late-night Hawaiian fare, and colorful drinks every night until 2:00 a.m. Baby Ketten has a more obscure selection of singable indie tunes, and rotates nights and locations.

Shop Information

[1] **Know Your City**
Ⓐ 800 NW 6th Ave. #331 Ⓣ (503) 592-0337
Ⓗ M-F 9 a.m.-5 p.m.
Ⓦ knowyourcity.org/tours

[2] **Laurelhurst Park**
Ⓐ SE Cesar E Chavez Blvd. & Stark St.

[3] **Alibi Tiki Lounge**
Ⓐ 4024 N Interstate Ave. Ⓣ (503) 287-5335
Ⓗ 11 a.m.-2 a.m. daily
Ⓦ alibiportland.com

[4] **Baby Ketten Karaoke**
Ⓣ (503) 200-0000
Ⓦ babyketten.com

Eat your way around Portland!

Tips for seeing and eating the best parts of Portland.

JENNA CHEN

Yoga Instructor & Dancer

After five years of living in Portland, I am happy to share parts of this unique city that I love so much. As a former collective manager at People's Food Co-op, I became steeped in our local food scene and learned what it means to truly eat locally and build resilient community. As a yoga teacher and dancer, I treasure the abundance of natural and physical spaces in Portland and their accessibility by bike and public transit. This town is a gem, savor every last drop!

DAY 1

10:00 AM People's Food Co-op

After breakfast and coffee, take your time walking down Hawthorne street and be sure to stop at Powell's Books on Hawthorne and Red Light. [1]. From Hawthorne walk south a few blocks to Division Street, a newly developed strip with more coffee, boutiques and even a female-friendly sex shop, She Bop [2]. Walk a couple more blocks south to Clinton St. and follow this bike thoroughfare to People's Food Co-op (p. 76), the oldest food co-op in town with a weekly farmers' market every Wednesday. Check peoples.coop for more community room events.

12:00 PM The Portland Mercado [3]

Have lunch at the Portland Mercado, the first Latino public market and community center that opened in 2015. They provide affordable retail space for small businesses to launch and grow and are a hub for Latino culture in Portland. Try a variety of authentic cuisines from Latin America in an up and coming part of town.

1:00 PM Mt. Tabor (p. 244)

Catch a ride to Mount Tabor, an inactive volcano in SE Portland with one of the best views of the city. You can walk, hike, or drive up to the top and sit among the tall trees.

3:00 PM The Commons Brewery (p. 96)

Relax and taste some local beers at The Commons Brewery, brewed and bottled in the same building as the tasting room. Then walk over to Mother Foucault's bookshop (p. 244), a cozy shop filled with old classics and tons of character.

4:00 PM Waterfront Biking or Walking

Rent a bike from one of the many local bike shops or hop on an orange Biketown bike and pedal around the waterfront and over a couple bridges. The Steel – Hawthorne bridge loop has great views of the Willamette River and downtown Portland.

7:00 PM Laurelhurst Market [4]

Laurelhurst Market is a restaurant and full service butcher shop that boasts some of the city's best and most ethically sourced meat with suitable pairings. Get dinner here and stroll around the Laurelhurst neighborhood, from vintage shops to another beautiful tree-lined park, this neighborhood is beautiful and full. Looking for desert? Pix Patisserie [5] is right down the street, Salt and Straw Ice Cream (p. 68) isn't too far, Lauretta Jean's [6] for pie, or Voodoo Doughnut's Eastside location, which is much less crowded than the downtown one, are all great options.

8:00 PM SE Nightlife

If you're looking to go dancing, Holocene (p. 141) or the Goodfoot [7] are your best bet on the Eastside. Check out who's on the bill at the newly renovated Revolution Hall for live music or catch a movie at the historic Hollywood Theatre.

DAY2

9:00 AM **Pip's Original** [8]

This cafe, known for its mini doughnuts and unique chai tea flavors will not disappoint. Get the chai flight and try all the doughnuts. There may be a line, but it's worth it!

11:00 AM **Farmers' Market**

Portland is famous for its bustling farmers' markets. There are many different markets on multiple days of the week, check portlandfarmersmarket.org to see which one fits your schedule. This is a great opportunity to talk with the people who grow, make and sell the food we eat and love. Get something local to munch on and sit and take in the energy of the market.

12:00 PM **Rose Garden** [9]

The MAX will take you directly to the International Rose Test Garden where over 500 varieties of roses grow. The best time to visit is from April through October. You could spend hours here smelling all the different roses, but when you've had enough the Japanese Garden (p. 234) is an award-winning oasis that is worth a peak.

2:00 PM **Lunch in Downtown**

Take public transit back into downtown where you have a myriad of lunch choices to choose from. Nong's Khao Man Gai (p. 81) is simple but delicious Asian comfort food from a food truck. Lardo (p. 81) , Tasty n Alder [10], and Jake's Famous Crawfish [11] offer more American fare. Don't forget to stop by the famous downtown Powell's Books (p. 236) location, the oldest and biggest independent bookstore in the country, newly remodeled and a Portland must.

4:00 PM **Portland Art Museum** (p. 122)

Staying on the west side of the city, take the bus or the streetcar to the Portland Art Museum. The Portland Art Museum is a beautiful building set in the Park Blocks of the city, surrounded by beautiful trees. Take some time here to be silent and absorb some art.

6:00 PM **Little Bird Bistro** (p. 66)

Eat dinner at Little Bird Bistro for a delicious French American meal unlike anything you've tasted before.

Shop Information

[1] **Red Light**

Ⓐ 3590 SE Hawthorne Blvd. Ⓣ (503) 963-8888
Ⓗ M-Th 11 a.m.-8 p.m., F-Sa 11 a.m.-9 p.m.,
   Su 12 p.m.-7 p.m. Ⓦ redlightclothingexchange.com

[2] **She Bop**

Ⓐ 3213 SE Division St. Ⓣ (503)-688-1196
Ⓗ Su-Th 11 a.m.-7 p.m., F-Sa 11 a.m.-8 p.m.
Ⓦ sheboptheshop.com

[3] **The Portland Mercado**

Ⓐ 7238 SE Foster Rd. Ⓗ 10 a.m.-9 p.m. daily
Ⓦ portlandmercado.org

[4] **Laurelhurst Market**

Ⓐ 3155 E Burnside St. Ⓣ (503) 206-3097 (Restaurant)
Ⓗ 5 p.m.-10 p.m. daily (Restaurant)
Ⓦ laurelhurstmarket.com

[5] **Pix Patisserie**

Ⓐ 2225 E Burnside St. Ⓣ (971) 271-7166
Ⓗ M-F 4 p.m.-12 a.m., Sa-Su 2 p.m.-12 a.m.
Ⓦ pixpatisserie.com

[6] **Lauretta Jean's**

Ⓐ 3402 SE Division St. Ⓣ (503) 235-3119
Ⓗ Su-Th 8 a.m.-10 p.m., F-Sa 8 a.m.-11 p.m.
Ⓦ laurettajeans.com

[7] **The Goodfoot**

Ⓐ 2845 SE Stark St. Ⓣ (503) 239-9292
Ⓗ 5 p.m.–2:30 a.m. Ⓦ thegoodfoot.com

[8] **Pip's Original**

Ⓐ 4759 NE Fremont St. Ⓣ (503) 206-8692
Ⓗ 8 a.m.-4 p.m. daily Ⓦ pipsoriginal.com

[9] **Portland International Rose Test Garden**

Ⓐ 400 SW Kingston Ave. Ⓣ (503) 823-3664
Ⓗ 7:30 a.m.-9 p.m. daily

[10] **Tasty n Alder**

Ⓐ 580 SW 12th Ave. Ⓣ (503) 621-9251
Ⓗ Su-Th 9 a.m.-10 p.m., F-Sa 9 a.m.-11 p.m.
Ⓦ tastynalder.com

[11] **Jake's Famous Crawfish**

Ⓐ 401 SW 12th Ave. Ⓣ (503) 226-1419
Ⓗ M-Th 11:30 a.m.-10 p.m., F-Sa 11:30 a.m.-11:00 p.m.,
   Su 10 a.m.-10 p.m.

Art, books, and wilderness

Portland is a casual town surrounded by a diverse ecology, and carrying a great book to these places can make for an enriching vacation and give context to this place and its people.

Isao Nishiyama

Isao Nishiyama

BLAIR SAXON-HILL AND JOHN BRODIE

Artists and co-owners of Monograph Bookwerks

Blair Saxon-Hill has lived in Portland for twenty years and is an artist and the co-owner of Monograph Bookwerks in the Alberta district of NE Portland. In 2016, she was an Oregon Arts Commission Fellow and a Hallie Ford Foundation Fellow.
John Brodie was born in Portland and has been a practicing artist for over twenty-five years. He was included in Disjecta's PDX2010: A Biennial of Contemporary Art.

DAY 1

9:00 AM Sweedeedee (p. 42)

Wake up at 9:00 a.m. (other than coffee shops and breakfast spots, nothing really opens until 11:00 a.m. in Portland. So don't worry, you have two hours!). Go directly to Sweedeedee, where you will have a jolt of true Portland culture. Help yourself to coffee while you wait. After breakfast, cruise in to Mississippi Records (p. 136) next door—even if you're not into records, this place is fantastic. Downstairs is the Portland Museum of Modern Art (p. 127), with consistently great art exhibitions.

12:00 PM Salvage Works [1]

Due to public outcry, Portland is now the first city in the country to ban the demolition of homes built in 1916 or before. Before homes are deconstructed, as of October 2016, the materials inside are to be salvaged. Salvage Works is a key partner in the reuse of Portland's historical architectural materials. Head to North Portland's Kenton neighborhood and visit Salvage Works, a huge warehouse of reclaimed lumber plus a storefront of custom furniture and vintage objects.

1:00 PM Disjecta Contemporary Art Center (p. 127)

Just down the street from Salvage Works is Disjecta Contemporary Art Center. With an active events calendar and a large-scale exhibition space, Disjecta presents exhibits and performances by local and national artists. Stroll to the corner of North Interstate and North Denver Avenues for a photo-op with Portland's thirty-seven-foot tall statue of mythical logger Paul Bunyan (erected in 1959).

3:30 PM Bookstores and a Bookmaking Resource Center

Visit two uncommon bookstores specializing in rare books and ephemera on avant-garde artists, political and counterculture movements, and poetry - Division Leap (by appointment only, p. 244) and Passages Bookshop (p. 241). Or head to the Independent Publishing Resource Center's (IPRC, p. 240) new location. The IPRC is a DIY print, art, and bookmaking resource center for letterpress, screen printing, zine, and bookmaking and includes a retail space.

5:00 PM Mother Foucault's Bookshop (p. 244)

A few blocks from the Independent Publishing Resource Center is an iconic Portland bookstore and one of our favorites, Mother Foucault's specializing in literature, poetry and philosophy. They host plenty of regularly scheduled readings, musical events, chess games, wine drinking, and resident writers—so stop in for the unexpected and meet great poets.

7:00 PM Music and Art

You are near several music and art venues. Check the schedules of Yale Union (p. 126), Holocene (p. 141), Revolution Hall [2], Bunk Bar [3], and Doug Fir Lounge (p. 143). Otherwise, you can get a drink at: Angel Face (for an enchanting experience (p. 115), Dig A Pony [4], Beer Bar (for the true beer lover who wants to sit in a great interior with a menu that includes sour beers), or Rontoms (for a patio that is much bigger than you'd imagine from the exterior, (p. 147). And when you get hungry, you can eat at Luce (p. 82), Navarre [5], PaaDee [6], or Wolf & Bears [7] (a food cart Captured Beer Bus [8] five steps away)

DAY2

8:00 AM **Woodlawn Coffee & Pastry** [9]

Start off early and head to Woodlawn Coffee & Pastry on NE Dekum to get coffee and a house-baked yummy treat. After relaxing with your coffee and hanging with the locals, go just a few blocks down to P's & Q's Market (p. 52). This spot is a true charmer. Here you are going to stock up on lunch and snacks for your mini-adventure into the wilderness.

9:00 AM **Bagby Hot Springs** [10]

You are headed to Bagby Hot Springs in a car (hopefully with a new Portland friend!). A must-see hot springs in a beautiful section of the Oregon wilderness. After driving two and a half hours, you will have experienced a bit of the Oregon landscape. Then hike on a well-maintained trail for forty-five minutes before soaking in a gravity-fed natural hot spring, all for a $5 admission fee. We know it sounds like a trek, but trust us, it's worth every minute. An alternate place might be to register for a class at Wildcraft Studio to learn regional natural dyeing, foraging local foods, screen-printing, and more. Just ninety minutes by car from Portland in White Salmon, Washington.

4:00 PM **People's Food Co-op** (p.76)

Refreshed and ready for an organic snack or juice back in Portland? Go to the best co-op grocery in town—People's Food Co-op. If you're lucky, it's a Wednesday and you can experience the year-round, all-organic farmer's market.

5:00 PM **Keller Fountain Park** [11]

Speaking of falling water, now that you're back in the city, check out the Northwest-inspired landscape design and fountains of Lawrence Halprin. To do so, start at SW 3rd & Clay (Keller Fountain) and walk south to see a multi-city block sequence of Halprin-designed urban parks. These parks include the well-known Keller (Forecourt) Fountain Park, the lesser-known and hidden Pettygrove Park, and the Lovejoy Fountain Park.

7:00 PM **PSU Bowling Alley** [12]

Bowling! Truly a secret spot, the PSU bowling alley is an old-school bowling alley in the basement of the Portland State University campus next to the South Park Blocks in Southwest Portland. With only six lanes, and unknown to many, it's a casual and fun hangout spot for students and those in the know. They also have video games and billiard tables.

10:00 PM **Skyline Tavern Project** [13]

Hopefully you still have the car and can visit the Skyline Tavern Project, an old Portland haunt now under new ownership. This hilltop bar is known for its epic views and is bound to become a new Portland hotspot. Part city, part wilderness.

Shop Information

[1] **Salvage Works**
Ⓐ 2024 N Argyle St. Ⓣ (503) 899-0052
Ⓗ M-Sa 9 a.m.-6 p.m., Su 11 a.m.-4 p.m. Ⓦ salvageworkspdx.com

[2] **Revolution Hall**
Ⓐ 1300 SE Stark St. Ⓣ (971) 808-5091
Ⓗ check show times Ⓦ revolutionhallpdx.com

[3] **Bunk Bar**
Ⓐ 1028 SE Water Ave. Ⓣ (503) 328-2865
Ⓗ Su-M 11 a.m.-10 p.m., Tu-Th 11 a.m.-12 a.m.,
F-Sa 11 a.m.-1 a.m.
Ⓦ bunksandwiches.com

[4] **Dig A Pony**
Ⓐ 736 SE Grand Ave. Ⓣ (971) 279-4409
Ⓗ 4 p.m.-2 a.m. Ⓦ digaponyportland.com

[5] **Navarre**
Ⓐ 10 NE 28th Ave. Ⓣ (503) 232-3555
Ⓗ See website for hours. Ⓦ navarreporland.com

[6] **PaaDee**
Ⓐ 6 SE 28th Ave. Ⓣ (503) 360-1453
Ⓗ 11:30 a.m.-3 pm, 5 p.m.-10 p.m. daily
Ⓦ paadeepdx.com

[7] **Wolf & Bears**
Ⓐ SW 10th Between Alder & Washington
Ⓣ (503) 810-0671 Ⓗ 11 a.m.-4 p.m. daily
Ⓦ eatwolfandbears.com

[8] **Captured Beer Bus**
Ⓐ 113 SE 28th Ave. Ⓣ (509) 954-2136
Ⓗ 12 p.m.-9 p.m. daily Ⓦ capturedbeerbus.com

[9] **Woodlawn Coffee & Pastry**
Ⓐ 808 NE Dekum St. Ⓣ (503) 954-2412
Ⓗ 6:30 a.m.-5 p.m. daily Ⓦ woodlawncoffee.com

[10] **Bagby Hot Springs**
Ⓐ Estacada, OR Ⓣ (503) 860-4705
Ⓦ bagbyhotsprings.org

[11] **Keller Fountain Park**
Ⓐ SW 3rd Ave. & Clay St.

[12] **PSU Bowling Alley**
Ⓐ 1825 SW Broadway Ⓣ (503) 725-4529
Ⓗ M-Sa 12 a.m.-10 p.m., Su only by reservation
Ⓦ pdx.edu/gameroom/bowling

[13] **Skyline Tavern Project**
Ⓐ 8031 NW Skyline Blvd. Ⓣ (503) 286-4788
Ⓗ 12 p.m.-12 a.m. daily Ⓦ skytav.com

My usual routine

Portland has become known globally as a city that encourages healthy, well-balanced lifestyles, support of local/independent business, and unique artisan crafts. These elements, among many others, are why I choose to live in Portland. These are my recommendations for your next visit.

ARTHUR HITCHCOCK

Freelance Photographer / Producer

Arthur Hitchcock is a photographer, multi-disciplinary artist, and producer. He was born in the Midwest, grew up in Long Beach, CA, and is now pursuing a fully nomadic lifestyle with a home base in Portland, OR.

DAY 1

9:00 AM Pip's Original [1]

After gathering your photographic supplies for your travel scrapbook, head over to Pip's Original for some freshly made mini-doughnuts and delicious chai tea. All recipes are developed by the owners, Nate and Jaime Snell, and they are incredible. I can personally recommend just about everything on the menu, but a nice first-time order would consist of Nutella and sea salt doughnuts with the Heart of Gold chai. Try to arrive before you feel really hungry, because this place can get busy!

11:00 AM The Good Mod (p. 194)

After breakfast, make your way to The Good Mod for a showroom and workshop tour. The Good Mod offers an enormous selection of classic mid-century/Danish modern furniture, art, and custom design/build services. They recently co-designed and fabricated a large portion of Airbnb's Portland CX Hub, a one-of-a-kind office in downtown Portland. If you are there earlier in the week, you might see me photographing the furniture! The entrance can be found on West Burnside, hidden away from the bustle of downtown. On the fourth floor, your adventure into design awaits. The showroom is always filled with beautiful light, and is in an older warehouse-like space. Be sure to take lots of photographs.

12:00 PM Grassa [2]

Only a block away from The Good Mod is my usual and favorite lunch spot, Grassa. They offer made-that-morning pasta that is local, often organic, and delicious. There are choices for lighter or heartier meals; I usually go for the lighter options. The spaghetti aglio oglio is my staple. Grassa is structured so you pay beforehand, which is nice when you have a busy day in Portland ahead of you. Comfortable and utilitarian in its design/branding, with beautiful large windows for great street views.

1:00 PM Sauvie Island [3]

If you have access to a car, then this is the perfect opportunity to explore Portland's natural beauty. My favorite local escape is Sauvie Island. Just a short drive up Highway 30 west, you can find this river-surrounded island filled with blooming flowers, local farms, and multiple beaches. Best plan of action is to drive the entire loop of the island in either direction and stop anywhere that interests you. There are too many scenic stops to list! Bring a friend, some whiskey or beer, and have a photoshoot in the golden hour before sunset. At some point in your leisurely drive, call and make dinner reservations at DOC. They get busy, and that is your next stop.

6:00 PM DOC (p. 58)

Prepare yourself for the best meal in Portland. Two dinner seatings are available at DOC in Northeast Portland. Since you have been busy all day, go for the earlier 6:00 p.m. seating. They have a prix fixe menu, so enjoy six-plus courses of predetermined goodness. The menu changes every week, so you are guaranteed something new every visit. Featuring the best of local and foreign cuisine, each course is specifically curated to complement the next. Intimate seating and low light make this a great place for a date or a group of friends. You enter through the small but efficient kitchen and get to watch these talented chefs prepare everything throughout the evening. Tip: Get the wine pairing.

10:00 PM Expatriate (p. 115)

Just a quick walk across the street from DOC is a local favorite cocktail bar, Expatriate. Great ambience and a candlelit bar counter make for a fantastic end-of-evening drink. Music is always top notch, bartenders specialize in quick flair service, and they DJ between creations. Finish your first day in Portland with friends and know that you did everything a local creative would do.

DAY2

9:00 AM Miss Delta [4]

Check out what's happening on Mississippi Avenue in North Portland. This local-business-lined street is perfect for shopping after breakfast at Miss Delta. Miss Delta offers Southern-inspired American dishes with options for breakfast and lunch. If you think you can handle it, get the praline butter waffles with fried chicken. Simply amazing. There is always little to no line for this breakfast spot, which is rare in Portland these days.

11:00 AM Mississippi Avenue

Cruise down Mississippi Avenue to see an assortment of local establishments such as Flutter [5] (women's clothing and curios), Paxton Gate (p. 227) (taxidermy and scientific items), and Land [6] (screenprints and stationery), and Pistils Nursery (p. 223). My favorites are Paxton Gate and Pistils. Paxton Gate is a wonderfully weird and interesting store with beautiful locally made jewelry and exotic taxidermy creations. Pistils is a beautiful plant nursery and garden supply that always makes me feel refreshed and inspired by nature.

1:00 PM Nong's Khao Man Ghai (p. 81)

Head back downtown to the food cart pod on 10th and Alder. This is one of the busiest hubs downtown. Locals and visitors flock to the carts to dine on quickly created fresh food, designed to be eaten outside or on the go. My friends and I frequent our friend Nong's cart almost every day. Nong's Khao Man Ghai specializes in a simple Thai chicken and rice dish with broth. Can't go wrong with that! Say hi for me!

2:30 PM Blue Sky Gallery (p. 130)

A close walk away is one of my favorite galleries, Blue Sky Gallery. Peruse some beautiful photographic work from contemporary artists. Be sure to look at the Drawers, a collection of local work available for purchase.

3:30 PM Bailey's Taproom (p.117)

After viewing some contemporary photography, walk back across Burnside to Bailey's Taproom to grab some local beer. Featuring more beer choices than you will know what to do with, this will help you wind down your busy afternoon.

5:00 PM Departure (p. 82)

Prepare for dinner at Departure: excellent Pan-Asian cuisine by one of the city's top chefs. Located on the top floor of The Nines hotel, be sure to check out the balcony and look out over downtown Portland. Grab some inventive sushi from Chef Gregory and a wild global cocktail from the bar and get ready to spend the evening not wanting to leave this city.

10:00 PM Kask [7]

Celebrate your last evening in style at Kask, one of the city's best cocktail bars, and one of my downtown regular choices. Grab a neat Bowmore Scotch to start, and a Doctor's Order to finish. Low lighting, rugged Pacific Northwest-style interior. Bar, tabletops, and seating adorned with old-growth hardwoods from our local forests. After a calm evening in this quiet cocktail bar, head on back to your Airbnb and sleep well knowing a little bit more about Portland.

Shop Information

[1] Pip's Original

Ⓐ 4759 NE Fremont St.   Ⓣ (503) 206-8692
Ⓗ 8 a.m.-4 p.m. daily
Ⓦ pipsoriginal.com

[2] Grassa

Ⓐ 1205 SW Washington St.   Ⓣ (503) 241-1133
Ⓗ 11 a.m.-10 p.m. daily
Ⓦ grassapdx.com

[3] Sauvie Island

Ⓐ 15000 NW Sauvie Island Rd.

[4] Miss Delta

Ⓐ 3950 N Mississippi Ave.   Ⓣ (503) 287-7629
Ⓗ M-F 10 a.m.-10 p.m., Sa-Su 9 a.m.-10 p.m.
Ⓦ missdeltapdx.net

[5] Flutter

Ⓐ 3948 N Mississippi Ave.   Ⓣ (503) 288-1649
Ⓗ Su-W 11 a.m.-6 p.m., Th–F 11 a.m.-7 p.m.,
   Sa 10 a.m.-7 p.m.
Ⓦ flutterpdx.com

[6] Land

Ⓐ 3925 N Mississippi Ave.   Ⓣ (503) 451-0689
Ⓗ 10 a.m.-6 p.m. daily   Ⓦ landpdx.com

[7] Kask

Ⓐ 1215 SW Alder St.   Ⓣ (503) 241-7163
Ⓗ Tu-Th 5 p.m.-10 p.m., F-Sa 5 p.m.-11 p.m.,
   Su 5 p.m.-10 p.m.
Ⓦ superbitepdx.com/kask

Casual and mostly kids-friendly

Our daughter is three so we go on lots of walks, spend time in parks, and when we eat out, we go to pretty casual places. We don't travel much but when we do, we look for similar things to do.

MAY BARRUEL

Owner, Director at Nationale

An art gallery and specialty shop in Southeast Portland. We primarily focus on emerging Portland-based artists, and we are dedicated to promoting the arts through exhibitions, performances, and a selection of carefully chosen goods. Originally from France, I moved to Portland in 2000 and live in Southeast with my boyfriend, Ty, and our daughter, Lou.

DAY 1

10:00 AM   Little T American Baker (p. 80)

We walk through Ladd's Addition and check out all the roses on our way to breakfast at Little T American Baker. Coming from France, I am especially biased towards a good croissant, and Little T's is my favorite. I also love their savory breakfast sandwiches, like the eggs/cheese/bacon on whole wheat croissant or the Croque Madame on brioche. I've never had anything I didn't love from this place, it is hands down my go-to restaurant in Portland.

11:00 AM   The Crystal Springs Rhododendron Garden

Hop on the #10 bus to go to the Crystal Springs Rhododendron Garden. Free in the winter and on Mondays and Tuesdays the rest of the year. Otherwise $4, a modest fee for such a beautiful place.

1:00 PM   Nationale (p.124)

Head back to Division St. We usually walk up the street to go catch up on things at Nationale and grab lunch at Taqueria Lindo Michoacan [1], Roman Candle [2], or the wonderfully cozy Lauretta Jean's [3]. Make sure to split a piece of pie for dessert!

3:00 PM   Exiled Records (p.139)
& Crossroads Music (p.147)

Head over to Hawthorne in search of records. Exiled Records and Crossroads Music always have great selections.

4:00 PM   Sewallcrest City Park [4]

By this time, we need a little break from all the food and walking we've been doing. We stop by Sewallcrest City Park to either read in the grass or play and run around.

5:00 PM   Mother Foucault's Bookshop (p. 244)

We visit our friend Craig at Mother Foucault's Bookshop and are immediately transported into a different place and time. Think Shakespeare and Company in Portland.

6:00 PM   Laurelhurst Theater (p.129)

Catch a movie at Laurelhurst Theater (21 or older after 5:30 p.m.).

8:30 PM   Dove Vivi [5]

Dinner at Dove Vivi. Their cornmeal crust pizza is inimitable.

10:00 PM   Angel Face (p.115)

Nightcap at Angel Face with a Manhattan and their perfect Tarte Tatin.

DAY 2

9:30 AM   Stumptown Coffee Roasters Belmont (p.116)

Today we're heading to Northeast Portland to see some art but most places open a bit late so we grab coffee at Stumptown Belmont and start the day off with a walk in Laurelhurst Park [6]. Something about it reminds me of our trip to Victoria, Canada.

11:00 AM   Sweedeedee (p. 42)

Breakfast at Sweedeedee. Everything on the menu is delicious, healthy, local, and made in-house.

12:00 AM   Portland Museum of Modern Art (p.127)

We're here to see the art show next door at PMoMA.

Conveniently, it's located in the basement of Mississippi Records (p.136), so more record shopping!

12:30 AM Monograph Bookwerks (p.238)

In the mood for great art books, we head to Monograph Bookwerks and Ampersand Gallery & Fine Books (p. 240), where we also check out their current art show.

1:30 PM Lowell (p.214)

On the way toward downtown, we stop by Lowell and say hi to our favorite person in town, Maya. We find a little porcelain cat to add to our growing collection.

2:00 PM Adams and Ollman (p.126)

Our next stop is Adams and Ollman, for more art viewing. Amy and the gallery used to be our neighbors when we were all on Burnside.

2:30 PM Addy's Sandwich Bar [7]

We walk over to Addy's Sandwich Bar and grab lunch. I especially love Addy's handmade pâté that she serves with cornichon and mustard on LittleT baguette. It feels like home once again!

3:30 PM Hilary Horvath Flowers [8]

On the way back to the Pearl District, we stop by Hilary Horvath Flowers and Alder & Co (p.218).The space looks and smells beautiful. We grab a little bit of lily of the valley to celebrate this warm spring weather.

4:00 PM Galleries

We get coffee from Heart Roasters (p.113) across the street and head toward PDX Contemporary Art (p.130) and Open Gallery, two of our favorite galleries in town.

5:00 PM Forest Park (p.167)

Because we are so close to Forest Park, we decide to go for an impromptu hike.

6:30 PM Slammer Tavern [9]

On the way back to SE, we stop for a drink at the Slammer Tavern (21+) and catch the end of a Blazers game. I run over to Haunt [10] to visit my old neighbor and friend, the designer Holly Stalder.

8:30 PM Nong's Khao Man Ghai (p. 81)

We order Nong's Khao Man Ghai to go and then stop by Clinton St. Video [11] to grab a DVD so we can spend the evening relaxing at home.

Shop Information

[1] Taqueria Lindo Michoacan
Ⓐ 4035 SE Division St. Ⓣ (503) 313-6864
Ⓗ M-Sa 10:30 a.m.-7 p.m.

[2] Roman Candle
Ⓐ 3377 SE Division St. Ⓣ (971) 302 6605
Ⓗ 7 a.m.-4 p.m. daily Ⓦ romancandlebaking.com

[3] Lauretta Jean's
Ⓐ 3402 SE Division St. Ⓣ (503) 235-3119
Ⓗ Su-Th 8 a.m.-10 p.m., F-Sa 8 a.m.-11 p.m.
Ⓦ laurettajeans.com

[4] Sewallcrest City Park
Ⓐ SE 31st Ave. & SE Market St.

[5] Dove Vivi
Ⓐ 2727 NE Glisan St. Ⓣ (503) 239-4444
Ⓗ 4 p.m.-10 p.m. daily Ⓦ dovevivipizza.com

[6] Laurelhurst Park
Ⓐ SE Cesar E Chavez Blvd. & Stark St.

[7] Addy's Sandwich Bar
Ⓐ 911 SW 10th Ave. Ⓣ (503) 267-0994
Ⓗ M-F 9 a.m.-4 p.m.
Ⓦ addyssandwichbar.com

[8] Hilary Horvath Flowers
Ⓐ 616 SW 12th Ave. Ⓣ (503) 789-1509
Ⓗ M-Sa 11 p.m.-6 p.m., Su 11 p.m.-4 p.m.
Ⓦ hilaryhorvath.com

[9] Slammer Tavern
Ⓐ 500 SE 8th Ave. Ⓣ (503) 232-6504
Ⓗ M-Sa 3 p.m.-2:30 a.m., Su 10 a.m.-1 am

[10] Haunt
Ⓐ 811 E Burnside St.,Suite 114 Ⓣ (503)928-7266
Ⓗ W-Su 12 p.m.-5 p.m.
Ⓦ hollystalder.com/haunt-

[11] Clinton Street Video
Ⓐ 2501 SE Clinton St. Ⓣ (503) 236-9030
Ⓗ M-Th 2 p.m.-10 p.m., F-Su 12 p.m.-10 p.m.

My Portland

Commentary by

Jeff Hammerly
Senior International Tourism and Communications Manager, Travel Portland

Portland-proud, weird, and above all pro-community

I am one of the Portland "freaks." A mild freak, to be sure, but a freak. No driver's license until I was twenty-eight years old. No car till I was thirty-four. I rode everywhere on bicycle (and, to be fair, in the front and back seats of friends' cars). I was a Bikey (and let's make a clear distinction here between "Bikey" and "Bike Nazi," the latter, unfortunately, becoming more common among those—particularly newcomers—who have only a superficial grasp of what it means to be blessed by existence in this time and place). I have owned only two cars in my sixty years of life. I was Portland before it was (is) the weird place it is today. I still am. We were anti-corporate, pro-environmental, pro-preservation, and above all, pro-community.

It's a funny thing to age. To some folks (younger, perhaps?), Portland freaks in my age bracket (and mind you, we may now wear a suit on occasion) may look to be part of a generation disconnected from what's happening in Portland. Don't be fooled. Portland made us who we are now, and we helped make it what it is today.

There is the Portland with its standard palatable places for first-time visitors (and where everyone should go at least once!):

- **Walk/bike Waterfront Park** (p.244)
- **Eastbank Esplanade Loop**
- **Vera Katz Eastbank Esplanade** [1]
- **Portland Farmers Market** (p. 78)
- **International Rose Test Garden**
- **Portland Japanese Garden** (p. 234)
- **Food cart pods**
- **Brewpubs**
- **Timbers / Trail Blazers games** (p. 182)
- **Powell's City of Books** (p. 236)

And to catch a lovely view:

- **Portland Aerial Tram** [2]
- **Pittock Mansion** (from the garden) [3]
- **Mount Hood** (p. 172)

And my other personal favorites:

- **Mount Tabor Park** (on no-car day)
- **Bars with dartboards**
- **Laurelhurst Theater** (cheap movie and beer) (p.129)
- **Hollywood Theatre** (p. 131)
- **People's Food Co-op** (p. 76)

This is the lifestyle we hippies chose in the 1960s! Although it has been transformed, perhaps some would say, transmuted, it's more mainstream and therefore more powerful than ever. It has given birth to the New Seasons and Whole Foods of the world.

- **Portland Homestead Supply** [4]
- **Pretty bicycles anywhere in the city**

A pretty bicycle is the pinnacle of design beauty.

- **Tall Douglas-fir trees in all Portland parks**

Visitors get to use the fabulous public spaces without paying any fees or taxes. Use them! And relax, Portland-style.

- **African music concerts at Star Theatre** [5]

When the soul, R&B, soukous, jit, marimba, rai, reggae, or African hip hop are flying at the Star, there's no place better in the world to be for an evening.

- **Trail runs and rides in Forest Park**
- **Walks and rides through residential neighborhoods throughout the city, especially the east side.**

Portland is a city where our urban dreams of activity, creativity, grit, involvement, and flavor meet our suburban longings for tranquility, order, pastoralism, and independence to shape our smaller world (backyards) in our own image. Portland is the embodiment of the creative, independent, and blessed middle-class. As a Japanese friend once told me, "Portland is the city that shows what America could be, should be."

Shop Information

[1] **Vera Katz Eastbank Esplanade**
Ⓐ Steel Bridge to SE Caruthers.
Ⓦ portlandoregon.gov/parks

[2] **Portland Aerial Tram**
Ⓐ 3303 SW Bond Ave.
Ⓗ M-F 5:30 a.m.-9:30 p.m.,
    Sa 9 a.m.-5 p.m.
Ⓦ gobytram.com

[3] **Pittock Mansion**
Ⓐ 3229 NW Pittock Drive
Ⓣ (503) 823-3623
Ⓗ hours vary by season
Ⓦ pittockmansion.org

[4] **Portland Homestead Supply**
Ⓐ 8012 SE 13th Ave.
Ⓣ (503) 233-8691
Ⓗ Tu-Sa 10 a.m.-6 p.m., Su 11 a.m.-5 p.m.
Ⓦ homesteadsupplyco.com

[5] **Star Theater**
Ⓐ 13 NW 6th Ave.
Ⓣ (503) 248-4700
Ⓦ startheaterportland.com

EVENTS *in* PORTLAND

Travel Portland

1 JANUARY

ChocolateFest

Love chocolate? You won't want to miss ChocolateFest, a weekend dedicated to sampling and savoring everything from artisan truffles to drinking chocolate from more than eighty exhibitors at the Oregon Convention Center.
chocolatefest.org

Fertile Ground Festival

Founded in 2009, Fertile Ground is focused on new Portland art. The eleven-day, citywide festival showcases play premieres, art installations, events, and even in-progress projects, all created by local artists.
fertilegroundpdx.org

Chamber Music Northwest Winter Festival

Known for its popular summer series, Chamber Music Northwest also presents a suite of concerts in late January/early February.
cmnw.org

2 FEBRUARY

Portland International Film Festival

Held by the Northwest Film Center, the Portland International Film Festival is the granddaddy of Portland's twenty-plus annual film festivals, filling two weeks with 100 local premieres from around the globe.
nwfilm.org/festivals/piff

Portland Jazz Festival

Celebrating both the jazz genre and Black History Month, the Portland Jazz Festival is packed with more than 150 concerts, including performances by major international artists and scores of free shows showcasing local talent.
pdxjazz.com

Chinese New Year at Lan Su Chinese Garden

The two-week Chinese New Year celebration, held in late January and early February at Lan Su Chinese Garden, includes lion dances, children's activities, martial arts, and cultural and historical demonstrations. The festivities culminate with a traditional lantern-viewing ceremony.
lansugarden.org/things-to-do/events/chinese-new-year

3 MARCH

Portland Dining Month

Every March, more than 100 of some of the city's best restaurants offers three-course, pre-fixe menus at a great value of just $29.
travelportland.com/dining-month

Portland Saturday Market

The nation's longest-running open-air arts and crafts market, the Portland Saturday Market features artisans selling their wares in a scenic riverside setting—open Sundays, too. Runs March through December. (or Christmas Eve).
portlandsaturdaymarket.com

POW Fest

The annual Portland Oregon Women's (POW) Film Festival focuses on the art and cinematic contribution of women filmmakers from around the world. Spanning four days, the roster of events comprise an exhibition of films made by women, moderated filmmaker panels, and filmmaker workshops.
powfest.com

St. Patrick's Day

Led by Kells Irish Pub, this annual St. Patrick's Festival includes live music, amateur boxing, Irish dance performances, and plenty more inside the large pub and special festival tent outside. You might also catch locals and visitors—around 35,000 of them—taking to the street for the Shamrock Run, the second-largest running and walking event on the West Coast and a Portland tradition since 1979.
kellsportland.com/st-patricks-festival

4 APRIL

Wooden Shoe Tulip Festival

The month-long Wooden Shoe Tulip Festival showcases more than forty acres of tulips and daffodils in bloom at the Wooden Shoe Tulip Farm in Woodburn, forty-five minutes south of downtown Portland. Weekend events include food, wine, pony rides for the kids, and, of course, tulip viewing.
woodenshoe.com/events/tulip-fest

Soul'd Out Music Festival

The annual Soul'd Out Music Festival has drawn a diverse

range of acts, like Questlove, Yasiin Bey, Diana Krall, and many other internationally known performers. The ten-day festival packs some of the city's best venues, including the Arlene Schnitzer Concert Hall, Doug Fir, Wonder Ballroom, Alhambra Theatre, and Holocene.
souldoutfestival.com

5 | MAY

Portland Farmers Market

Most of the area's farmers' markets open in May. Among the items featured are fresh produce, flowers, seafood, breads, and berries. There are three Portland Farmers Markets in downtown Portland: Saturdays, in the South Park Blocks at Portland State University; Mondays, at Pioneer Courthouse Square; and Wednesdays, in the South Park Blocks at Salmon Street. In addition to shopping, the markets feature chef demonstrations and other entertainment.
portlandfarmersmarket.org

Bridgetown Comedy Festival

The popular Bridgetown Comedy Festival has drawn top comics like Reggie Watts and Janeane Garofalo, and was voted the nation's best comedy festival in the 2010 *Punchline Magazine* readers' poll. Spanning a weekend, the fest is held at at multiple Southeast Portland venues, including Doug Fir Lounge.
bridgetowncomedy.com

Portland Rose Festival

Since 1907, the Portland Rose Festival has been the city's quintessential event. The family-friendly fest kicks off Memorial Day weekend and includes the Grand Floral Parade, dragon boat races, concerts, and more.
rosefestival.org

6 | JUNE

World Naked Bike Ride

Portland's version of the World Naked Bike Ride is the largest in the world. In 2015, more than 10,000 cyclists took to the streets in this free, clothing-optional nighttime ride through the city.
pdxwnbr.org

Portland Pride

Portland Pride, the city's annual lesbian, gay, bisexual, and transgender (LGBTQ) community celebration, features a parade, live entertainment, and family events at Tom McCall Waterfront Park.
pridenw.org

Portland International Beer Festival

The Portland International Beer Festival draws more than 200 brews from at least fifteen countries to a beer garden setting in the Lloyd District's Holladay Park.
portland-beerfest.com

7 | JULY

Waterfront Blues Festival

The Waterfront Blues Festival—the largest blues festival west of the Mississippi River—rocks crowds on the riverbank of Tom McCall Waterfront Park and on the water itself with five days of top national acts, as well as spectacular fireworks on July 4, all in support of the Oregon Food Bank.
waterfrontbluesfest.com

Oregon Brewers Festival

Craft breweries from around the United States bring more than eighty beers to the Oregon Brewers Festival, the largest gathering of independent brewers in North America, held in downtown Portland's Tom McCall Waterfront Park.
oregonbrewfest.com

PDX Pop Now!

The all-ages PDX Pop Now! festival highlights as many as fifty local independent artists at a single venue over two days. The volunteer-driven nonprofit behind the festival also produces an annual compilation CD of local music.
pdxpopnow.com

The Big Float

Every summer, the Big Float celebrates the river that runs through the center of the city with a flotilla of inner tubes and inflatable toys, and a beach party just south of the Hawthorne Bridge in downtown's Tom McCall Waterfront Park.
thebigfloat.com

Portland Zine Symposium

Portland's DIY culture is alive and well, and you can catch it in all its glory at this annual gathering of underground media connoisseurs. The Portland Zine Symposium is a free two-day event focused on skill-sharing that includes workshops, panel discussions, and 150-plus tables of people buying, selling, and trading zines.
portlandzinesymposium.org

8 | AUGUST

Pickathon

Since 1999, the Pickathon Festival, a celebrated multi-stage, campout music festival at the lush Pendarvis Farm just outside Portland, has attracted headliners like Jeff Tweedy and Yo La Tengo while establishing itself as the nation's greenest music festival.
pickathon.com

MusicfestNW

Founded in 2001 to showcase local musicians and bring in national acts, MFNW features a weekend of concerts on two stages in downtown's Tom McCall Waterfront Park.
Portland.projectpabst.com

PDX Adult Soapbox Derby

Fearless grown-ups hurtle down an extinct volcano in homemade improvised vehicles during the PDX Soapbox Derby. It could be a recipe for disaster, but instead it's a beloved annual event held in Mount Tabor Park, which offers spectacular views of downtown. Spectators bring their own beer and cheer on the fastest—and kookiest—gravity-powered cars. **soapboxracer.com**

Bridge Pedal

The Providence Bridge Pedal is an annual bike ride across Portland's bridges that cements Portland's bike-friendly status. Ten bridges are partially closed to cars, affording bicyclists rare views and a choice of relaxed rides ranging in distance from fourteen to thirty-six miles. **providence.org/bridge-pedal**

9 SEPTEMBER

Time-Based Art (TBA) Festival

During the Time-Based Art Festival, presented by the Portland Institute for Contemporary Art (PICA), visual artists, musicians, dancers, and other creative people from all over the world push boundaries with installations, performances, and interactive art experiences. **pica.org/programs/tba-festival**

Feast Portland

International culinary festival Feast Portland taps into the wealth of renowned Portland chefs and welcomes noted culinary stars from around the world to make the most of Oregon's bounty. Find events at restaurants around town, plus happenings at Director Park, Pioneer Courthouse Square, and the Portland Art Museum. **feastportland.com**

10 OCTOBER

Portland Trail Blazers Basketball

Winners of the 1977 NBA Championship, the Portland Trail Blazers play at the Moda Cente. Blazers faithful take in games from October to April at the nearby Spirit of 77 and other Blazers-loyal sports bars. **nba.com/blazers**

Portland Fashion Week

Portland Fashion Week, the world's only comprehensively sustainable fashion week, features independent, eco-couture, street, and active wear offerings from North American and international designers, all at downtown's Pioneer Courthouse Square. **portlandfashionweek.net**

Haunted houses

Portland likes its scares as much as any other city and has the haunted houses to prove it. Some of the biggest annual options include Fright Town at Memorial Coliseum and the 13th Door and Fear Asylum in nearby towns Beaverton and Milwaukie, respectively. **fearpdx.com**

Portland Fermentation Festival

Celebrate pickling season by sampling fermented foods and drinks such as kraut, kombucha, kimchi, and miso and taking workshops on how to make them. Get recipes and tips from professionals and home fermentation enthusiasts. **portlandfermentationfestival.com**

Portland Queer Film Festival

Now in its twenty-first year, the annual Portland Queer Film Festival feature, documentary, and short films that offer glimpses into the lives of lesbian, gay, bisexual, and transgender people and communities in different parts of the world. The festival attracts thousands of filmgoers during its ten-day run at Northwest Portland's Cinema 21. **pdxqueerfilm.com**

West Coast Giant Pumpkin Regatta

Watch giant pumpkins race across the lake at Tualatin Commons, twenty-five minutes southwest of Portland, as boaters navigate these oversized gourds toward the finish line of the West Coast Giant Pumpkin Regatta. This free, wacky, entertaining event is the only one of its kind on the West Coast. **tualatinoregon.gov/recreation/west-coast-giant-pumpkin-regatta-official-page**

11 NOVEMBER

Wordstock

After ten years, Portland's premiere literary festival experienced a renaissance. Now a one-day event, Wordstock is the largest celebration of literature in the Pacific Northwest. It includes a book fair, headlining local and national author events, panels, on-stage conversations, and readings, all at the Portland Art Museum and nearby venues. **literary-arts.org/what-we-do/wordstock**

Tree Lighting Ceremony

On the day after Thanksgiving, thousands of people gather in downtown's Pioneer Courthouse Square (better known as Portland's living room) to celebrate the official start of the holiday season with the ceremonial lighting of a spectacular seventy-five-foot-tall tree provided by Stimson Lumber Company.

12 DECEMBER

Holiday Ale Fest

Packed with revelry and cheer, this winter beer festival is held right under the city's holiday tree in Pioneer Courthouse Square. The five-day Holiday Ale Fest celebration features more than forty of the Pacific Northwest's best-tasting seasonal suds, many not available anywhere else. **holidayale.com**

Holiday light displays

Some of Portland's bright spots include ZooLights, a display of more than a million lights at the Oregon Zoo, an awesome display at the Grotto, and the Christmas Ship Parade, featuring brilliantly decorated boats on the Willamette and Columbia rivers.

SOUTHWEST AREA

SW MAP

NORTHWEST AREA

NORTH AREA

N MAP

NORTHEAST AREA

NE
MAP

SOUTHEAST AREA

AFTERWORD

The elements that we believe make up a good guidebook:

-Encourages and generates a strong sense of curiosity for a place during the planning stages of a trip.
-Is as dependable as an old friend once the reader arrives at that destination.
-Instantly brings back memories of the reader's journey when they page through the guidebook after their trip.

Portland is a unique city with a rich culture and diverse population that is ripening and growing at a speed unlike most of our world's cities.

We hope that our elements of a good guidebook listed above are fulfilled during and after your journey to this rare gem of a city.

We would also like to use this space to give thanks to Travel Portland, Hawthorne Books, all of our amazing friends in Portland who helped make this guidebook possible, and you for choosing *True Portland* as a guidebook for your travels.

BRIDGE LAB

media Surf

TRUE PORTLAND

The unofficial guide for creative people

Annual 2017

Publisher
Teruo Kurosaki
BRIDGE LAB

Supplier
Media Surf Communications Inc.
Midori.so 3F 3-3-11 Aobadai, Meguro-ku, TOKYO, JAPAN
info@mediasurf.co.jp

Editor
Yusuke Tanaka, Daisuke Horie, Akihito Matsui (Media Surf Communications Inc.)
Etsuyo Okajima (Freedom University) / Takeshi Okuno

Assistant Editor
Jun Kuramoto, Kaede Sakai
(Media Surf Communications Inc.)

Art Director / Designer / Illustrator
Shinpei Onishi

Designer / Illustrator
Aya Kanamori

Designer
Taro Kimura

Writer
Mari Sekizawa
Tomohiro Mazawa (Media Surf Communications Inc.)
Mana Morimoto

Photographer
Arthur Hitchcock / Christine Dong
Dina Avila / Satoshi Eto (Columbia Sportswear Japan)
Travel Portland

Translator
Fulford Enterprises, Ltd

Cooperator
Yuzu Abe, Midori Sasaki, Kosuke Takagi,
Wataru Tanaka, Jumpei Takeda, Hirotaka Haibara,
Kouta Wakana, Viola Kimura, Lynn Watanabe (Media
Surf Communications Inc.)
Katsu Tanaka / Mayuko Kawano (Airbnb)
Miho Koshiba (Mirai Institute K.K.)
Tomomi Shibasaki / Yoshiko Takemoto
Tatsuya Mizuno / Nobuhiko Mochizuki

Travel Portland
Icebreaker (GOLDWIN INC.)
Columbia Sportswear Japan

Special thanks to
Yoshio Kurosaki and Nikki Kurosaki
Steve Bloom (Japanese Garden)
and all the Portlanders we met!

website ⇒ truepdx.com

- -

English Edition

Publisher
Rhonda Hughes

Editor
Liz Crain

Proofreaders
Linley Barba / Jessica Knauss / Michelle J. Robbins

BRIDGE LAB

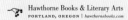